AF279488

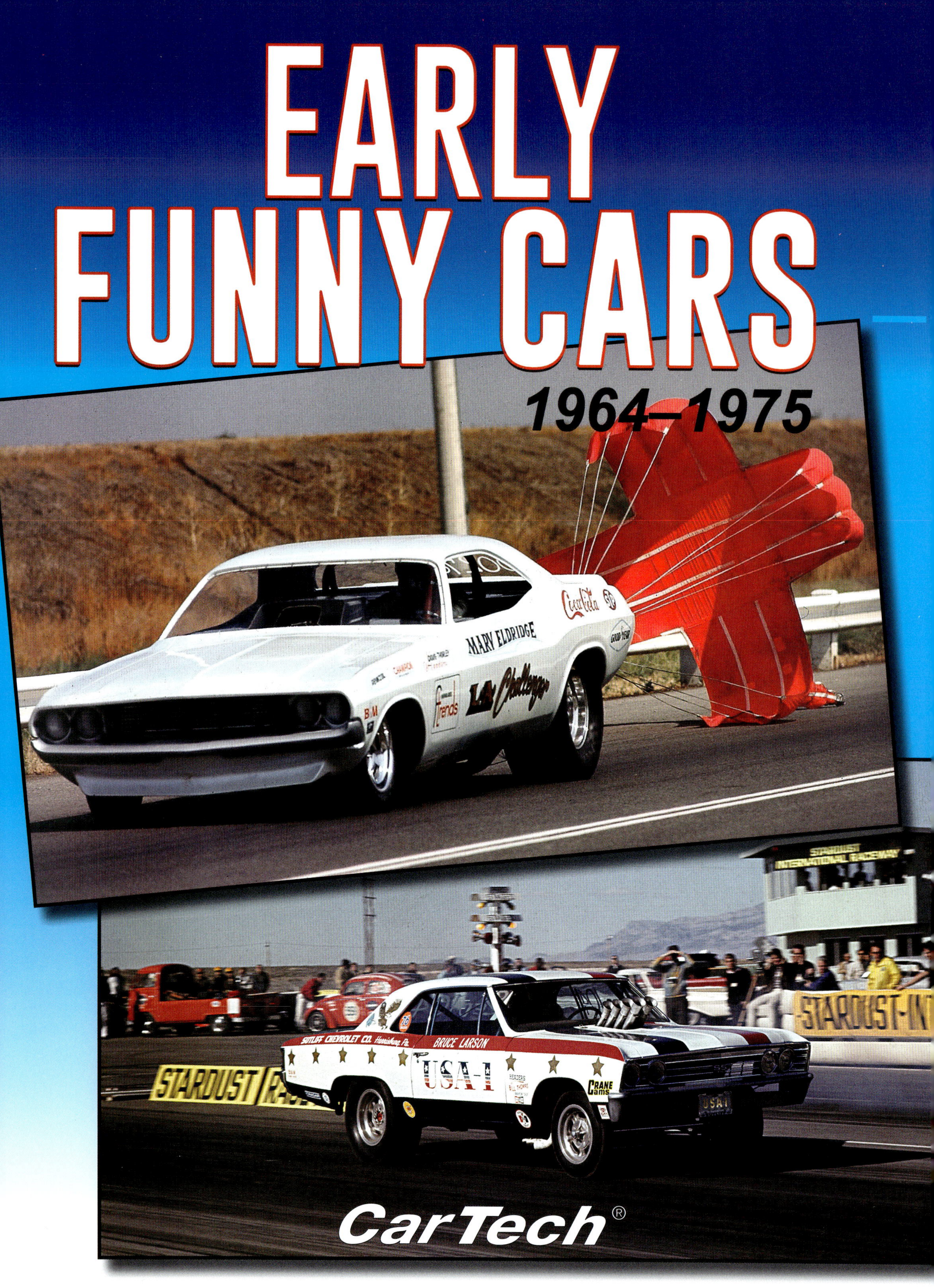

EARLY FUNNY CARS
1964–1975
CarTech®

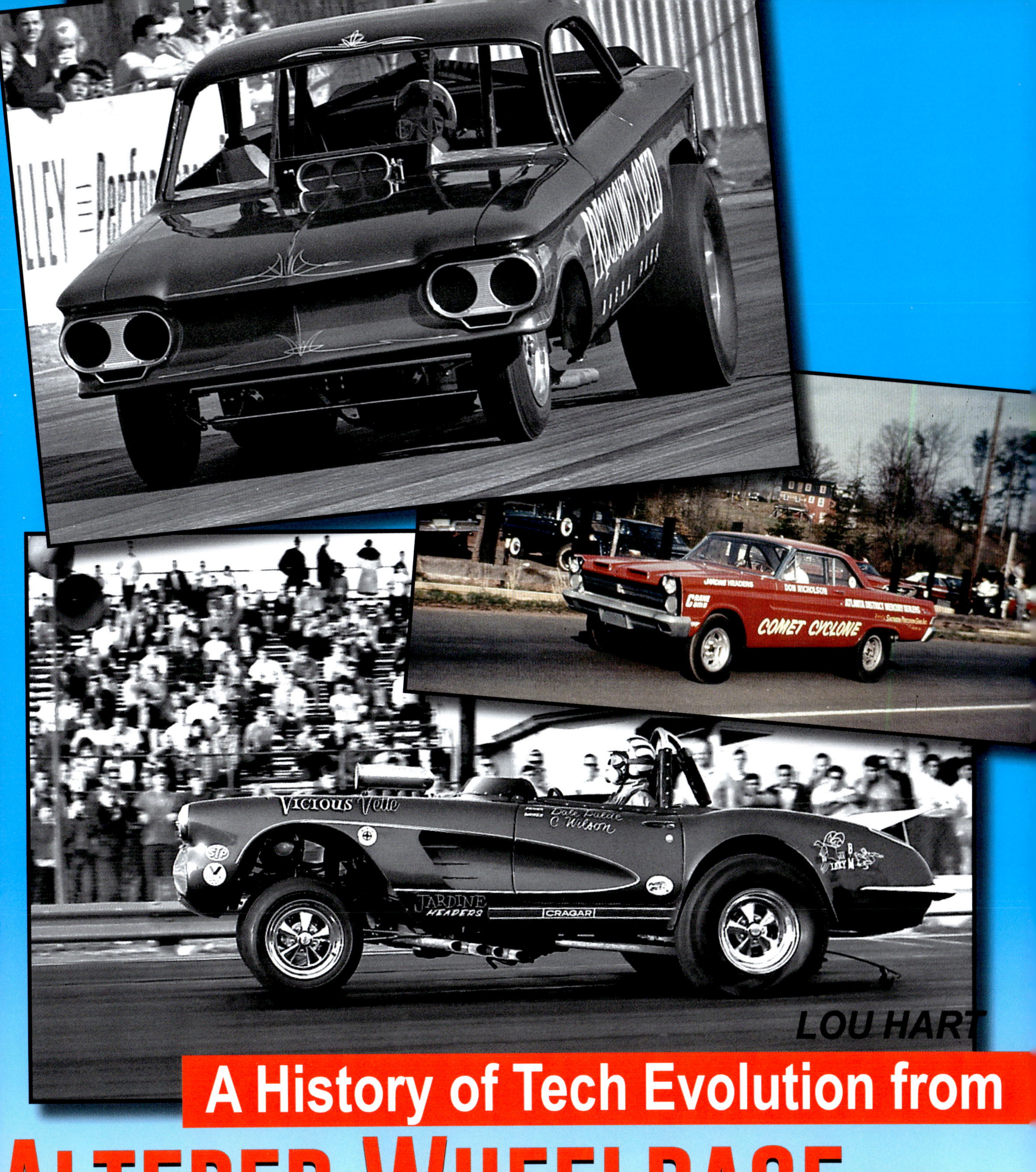

LOU HART
A History of Tech Evolution from
ALTERED WHEELBASE TO
MATCH RACE FLIP TOPS

CarTech®, Inc.
6118 Main Street
North Branch, MN 55056
Phone: 651-277-1200 or 800-551-4754
Fax: 651-277-1203
www.cartechbooks.com

Edit by Wes Eisenschenk
Layout by Monica Seiberlich

ISBN 978-1-61325-698-5
Item No. CT683

Library of Congress Cataloging-in-Publication Data Available

Written, edited, designed, and printed in the U.S.A.
10 9 8 7 6 5 4 3 2 1

PUBLISHER'S NOTE: In reporting history, the images required to tell the tale will vary greatly in quality, especially by modern photographic standards. While some images in this volume are not up to those digital standards, we have included them, as we feel they are an important element in telling the story.

All images are courtesy of Lou Hart or the Lou Hart Collection (including photos from Tom West, Alan Earman, Jake Johnston, and the estate of Steve Rollins) unless otherwise noted.

DISTRIBUTION BY:

Europe
PGUK
63 Hatton Garden
London EC1N 8LE, England
Phone: 020 7061 1980 • Fax: 020 7242 3725
www.pguk.co.uk

Australia
Renniks Publications Ltd.
3/37-39 Green Street
Banksmeadow, NSW 2109, Australia
Phone: 2 9695 7055 • Fax: 2 9695 7355
www.renniks.com

Canada
Login Canada
300 Saulteaux Crescent
Winnipeg, MB, R3J 3T2 Canada
Phone: 800 665 1148 • Fax: 800 665 0103
www.lb.ca

Table of Contents

Dedication

There are no words for how blessed I am to have known my mentor and friend Tom West! Without his inspiration, I could not have pulled this project together. The unbelievable libraries of his imagery (not just on Funny Cars but also all he captured behind the camera), his knowledge, creativity, artistry, and passion lives on with this book. We cannot forget what he accomplished in the hobby/ model kit industry, which will always have a part in our lives.

Tom stepped up to offer pointers to me as a 16-year-old kid starting out with a not-so-great school camera. Over the years, he was a brother-like figure in my life, and

it is truly an honor to keep Tom's memory and works alive. He shared many of his awesome stories over the phone and over shared meals. I'm forever grateful for his friendship. Thank you to the family of Tom West: his beautiful mother, Hilda West; daughter, Lauren Cruz; and son, Josh, for their undivided support.

Rest in Peace, Tom, and Godspeed!

This book is also dedicated to all of my peers who are no longer with us. Their lives have left me with lasting memories of their work and impressions that words can't describe. They'll always be in my mind and heart.

Acknowledgments

I wish to extend my deepest gratitude to Dale Pulde and Valerie Harrell for their valuable time at the peak of their busiest schedules and for putting up with my calls for the foreword in the book.

To my heroes on or off the drag strip, who I followed through of the golden age of nitro Funny Cars, who lived it and experienced the greatest times in Funny Car history, I thank you for your stories, rivalries, memories, and contributions in this book. Thank you all for this amazing ride through Funny Car history: Jay Howell, Dave Boncosky, Al Bergler, Jake Johnston, Roland Leong, Randy Walls, Bruce Larson, Jim Shue, Dale Pulde, Mike Thermos, Steve Montrelli, Walt Stevens, and Kenny Youngblood.

It was a tough ride in 2020, but words cannot express my love and appreciation to all my close friends and their positivity, including my high school best friend and buddy of more than 50 years, Dale Kunesh; lifelong friends Steve and Marie Delgadillo for their time; my great friend and the "Funk & Wagnall" of Funny Car knowledge, Tim Pearl; and my pal and Funny Car shoe Cory Lee. They all helped me with their time and contributions, enabling me to complete this project.

Recognition also goes out to Mike and Geri Golonka for their time to cement the facts of the Coca-Cola series;

Dennis Doubleday; Paul Johnson, for allowing me to pick and choose from his mass collection of negatives on the early days of A/FX; Dave Wallace; Tony Thacker; Greg Sullivan; Steve Condit; Ross Howard; David Paine; Kathy Beebe-Harris; Franca LaBarbera; Lloyd Wolfe; Kleet Norris; Stormy Byrd; and all my friends for their support for this project.

To all my colleagues, especially the celebrated "Dean" of drag racing photographers, Mr. Steve Reyes, with his awesome photographs and historical information, including all of the fun stories he shared from the early to adolescent days of Funny Cars. Thank you, Steve!

Finally, I cannot say thank you enough to my wife and "warden," Dawley, for her love, support, and the few if-looks-could-kill glares for putting up with all my shenanigans on taking over the entire home, which was scattered with photos, negatives, and endless piles of reference materials. Also, special thanks to my daughters, Kelly, Amber, and Teri; sons-in-law, Matthew Yax, Juan Flores, and Mike Medra; and the grandkids. Thanks, kids, for letting "Dad be Dad" and understanding my love and passion for drag racing, which has been a huge part of my life. Lastly, I especially want to thank my son Brandon, for giving me encouragement through this project.

Foreword by Dale Pulde

Several months ago, my longtime friend Lou Hart mentioned that he was writing a book about the early Funny Cars, where it all started. Being as it was with Lou, I said, "Sure! Let me know what you need."

In today's world, so many of the younger generation of Funny Car fans have no real idea about how the crazy, wild Funny Cars came to be or where it all began. For instance, I worked with a Funny Car driver in the 1990s who had no idea about the old drivers, the history of the past cars, or how the class evolved. I told him that this all started with guys getting their hands on a perfectly good running car and cutting it up just to race a car.

We had ideas about how to make it work and what we should try. We scribbled them down on napkins over Cokes and burgers at the local hangout. We learned without the aid of today's electronics or computers. Our "technology" was

all brains and brawn that either worked or failed, and we persevered! It wasn't all glamorous or golden times; it also had its shares of setbacks, failures, and disasters.

This book covers the roots, trials, and tribulations of the dedicated competitors in the early Funny Car years that evolved through the early 1960s through the early 1970s. It includes the life of being on the road for months, struggling at times to make a living, and the friendships that were made along the way.

Sit back, relax, and learn about the lives and times of what we did in my pal Lou Hart's new book, *Early Funny Cars 1964–1975: A History of Tech Evolution from Altered Wheelbase to Match Race Flip Tops!*

Dale Pulde
Legendary Funny Car driver,
crew chief, and tuner

Bill "Golden" Maverick gets the jump on Arkie Spoon at Pomona. Maverick's Top Stock Dodge scored three wins on the weekend, two at Fontana, and the finale at Pomona, running an ET of 11.34 at 127.85 mph. Spoon later left the Mopars and went on to run a Mercury Comet. (Photo Courtesy Tony Thacker/TorqTalk.com)

Chapter One

1964-1965

Quarter-Mile Madness: Mixing Aspects of A/FX and X/S

The 1960s were pivotal years in America. The decade included the space race with the Soviet Union, the assassination of President John F. Kennedy, the Civil Rights Movement, the Vietnam War, the rock and roll invasion with the Beatles, and regular gasoline averaged 24 cents a gallon.

The drag racing "boomers" yearned to have their own identity. The early hot rodders were now older and more involved in organized motorsports. While the rail jobs were still the kings and darlings on the drag strip, the "big names" frequently broke the 200-mph barrier. Nothing was coming close to their performances with the street-legal vehicles.

Birth of the Chrysler 426 Orange Monster

The Chrysler-Plymouth-Dodge Division has done more for hot rodding than any other make in the performance picture. The history of the hemispherical engine has been around since 1904, when the Welch passenger engine was introduced. The hemispherical design also played an important role in the aircraft industry after Austro-Daimler was introduced in the early years of the 20th century.

The popularity was slow to catch on with the hemispherical chambered designs because the early examples were rough, more costly, and complex to build. The engines also gave away 70 ci or more.

In 1951, Chrysler's Firepower engine overcame most of the disadvantages and flaws. Overnight it was the most talked about engine available on the market; it was the performance engine. These engines found their way into both stock car racing and drag racing, running either on gasoline or fuel dragsters, and they were dominating everything on the track.

Chrysler Racing held the edge when the Mopars won most of the big meets of the 1963 season, running their known 413 and 426 Max Wedge engines. So, with the start of a new season looming, the company wanted to take racing to another level. Chrysler engineers spent months behind closed doors designing a more powerful and durable engine to continue their winning ways. At the same time, they were making a statement to the racing world once and for all to prove that they were serious players at the tri-ovals, super speedways, and quarter mile! This new breed of a racing engine produced higher horsepower and massive

The engine that changed the structure in drag racing was the Chrysler A990 426 Race Hemi. It was available in 1964 and 1965 but only in the Dodge Coronet and Plymouth Belvedere branding. Both cars featured lightweight aluminum body pieces to save weight. Eventually, these engines morphed into the expanding world of the factory A/FX classes, which were the precursor to the Funny Car class. Hilborn built elaborate fuel injection systems that pumped nitromethane to the combustion chambers. The injectors bolted to the magnesium intake manifolds and were fitted with lengthened or shortened aluminum air tubes. (Photo Courtesy Paul Johnson)

The gearheads and car nuts were the backbone of drag racing. Looking back at the days of the flathead 6 and the fluid drives, this breed could get more power from a V-8 than from a flathead engine. This group of young men was comprised of hardcore hot rodders and cruisers, who spent their Saturday mornings working on their crudely built, jazzed-up jalopies. Their nights were spent driving up and down the main street boulevard and hanging out at the local burger joints with their steady girls.

On the other hand, there were also a few renegade rodders who terrorized the high roads and city streets with their shenanigans. This led them to being on a first-name basis with local law enforcement.

The majority of rodders belonged to organized car clubs. Their first rule was safety, and members pledged not to race on the streets and to only do so at regulated, sanctioned drag strips. These diehards stretched the limits of their wayward machines, still craving the need to go faster with style. No longer wanting the image of the large, bulky, family four-door sedan, this generation wanted more substance and flash!

torque, and it changed racing history in both NASCAR and drag racing.

The engine research lab in Highland Park cast the first 426 Hemi sample engines, which promptly failed when the cylinder walls overheated and cracked under stressful testing. It was determined that the walls were too thin. With time being of the essence, the engineers, led by Tom Hoover and engine development manager Bill Weertman, went back to the drawing board and made all the necessary changes to strengthen the blocks. The team carefully reassembled several new Orange Monster prototypes.

After successful tests in the shop on the dynamometers, these engines were released to the Mopar NASCAR teams to test. Hoover toiled with the Chrysler teams to work out any defects and faults prior to their highly anticipated debut at the 1964 Grand National Daytona 500.

Hoover's work paid off when the factory-backed Plymouth teams of Richard Petty, Jimmy Pardue, and Paul Goldsmith successfully finished 1-2-3, all driving 1964 Plymouths prepped with the new Race Hemi. The dominance in the race ushered in a new phrase "Win on Sunday, sell on Monday."

Plymouth dealerships were flooded with potential buyers wanting to get their hands on these fast Hemi cars. Although these engines were not available to the public for another year, the demand was overwhelming, and deposits were laid down. The drag racing Super Stock Dodges and Plymouths were next in line to get the new engine makeovers, but delays in the program kept the 413 and 426 Wedge engines in competition. The march of the Chryslers did not skip a beat, as both brands continued to dominate in both American Hot Rod Association (AHRA) and National Hot Rod Association (NHRA) national events.

Al Vanderwoude's 1964 Plymouth, the Flying Dutchman, *was one of the first entry-level leaders of the Funny Car Factory Experimental insurgence that perhaps was one of the most unconventional cars built. The rear axle was positioned directly behind the front doors. (Photo Courtesy Tony Thacker/TorqTalk.com)*

Super Stock Evolves

Let's look back to how this craze started. The early years in the Super Stock class morphed into the ranks of A/Factory Experimental (A/FX) classes when teams experimented with an array of modifications, including different engines, fuel systems, gear ratios, and adding larger tires. After chopping off the excess weight to run quicker and altering both front and rear suspensions, these cars started to move!

Then, out of the blue, someone had the idea to bolt on a supercharger to a large-cubic-inch engine and stuff it into a stock, steel-bodied production car. Some thought it was an insane idea, but the perseverance of those few who dared planted the seed, and the rest is history!

Race on Sunday

When Detroit's Big Three caught a glimpse of what things were about to be, Chrysler, Ford, and General Motors aimed and took their pitch toward the 18-to-25 age group. They nailed it when they released their lines of subcompact performance models built with more

Bill Hanyon launches off the line at Pomona in the Milne Brothers A/FX Plymouth slightly behind the Yeakel Plymouth Center Plymouth driven by Bruce Morgan. The Plymouths were powered by a 426 Wedge motor with dual Carter carburetors that were mounted to the factory cross-ram intake manifold. A TorqueFlite automatic transmission transferred power to the rear wheels on each machine. Hanyon's ET of 11.87 at 121.29 mph qualified the big Mopar. (Photo Courtesy Paul Johnson)

Ronnie Sox of Greensborough, North Carolina, was the one to beat from the East Coast during this rare West Coast appearance. He captured the A/FX title here at Lions when he defeated Al Means in his Ford Thunderbolt. The torrid 427-ci Mercury Comet out of Brinsfield Lincoln-Mercury turned in an ET of 11.33 at 121.52 mph in the final round, which was good enough to set a new Lions Drag Strip ET track record. (Photo Courtesy Paul Johnson)

"Dyno" Don Nicholson from Atlanta, Georgia, found California to his liking when he brought his Atlanta District Mercury Dealers drag racing beach wagon Marauder to Lions Drag Strip for the West Coast Stocker's Championships. Nicholson showed why his Comet was the top of the class when he defeated the Blairs Speed Shop Plymouth, running an event-best ET of 11.47 at 122.78 mph to 12.0 at 119.78 mph. (Photo Courtesy Paul Johnson)

powerful, larger cubic inch V-8 engines with higher compression, multiple carburation, and 4-speed transmissions.

Sales flourished and demand exceeded expectations. As these cars arrived at the dealerships, they rapidly rolled out of the showroom and into the waiting hands of these rodders. The cars quickly changed from the stock appearance and were modified with customized body parts, exhaust systems, hotter cams and carbs, retuning, and refining of what Detroit built.

The Chrysler 413 Wedge, Chevy 409, Ford 390, and Pontiac 389 were the hot ticket out of Michigan. Aftermarket speed shops and mail-order warehouses sold thousands of high-performance parts through their doors, giving the rodders a taste of what they desired: speed and power. These youngsters were brought up during the intense car-conscience era that was the preamble for the Funny Car. Drag racing was back into its own, and it was big. Racers and spectators could now relate to a car that had nearly half the power of a rail but was more identifiable.

Butch Leal pulls his Mickey Thompson–prepared Ford Thunderbolt off the line against a new A/FX Plymouth at Fremont Drag Strip. Leal's Ford ran a low-riser 427-ci engine with a 4-speed transmission. Leal's Thunderbolt ran a best ET of 10.90 at 128 mph. (Photo Courtesy Paul Johnson)

Lightning Strikes Twice as Ford "Bolts" Back at Chrysler

Ford's administration took quick action not to fall further behind Chrysler in the Stock and Super Stock ranks. In 1964, the automaker entered the drag racing scene when Ford unveiled its Total Performance packages for full- and mid-sized models.

There were two new prototypes. One was a 1964 427 Fairlane Thunderbolt. In competition-sanctioned events against cars in its class, it proved to be an immediate success. Turning the quarter mile with times less than 12 seconds and top speeds over 120 mph, many of the country's previously unbeaten Super Stock drag cars were quickly eliminated by Ford's new Fairlane. The car earned the 1964 NHRA Manufacturers Cup.

Ford shipped a total of 100 289-ci K-code Fairlanes to Dearborn Steel Tubing to convert the small-block Fairlanes over to Thunderbolts. The Thunderbolts were powered with a 427 high-riser engine with dual 4-barrel carburetors. Forty-nine models ran 4-speeds and 51 automatic 4-speed transmission cars were built (100 total). They featured a lightweight fiberglass front end and a fabricated exhaust system that consisted of steel tubing of 31-inch pipes from each port downsized to 14-inch collector cans that ran out a single muffler.

Several of the T-Bolts ended up in the hands of independents. "Quick Draw" Foster and Emmet "Rattlesnake" Austin were just a few racers who instilled fear in their opponents.

The Thunderbolts were the fly in the ointment for Chrysler right from the start. Gas Ronda defeated follow teammate Butch Leal in the finals at NHRA Winternationals, and later in the year, Ronda captured the NHRA Super Stock Championship for Ford.

Instead of shelling out the big dollars to order complete vehicles through Ford dealers, Ford engines and engine components were offered to the do-it-yourselfer drag car builders in the form of Cobra kits and 427 engine options.

Ford's other entry was the heavier 1964 "A" Stock Galaxie 500 to run in the Stock class. The "A" Stock Galaxies were metal fastbacks that were bolted on factory lightened frame and assembled with a fiberglass hood, decklid, and fenders. The powertrain ran nearly the same components as the Thunderbolts: a 427-ci high-riser engine, dual Holley carburetors, a heavy-duty locker rear end, and either a 4-speed or an automatic transmission with an NHRA-approved scattershield bellhousing.

The Fairlane protypes were tested at the Ford Proving Grounds in Dearborn, Michigan. They turned in runs with 11.50s ETs at 130-plus mph while the Galaxies were right behind running 12.80s at 118 mph. Ford manufactured a total of 50 lightweight fiberglass Galaxies.

The Stockers at the 1964 NHRA Winternationals were turning incredible times and speeds during all three days at Pomona, including "Wild" Bill Shrewsberry driving the Sachs & Sons 1964 A/FX Mercury Comet. Shrewsberry, from Long Beach, California, motored his way through the tough field to take home first place in the A/FX class with his Mercury. (Photo Courtesy Paul Johnson)

The 1964 NHRA Winternationals marked the first event for the new eliminator class Factory Experimental (F/X), which opened the door to what became Funny Cars and early Pro Stocks. Competition in the F/X Eliminator forced the limits toward the eventual push of carbureted, stock-body race cars. At the 1964 Nationals at Indy, Roger Lindamood's *Color Me Gone* S/SA Dodge ran against the Ramchargers machine, and those two names later became prominent in Funny Car racing.

Mercury was flying under the radar in the A/FX bracket with "Wild" Bill Shrewsberry at the wheel in the Sachs & Sons Mercury Comet. Running a 427 high-riser engine with dual 4-barrel carburetors, Shrewsberry and Jack Chrisman won A/FX class honors, but soon, the Comet with Chrisman changed the look and altered drag racing history.

Supercharged Factory Exhibitions

As Plymouth and Dodge continued the business-as-usual approach at circle tracks and on drag strips throughout the country, Dodge was now celebrating its golden anniversary with record sales (more than 30 percent from the previous year). Dodge decided to take a younger approach with its drag racing program.

While the cars were designed as a sales promotion gimmick, some thought the Dodge Chargers could have been the ultimate in factory-type drag racing. Advertising promoter Don Beebe approached Dodge with the idea of using rolling placards, a.k.a. the *Dodge Chargers*. The concept utilized a trio of steel-bodied Polara 330 production cars that were built on the West Coast by independent dragster contractors Dode Martin and Jim Nelson of Dragmaster.

Sponsored by the California Dodge Dealers, the cars were powered by an 850- to 900-hp supercharged dragster engine running on gasoline. The heavily modified cars toured, competing only against each other in exhibition runs throughout the country. The agreement included a lucrative mid-six-figure budget to run the planned eight-month schedule from March through October with drivers Jim Thornton, Jim Nelson, and veteran dragster driver Jimmy Nix.

Included were a fleet of top Dodge mechanics, ramp trucks with drivers, several identically painted street-driven Polaras for the team's use, spare engines that were to include the new 426 Hemi, transmissions, and a large inventory of factory racing parts. The cross-country tour began in California and circled back to the West Coast after the completed tour.

Select Dodge dealers throughout the country hosted the team with a festival-type atmosphere. The team had displays, performed demonstrations, and hosted meet-and-greet sessions, question-and-answer sessions, and autograph sessions for nearly a week before hitting the local drag strip to run the planned three-round match races. Strip owners benefited from the free advertising, which aired on local radio stations and in the newspapers, and how the appearance money was all paid by Dodge.

On race day, large groups of curious fans filled the grandstands and jammed the fences to catch a glimpse of these wild 10-second/130-mph machines. One appearance by the Chargers at Tucson Dragway set a new S/FX top speed record at 135.33 mph.

In the spring of 1964, the Dodge Division began a nation-wide tour of the Dodge Charger exhibition team Funny Cars that used a trio of steel-bodied S/FX Polara production cars that were each powered by a supercharged gasoline dragster engine. The three cars were built by the Dragmaster Company and sponsored by the California Dodge Dealers. The Chargers raced an eight-month program scheduled from March through October. The tour stopped at selected Dodge dealerships, providing a carnival-type atmosphere (food, prizes, and demonstrations) with drivers Jim Johnson and Jimmy Nix.

Drivers Jim Johnson and Jimmy Nix check out the blown 426 Wedge engine of a Dodge Charger prior to squaring off in one of their selected match races. The drivers drove identical cars, so the playing field was even until the starting light.

The flagship of the Dodge Chargers team was Jim John-son's Super Factory Experimental (S/FX) 1964 Dodge Polara. The Dodge Chargers tour worked flawlessly until a disaster during the eastern swing developed when book-ing dates could not be fulfilled and the cars could not run due to broken engines and transmissions. The unavailabil-ity of parts and a lack of funds caused the tour to end two months early.

The Chargers tour was received better than antici-pated, and Ford's management observed how much the positive results led to more sales for Dodge. This quickly led Lincoln-Mercury executives to take it a step further and form a team of their own with dragster trailblazer Jack Chrisman to drive and maintain the new super-charged nitro-fueled 427-ci S/FX Comet Caliente to chase down the Charger team.

While the Charger program received positive reviews in the early stages, the tour met disaster in August while appearing in the South. Problems occurred in the pro-gram when the promised 426-ci Race Hemis were never delivered. Mechanics were forced to piece together used parts from damaged and broken engines to assemble running motors. Transmissions blew up, rear ends broke, and the unavailability of parts and funding cuts caused the tour to end abruptly.

It's been said the tour ended at the Atlanta Speed Shop Dragway in Covington, Georgia, where the track management shelled out large amounts of money adver-tising "The Dodge Chargers . . . The Show of Shows."

The track ushered in the largest crowd of ecstatic spectators it had seen in two years, but things soon went sour when both cars were on site but never rolled off their tow rigs. When the question was asked if they were going make runs, one team member replied, "Nope, both cars have broken motors and there are no parts to repair them. So, no show today!"

While the management was dealing with this mess, the unruly crowd nearly started to riot by throwing bot-tles, trash cans, and anything in sight.

During the disruption, the unannounced and unad-vertised factory B/FD Mercury Comet of Jack Chris-man rolled through the gates of the Atlanta Speed Shop Dragway. Chrisman observed what was happening and quickly unloaded the car, fueled up, and towed the Comet up to the starting line area. Within minutes, he brought the 1,000-hp, nitro-fueled Mercury to life! The sound brought the unruly group running to the stands and fences to catch a glimpse of the Comet.

When the smoke blanketed the entire quarter mile, Chrisman unleased an unreal pass: a 10.51 ET at 142

Fresh from winning the A/FX class at the 1964 NHRA Winternationals with driver "Wild" Bill Shrewsberry, the first true Funny Car in drag racing now was hitting the strip with drag racing pioneer Charles "Jack" Chrisman at the helm. Chrisman successfully toured his factory-backed Mercury Comet in front of sold-out crowds throughout the country. The nitromethane-fueled Super Charged Cyclone cranked out 1,000-plus advertised horsepower from a blown 427-ci Mercury engine bolted to a direct-drive unit. Chrisman debuted the exhibition Sachs & Sons Comet on the West Coast on July 12 at Fremont Drag Strip when the Comet turned an ET of 10.38 at 148.27 mph on the Mercu-ry's maiden run. Chrisman (sans facemask) extirpates the slicks down the full length of the quarter mile at Fontana.

Jack Chrisman got spectators up on their feet when he pointed the Sachs & Sons Super Cyclone toward the finish line at Lions Drag Strip. The famous 2,800-pound factory-backed Marauder was one of the loudest vehicles on the exhibition circuit. When Chrisman cleared out the pipes and stabbed the pedal flat-blading, the force raised the decibel level up a point or two. If the wind was blowing in the right direction, the Howler was heard all the way to the Pike in Long Beach. Chrisman became the fastest passenger car in the quarter mile, stopping the clocks at 156.31 mph at the NHRA Nationals in Indianapolis. (Photo Courtesy Paul Johnson)

mph. The crowd went crazy and chanted for more. Chrisman brought the Cyclone back for the second pass, which netted a lower ET of 10.42 at 144 mph. There was a roar of approval for the Comet's efforts.

For the third and final run, Chrisman put his foot into it and ran a best 10.38 ET at 149 mph, annihilating the slicks down the quarter mile! This instantly vaulted Chrisman into the history books as the most popular exhibition attraction in drag racing. The first blown, nitro-burning Funny Car stole the limelight, which did not fare well with either the Chargers team or the Dodge top brass.

With this display of speed, quickness, and showmanship from the ace dragster driver, Chrisman figured out that the Chargers were sitting ducks. This brought Ford-Mercury's involvement up to the next level in drag racing. The manufacturer wars were on!

Orange Monster Lacks Landing Punch in Debut

With the success at the Daytona 500, Chrysler Performance now focused on the quarter mile and rolled out three Hemi-built cars for testing at Lions Drag Strip before the 1964 NHRA Winternationals in Pomona. The participating drivers testing were Al Eckstrand and Roger Lindamood in the new A/FX Plymouths.

The results were not quite as good as was predicted with the new engines. They were much slower in their performances when compared to the previous 426 Wedge cars. Several cars went through minor changes, including installing new camshafts, recurving distributors, and switching out the Carter AFB carburetors for Holley carburetors. The changes did not improve the results of the

Hemi cars, so the decision was made by both Chrysler's Robert McDaniel and Bob Cahill to shelve the cars for Pomona.

All was not a total disappointment for Chrysler, as the corporation's Super Stockers swept the Winternationals, running the reliable 426-R Max Wedge Stage III engine. Several refinements found their way into the drag 426 Monster engine. With wide open throttle bursts, the original tin-plated pistons were limited only to 15 seconds to prevent engine damage and required higher clearance.

Lawyer Al "Lawman" Eckstrand (right) receives help placing the Max Wedge scoop (the Race Hemi scoop hadn't yet been implemented) over the 426 Hemi below. Many firsts took place here at Lions Drag Strip in January 1964 with the Hemi in a new 2-percent Mopar, which featured the first-ever single-headlight setup in a Plymouth. Eckstrand's 1964 Plymouth 426 Max Wedge hardtop is behind him. (Photo Courtesy MotorTrend)

Dick Landy returned from a grueling tour through 31 states to pick up where he left off by taking an impressive win here in the A/FX class at Fontana. Landy's trademark was chomping on an unlit Dutch Masters cigar while he mashed through the gears. In the final round, the Dodge recorded a run of 11.00 at 123.11 mph to grab the trophy and cash. Landy said that the traction at Fontana was the best. (Photo Courtesy Paul Johnson)

From left to right are H.L. Shahan, Jim Thornton of the Ramchargers, Fred Cutler, Paul Bruns of Chrysler, Dave Koffel, Buddy Martin, Ronnie Sox, and an unidentified representative. The group is attending Chrysler's presentation of new factory-backed Plymouths and Dodges in Detroit. Chrysler built 50 of each model with the new 426-ci Race Hemi, which made the cars race ready for the public to purchase off the showroom floor.

With months of teardowns, blueprinting, balancing refinements, and hours of retesting, the results declared the new Hemis were ready to roll. They debuted in September at the 1964 NHRA US Nationals at Indianapolis. The outcome instantly changed the playing field when both Plymouth and Dodge brands captured class wins at the US Nationals: Roger Lindamood in Top Stock, Jim Thornton in Super Stock Automatic, and Dave Strickler topping the A/FX field. Chrysler products went on to win the AHRA Championship.

The Dawn of Super Cars in Drag Racing

By the end of 1964, both the Plymouth and Dodge divisions rolled out 12 specially modified 1965 Super Stock Plymouth Belvederes and Dodge Coronets. The cars were designed and built specially for acceleration competition in both NHRA and AHRA Super Stock racing.

Each sedan weighed approximately 200 to 400 pounds less than the other closest competitor and was equipped with the other version of the Orange Monster. This engine was the 426-ci Race Hemi that featured dual 4-barrel AFB carburetors with 1.60-inch primary and secondary bores, a cross-ram intake manifold, a unique cast-steel heat resistance exhaust system, and either a 4-speed manual or a TorqueFlite automatic transmission with a highly intricate torque converter. This transmission

helped the cars leave the starting line quicker.

For better weight transfer, the stock wheelbase was shortened or moved 10 to 15 inches rear and front. The cars also had lightweight aluminum front fenders, an aluminum hood with functional scoops, magnesium wheels, lightweight seats, a roll cage, deleted radio, heater, rear seat options, and relocation of the 105-pound battery to the trunk.

Notable racers Dick Landy, Ronnie Sox, Buddy Martin, Al Eckstrand, Dick Branster, Jim Thornton, Dick Landy, Butch Leal, H.L. Shahan, and Tommy Grove received these beasts that were well ahead of their time and nearly unbeatable. Also in line for these factory fliers were "Pee Wee" Wallace's *Virginian*, Pop Whitt's *Sly Fox*, Tom "Smoker No. 2" Smith, and Billy "High Gear" West, who were all driving Plymouths. On the Dodge side was Sam Kennedy's *Ram Charger* and Mrs. *"B"* Hemi Mopar.

SOHC 427s for Everyone

Mercury stepped up for 1965 and hired Bill Stroppe to prepare 100 Mercury Comets with the 427-ci overhead cam (OHC) engines just for drag racing, but the overall count was down to "limited availability" reserved for the top drivers in their drag racing program. Don Nicholson, Eddie Schartman, Jack Chrisman, and Dee Keeton were the first to receive the Comets.

One of the weapons from the arsenal of Plymouth was Butch Leal's California Flash 1965 Factory A-990 RO51 Belvedere. Leal had come from Ford to run the factory-altered Mopar equipped with a 4-speed manual transmission, which was 1 of 16 4-speed cars built to use in the 1965 racing scheme. Leal went on to win a high percentage of his open match races, and he won the Super Stock class title at the US Nationals. (Photo Courtesy Tony Thacker/TorqTalk.com)

Tommy Grove from Oakland, California, advanced to the third round during eliminations at the AHRA Winternationals driving the new Plymouth Melrose Missile. He ran a 10.95-second ET at 126.40 mph. In the semifinals, the factory Plymouth went up against the new SOHC Ford Mustang of Bill Lawton and lost, as Lawton's Mustang broke into the 10-second bracket. Lawton went on to win the class, defeating Les Ritchey, who was also driving a Mustang. (Photo Courtesy Tony Thacker/TorqTalk.com)

WHAT MAKES DRAG RACING...

As part of the 1965 Mercury factory press kit, this is an artist's detailed rendering of an A/FX Comet Caliente.

Problems surfaced for both Ford and Mercury's 427 single overhead cam (SOHC) engines. Devout bearing failure constantly bothered Ford's drag racing program and led the company to test forged aluminum rods that were originally designed for a 392 Chrysler Hemi.

Independents Unite

With all of the rumblings and noise from Dearborn and Detroit, GM's racing ban was still in effect for any factory-backed participation, including drag racing. The NHRA would not allow GM cars to run in the Super Stock classes if any of its specialty cars were not available from the showroom, so the NHRA created a new Factory Experimental (F/X) class where both Chevrolet and Pontiac could compete and race. The AHRA expanded the field with the A/Factory Experimental (A/FX), B/Factory Experimental (B/FX), and S/Factory Experimental (S/FX) classes to allow "Run what you brung" to the strip.

With General Motors already producing several compact high-performance A-Body models for public sale (Pontiac's GTO, Chevy's Chevelle, Oldsmobile's Cutlass, and Buick's Skylark), GM independent racers Arnie Beswick, Don and Roy Gay (Pontiac), Dick Harrell, Kelly Chadwick, and Steve Bovan (Chevy) built and campaigned highly competitive machines against the opposing Chrysler and Ford factory cars.

Chevrolet engineers developed its experimental 550-hp, 427-ci Mk. II Daytona engines to power their larger and heavier models. Meanwhile, another prototype (the Mk. I 427-ci engine with 430 hp) was developed for either Chevy II or Chevelle bodies that were equipped with aftermarket aluminum front end fenders, hoods, and doors, which brought the weight down to 3,000 to 3,200 pounds. Pontiac relied on carried-over versions of the 421 Super Duty 405-hp engines with dual 4-barrel carburetors. Parts for these engines were only available under the table or out the back door until the stock was depleted.

Arnie "the Farmer" Beswick

One of the most successful independent racers in the country at that time was Arnie "the Farmer" Beswick of Morrison, Illinois. In 1963, Beswick (driving 421-ci Pontiac Tempests) won several prestigious events, including the NASCAR Winternationals (yes, NASCAR had drag racing), the *Drag News* Invitationals, and the World Series of Drag Racing.

Arnie Beswick jumps off the line well ahead of his competition at Pomona. Beswick was one of the top GM independents without any type of major funding from the factory but was a thorn in the sides of the factory Chrysler- and Ford-employed superstars. (Photo Courtesy Paul Johnson)

NASCAR Goes Drag Racing

Bill France Sr., the president and founder of NASCAR, collaborated a deal with Bill Witzberger, owner of the Pittsburg International Dragway (PID), to form the NASCAR Drag Racing Division. With headquarters in Daytona Beach, Florida, the sanctioned body was established on the East Coast, running premier Top Fuel and Funny Cars races. When Chrysler and Richard Petty boycotted the 1965 NASCAR Grand National series due to the Hemi ban, he focused on drag racing and built a fuel-injected Petty-blue *43 Jr.* Barracuda.

A tragic day in Petty racing history was when Richard lined up against Arnie "the Farmer" Beswick at Southern Dragway near Dallas, Georgia. As both cars left evenly off the line, Petty's front suspension broke, and the car made a hard left turn. He lost control of the car, drove up an embankment, vaulted over a fence, and landed on top of a crowd of spectators. One person was killed and six others were injured. The accident was Petty's last run in his short career in drag racing.

The NASCAR Drag Racing Circuit suffered another tragedy when Top Fuel driver Gene Goldman lost his life at one of its big races.

Steve Bovan and Mike Hoag, employees at Blair's Speed Shop in Pasadena, California, built one of the most successful and memorable Chevy II Funny Cars that created havoc match racing throughout the country. Bovan and Hoag completely gutted the stock 1965 Nova, leaving nothing except the steel body shell. Hoag designed, fabricated, and built a tube chassis that was fortified to cradle the blown 396-ci engine and Art Carr transmission. At the US Nationals at Indy, Bovan competed with all the other "big" exhibition stockers in B/FD, which was the only class in which the NHRA would allow the car to run. The Chevy II recorded passes with a respectable ET of 9.50 at 150 mph, running on a ratio 25-percent nitro and 75-percent methanol.

Independent racer Tom Schlauch pulls off the line at Fontana in his The Brown One Pontiac Tempest, which was powered by a Super Duty 421-ci engine and tuned by Bob Hayes. Schlauch remains actively busy today, having built rare Pontiac race engines and cruising around in his 1969 Ram-Air V-equipped Trans Am. (Photo Courtesy Paul Johnson)

During the year, Beswick claimed the number-1 spot on the *Drag News* Mr. Stock Eliminator. His success carried over to the beginning of 1964, as he recorded his second consecutive win at the NASCAR Winternationals in Daytona Beach, Florida, and then traveled 3,000 miles across the country to California. There, he captured his class at the Smokers Meet in Bakersfield. This was all without the aid of factory support.

Bowtie Terrors

Chevrolet independents were considered to have little or no chance when going up against the high-dollar factory teams. Problems plagued the new 396 Porcupine-head engines with oil not getting to the upper cylinder head of the left side of the engine with the 425-hp versions. One of the underdogs that solved this issue was Huston Platt and his *Dixie Twister* Chevelle, which was thought of as the world's quickest and fastest F/X match racers that hailed out of Georgia. The self-supportive Huston ran a big-block, Porcupine-head, Mark V L78 396-ci engine that was rated at a stout 425 hp.

Pete Seaton, whose father was Louis Seaton, was one of GM's vice presidents who led the labor contract negotiations against the powerful United Auto Workers (UAW) union. Pete Seaton helped resolve the issues with his hard work that avoided a damaging strike. The long-standing connection he had with General Motors remained solid when he took his idea to go drag racing with some GM backing in his corner in running his first Chevelle Funny Car.

Dick Harrell, another stellar Chevy performer in the AHRA, once again was the one to beat in the match race league. Harrell teamed with Bill Thomas Race Cars on the West Coast, and together they built *Retribution II*, a 1965 Chevy II with a 427-ci Z11 engine. These were racers who knew how to make power on a shoestring budget and win their share.

AMC Drag Racing Development

The American Motors Corporation (AMC) viewpoint had been well known for quite some time that racing, speed, and performance was simply taboo. Bill Kraft, owner of a Norwalk, California, Rambler dealership since 1955, requested a visit to the executive offices of AMC President Roy Abernathy.

Kraft brought his vision of young prospective buyers owning an AMC car with higher punch and style. Kraft developed a two-door "Classic" that was built to compete

in drag racing's A/FX class. It had an AMC 418-ci engine from American Ambassador, four carburetors, a specially fabricated intake manifold, custom headers, mag wheels, and a 4-speed transmission.

Advertising Wars

From the street, strip, and showroom, Chrysler shook up the advertising wars. It primarily focused on the younger prospective buyers with full-page advertisements in magazines and newspapers, on billboards, and in commercials on local television, all displaying their various high-performance production models.

Drag News (a.k.a. the "Racer's Bible") was one of the top national weekly drag racing publications. It carried high-dollar advertisements from local and national high-performance dealers selling brand-new, race-ready cars available right out the door!

One particular advertisement on July 11, 1964, from Mr. Norman Kraus of Mr. Norm's Grand Spaulding Dodge in Chicago, went all out, announcing huge inventories of the new "Hemi-Ram, the only production car in America guaranteed to run in the 11s right off the showroom floor."

Norm also offered dozens of Ram Chargers, Street Rams, and 383-ci high-performance cars and parts. He was quoted as saying, "Wherever you live, I will pay your fare from anywhere to sell you a Hemi Ram Charger."

If you were lucky enough to purchase a Hemi Ram, the customer would automatically become a member of the Mr. Norm's Sports Club, which included car clinics, service and parts discounts, and dances and parties held at the dealership.

Dick Landy spent three phenomenally successful years on the Funny Car circuit. When the Funny Cars got further and further out there, a few Detroit manufacturers dropped their Funny Car programs to return to the Detroit iron for drag racing. Landy climbed out of the seat of his Funny Car and returned to his roots for 1967 with a pair of Dodge 440 Coronets in the SS/B class. (Photo Courtesy Paul Johnson)

Lou Baney, president of the Los Angeles Plymouth Dealers Association, oversaw one of the wildest Funny Car projects from the mid-1960s. Baney composed a team of the West's top talented body and chassis fabricators (Don Brown, Don Long, Pat Foster, Fred Susser, and Bob and Don Spar) and engine builder Dave Zeuschel to build the mid-engine, Hemi-powered Plymouth Hemi 'Cuda. Tom McEwen, selected to handle the driving chores in exhibition runs, heats up the big M&H slicks prior to making a test pass during filming secessions at Long Beach. The mid-engine 'Cuda experienced severe front end problems. When McEwen went full throttle, the front end bounced down the track. The weight of the front end was too light, which allowed air to enter through the open space from the engine compartment. The car lifted, went airborne in the traps with the speed in excess of 147 mph, and crashed back down. The most damage was done to the body. McEwen was rattled but walked away with minor injuries. After the incident, Baney rebuilt the car and made major changes by adding more weight to the front end and disc brakes.

Former AHRA Top Fuel Champion owner/driver Bob Sullivan journeys back on the return road in his Pandemonium V *Funny Car in front of the packed grandstands at the US Nationals in Indy. Sullivan and his wife, Shirley, pulled the nitro-powered 392 Hemi out of their dragster and dropped it into a stock, steel-bodied Barracuda that weighed 3,200 pounds (very heavy). The following year, Sullivan reduced the car's weight by removing the steel body parts and replacing them with fiberglass pieces to make it more competitive. Sullivan won a few races and lost more, but the crowds loved it. (Photo Courtesy Greg Sullivan)*

Jack Chrisman was "Mr. Entertainment" when he drove the Sachs & Sons Comet, blasting the tires the entire length in the quarter mile during exhibition runs. Chrisman returned in 1965, now a serious player match racing with his Super Comet Cyclone. *Jack swapped out the older 427 Wedge engine and replaced it with Ford's newest bullet, a blown 427 SOHC engine that was setback 25 percent in the chassis. Chrisman went on to race Funny Cars for nearly a decade, including being one of the founding members of the Coca-Cola Cavalcade of Stars. (Photo Courtesy Paul Johnson)*

A creative local television advertisement in Southern California by Dodge featured 76-year-old actress Kathryn Minner as the "The Little Old Lady (from Pasadena)," which was also a song created by surf rock icons Jan and Dean. Minner became the leading spokesperson for Dodge with the well-known slogan, "Put a Dodge in your Garage, Hon-ey."

Several other commercials featured Minner. She was at an oval track racing her Dodge Dart against a 180-mph Indy car and lead-footing the accelerator in Dick Landy's A/FX Dodge Dart down the boulevard. In another instance, "Wild" Bill Maverick is shown on the starting line of a drag strip in his A-100 *Little Red Wagon* exhibition wheel-stander as he races a Top Fuel dragster. The dragster starts off by pulling the front wheels high off the

"Dyno" Don Nicholson and mechanic genius Earl Wade campaigned a 1965 Mercury A/FX Comet Cyclone *that was one of fiercest and built by Bill Stroppe Engineering. The lightweight* Comet Cyclone *was nearly identical to the specifications of the previous year's altered-wheelbase model, which included Plexiglas windows and a fiberglass hood, front and rear bumpers, fenders, and doors. A factory Mercury 427 SOHC engine powered the Comet with a 4-speed manual transmission. (Photo Courtesy Paul Johnson)*

ground, and as the camera pans over to what should be Maverick in the *Little Red Wagon*, it shows the little old lady behind the wheel instead, blowing past the dragster and up on both rear wheels, reminding everyone that "Dodge builds tough trucks as well!"

"Dandy" Dick Landy's 111-inch wheelbase Coronet was the most controversial Factory Experimental machine built to date. Landy drove one of the first factory Dodge Hemi cars and took it upon himself to make several other modifications to obtain more speed and quicker times, including altering the wheelbase (sliding the front wheels forward 10 inches and rear wheels 15 inches). The original aluminum body parts (fenders, doors, bumpers, and hood) were scrapped and replaced with fiberglass components. A straight axle was added that was supported by leaf springs. This raised the front end by several inches while the back of the car was lowered. The awkward appearance was viewed by many as being the very first true Funny Car.

Dodge Swims and Darts into the Fold

Chrysler closed out the calendar year with another huge edge in competitive motor sports. Championships were won in the NASCAR Grand Nationals series, the Sports Car Club of America (SCCA) National Rallye Championships, and both NHRA and AHRA national sanctioned events. Looking ahead to 1965, it looked no different, as both Chrysler and Dodge factory engineers were developing two brand-new lighter models for the A/FX battles with the new Plymouth Barracuda and Dodge Dart.

The Barracuda and Mongoose

Former Bonneville and lakester rodder Lou Baney of Baney Plymouth in Los Angeles, California, was the president of the Southern California Plymouth Dealers Association and the United Drag Racers Association (UDRA). Baney searched for a different approach to showcase the new 1965 Plymouth Barracuda. Starting with a bone stock Barracuda Commando that was delivered to B&M Automotive in Van Nuys, California, it was completely dismantled, leaving only the body shell, dashboard, and upholstery intact.

However, this was not your ordinary match racer. It became the first rear-engine Funny Car. Power was supplied by a 1965 426 Plymouth Hemi, which was placed behind the driver out of his view. Tom "the Mongoose" McEwen was selected to drive the all-steel Barracuda for

Baney, and it debuted on February 7 at the NHRA Winternationals, making only exhibition passes.

After several weeks match racing around the Southern California strips, Baney and McEwen were back at Lions testing. McEwen climbed into the seat, stood on the loud pedal, and took off. At halftrack, the 'Cuda started to bounce the front wheels up and down. As the car entered the lights at 145 mph, it became airborne and crashed back down, causing substantial damage to the body.

McEwen walked away unscathed, but it was determined that the weight of the front end was too light and sat up too high, allowing air to enter underneath. Although the damage to the 'Cuda was basically structural, Baney got the go-ahead from the Plymouth Dealers Association for a new Hemi 'Cuda II with several safety and suspension upgrades. These changes included the addition of disc brakes and a heavier, lower front end. The Hemi 'Cuda II was later driven by "Fearless" Fred Goeske.

Pandemonium

Bob and Shirley Sullivan of Kansas City, Missouri, campaigned a Top Fuel dragster mostly on the AHRA circuit. The couple quickly noticed the rise in Funny Car exhibition popularity and decided to pull the motor out of their Top Fuel dragster and drop it into a brand-new steel-bodied 1965 Plymouth Barracuda.

Carrying on the *Pandemonium* name, the nitro-fed 392-ci Hemi cranked out quarter-mile runs with a 9.78 ET at 160 mph while smoking the tires all the way down the track, which delighted the fans. *Pandemonium* originally tipped the scales at 3,700 pounds, but when the popular Experimental class developed into a more competitive class, the car was lengthened 18 inches and the steel front clip was replaced with a fiberglass front end. The modifications trimmed the weight down to just under 3,200 pounds, which lowered the ET (9.43 seconds) and raised the top speed (177 mph).

Mercury hired guns "Dyno" Don Nicholson, "Fast" Eddie Schartman, and Jack Chrisman campaigned new Comet Cyclones for 1965. Each car was built with the new 427-ci SOHC engine fitted with alloy cylinder heads, dual Holley 4-barrel carburetors, and an aluminum low-rise intake manifold. The transmission was either a Ford C-6 automatic or a Toploader 4-speed manual. Chrysler and Ford engineers were loading up for 1966 with new compact models that took the manufacturer wars to a higher level.

Cecil County Drag-O-Way hosted the third annual Super Stock Nationals in front of 24,000 avid fans from more than 30 states. The race attracted more than 90 Funny stockers to the "The Traction Capital of the World." Bruce Larson's USA-1 *and Tommy Grove's* Ford Charger *Mustang were paired together in the 2,400-pound fuel class. Grove put away the Chevelle en route to take the Mr. Eliminator crown for the three-day event. (Photo Courtesy Lloyd Wolfe)*

Chapter Two

1966-1967

Funny Cars Hit the Scene

At Ford, the Thunderbolts and A-100 Galaxies were steps behind the dominant Chrysler cars. John Holman and Ralph Moody, contractors to Ford's successful Grand National NASCAR and earlier drag racing programs, were commissioned to build 10 specially prepared altered-wheelbase fastback Mustangs to compete in NHRA and AHRA A/FX classes.

Eight cars were built with the signature Ford 427-ci SOHC engine fitted with alloy cylinder heads and dual Holley 4-barrel carburetors bolted to an aluminum intake low-rise manifold. Ford's Toploader 4-speed manual transmission transferred power to the rear wheels. The two remaining Mustangs were built with the high-rise 427 Wedge motors.

Named the "Dollar Mustangs," these cars were made available to a select group of drivers for only $1.00 with the understanding that the cars would be returned to Ford when the automaker called. By mid-year, the Mustangs were dialed in to keep pace with the hot Mopars. However, with continued pressure to stay a step ahead with the Dodges and Plymouths, the decision was made to swap out the carburetors and replace them with a new mechanical fuel injection system developed by Stu Hilborn.

Along with the increased throttle responses, the Mustangs ran on nitro instead of gasoline, and several Mustangs changed over from the 4-speed to run a modified C-6 automatic transmission. With these changes, the Mustangs were able to stake their claim again over the Mopars for a brief time.

Dick Brannan dominated the seventh annual AHRA Winternationals Championships at Irwindale in February 1966, setting the low ET for unblown cars with a 9.21 at 149.50-mph qualifying pass. Brannan of Madison Heights, Michigan, won the unlimited stock bracket with his fuel-injected, nitro-burning Mustang.

John Holman and Ralph Moody's chronological history dates to late 1957, when they formed a partnership and combined their resources by building successful Ford NASCAR cars and engines. During the early Super Car wars in drag racing, Ford reached out to Holman-Moody in 1965 to build 10 K-coded altered-wheelbase A/FX Mustangs. Ford wanted to compete in the top Factory Experimental classes of drag racing by replacing the slower and heavier Thunderbolts and Galaxies. Eight Mustangs were equipped with the 427 SOHC engines, each with dual 4-barrel carburetors, while the other two Mustangs had 427 high-risers. The Mustangs were intended for match racing exclusively, so when the new super-light 1966 A/FX replacements arrived, they were now pure race cars with their stretched space frames and Hilborn fuel injection running on nitro.

Southern California's most potent factory-backed Ford that rolled out of the drag racing shops of Holman-Moody was the poppy red Mustang of Gas Ronda. Ronda, the high-performance manager at Russ Davis Ford in Covina, California, had been one of Ford's top chosen quarter-mile drivers since 1963. The tubed-framed, ultra-light Funny Car ran a Hilborn-aspirated 427 SOHC Cammer with prototype aluminum heads. Les Richey and Cliff Brian of Performance Associates in Covina handled tuning duties that took aim to unseat the powerful factory Mopars.

Les Ritchey's Performance Associates–sponsored A/FX Ford Mustang was one of early 10 factory-built Mustangs by Holman-Moody with a 427 SOHC Cammer motor, but he still ran the only one equipped with multiple Weber carburetors instead of the Hilborn stacks. Ritchey had received the engine four days earlier, yet posted runs of 10.50 at 130 mph, winning the A/FX class.

Larry Coleman's Holman-Moody A/FX Mustang battled the factory-backed big Plymouths and Dodges. Larry Coleman Enterprises, along with partner Bill Taylor, supplied the automatic transmissions for the Holman-Moody Mustangs that ran on the NASCAR Ultra Stock Circuit. The Mustangs were strong competitors, running well throughout the 1966 season but were fading out when the lighter tubular-frame "floppers" arrived on the scene that were developed by their counterparts at Mercury and Logghe. When Coleman commissioned Logghe for a new lightweight Funny Car, Hubert Platt was hired by Coleman to take up the driving chores of the Mustang.

Johnny Wright, Roy Terry, and Richard Gull formed this potent team with the Destroyer Chevy Malibu SS. The 2,900-pound B/XS car ran a slightly modified 427-ci Rat motor that was running on a 50-pound nitro solution pumped through the Hilborn port-injection system, which was matched to a Muncie 4-speed transmission. The trio shared driving time behind the wheel, but it was Wright who turned out the more consistent runs of 10.70s with speeds at 135 mph.

Burning the midnight oil for seven days a week behind his own plumbing business, Bill Rieck of Lompoc, California, entered the Funny Car wars with his Quarterbender *Dodge Dart. With many friends helping, the chassis was fabricated and constructed from 3x2-inch square steel that was stretched out to measure 118-3/4 inches in length. George Britting Engineering provided the dropped front axle and the front two leaf springs. Rieck installed a Dodge 426-ci Hemi mated to an Art Carr TorqueFlite transmission. The 1966 Dodge Dart 270 fiberglass body was a product of B&N Automotive in Dayton, Ohio, and featured modified rear fender wells moved forward 15 inches while the one-piece front clip was extended 13 inches. Jim Cockerill and John Hefner were crewmembers on the big turquoise Dodge that produced 160-mph blasts down the quarter mile.*

These changes gave Ford a winning record in match racing. In a 2005 interview of Gas Ronda recorded at the NHRA Museum, Ronda said, "In those days, Ford gave us two to three engines, a replacement car, and parts. I was conservative . . . I learned to make a run through the quarter mile balls out to turn a [good ET] and not hurt the engine."

Several area local independents threw their hats into the mix and built high-quality race cars without all of the fanfare or any backing from the factory. Many drivers arranged for and quietly acquired their parts out the back door and still dished out headaches to the high-dollar teams.

The seesaw battles between Ford and Chrysler tipped in Ford's favor at the 1965 NHRA Winternationals when Bill Lawton, from Cranston, Rhode Island, drove one of the Holman-Moody Mustangs that was racing under the Tasca Ford banner. He won the A/Factory Stock Experi-mental title at Pomona. Lawton singled in the final round when another Holman-Moody Mustang, driven by Len Richter, was unable to make the run due to breakage.

Starting to Get a Little Funny

Not one drag strip that was in the competitive business of providing spectators a great show would dare to bite the hand that fed them. The people demanded color and excitement, and track owners went out of their way to make sure that the fans received it.

While the Top Fuel dragsters were still the "kings of the quarter mile," the Funny Cars were in demand and were rapidly taking off. The game plan rapidly changed when Stock and Super Stock team owners and drivers realized that they could make more money match racing with a Funny Car. The rush was on when many sold off their older outdated iron to be replaced with newer advanced designs that were lighter, more powerful, and produced quicker times and faster speeds. The high-dollar factory and self-sustaining teams along with independents all kept their focus on one thing: winning.

The low-buck racers that were running on a shoestring budget either kept their older cars or bought the tried, used, and well raced cars. They would tear them down, overhauling the structure and appearance to squeeze out every unneeded pound to gain a tenth of a second or add a few miles per hour to the top speed of the car. Most of the earlier FX cars suffered with soft stock rear suspensions, little to no traction, and barely any drivability, so builders and drivers bolted the rear end to the frame and dropped several hundred pounds of weight. Over to the front end, A-frames were replaced to a modified tube-type straight axle package with a torsion bar suspension.

Another way to reduce weight was to acid dip the complete body or individual body parts. However, this also made the bodies flimsier, so they could easily get distorted, dented, or damaged either by leaning on or against them when wrenching, transporting, and racing.

Aluminum and Fiberglass

Many racers elected to remove the heavier steel body parts and replace them with lightweight fenders, bumpers, hoods, decklids, doors, and interior door panels made from either approved aluminum or fiberglass materials. Mechanics replaced tired engines with a new, powerful engine that was updated with freshly designed and manufactured internal and external parts, including

Richard "Doc" Spence designed, maintained, and drove his Skootin Cuda Plymouth Barracuda sponsored by the Site Brothers Plymouth dealership in Kansas City. The royal blue metal-flake 'Cuda ran a Plymouth 426-ci Hemi on an extremely potent mix (90-percent nitro and 10-percent methanol) that was fed through Hilborn injectors. At the 1966 AHRA World Championships, Spence captured the 1966 Mr. Stock Eliminator title at Lions Drag Strip.

pistons, crankshafts, connecting rods, camshafts, and aluminum cylinder heads. Carburetion was outdated and ditched. It was replaced with sophisticated fuel injection or supercharged systems that added major horsepower when burning nitro.

The AHRA's Traveling Amusement Show

With the success of the popular match racer Funny Cars, NHRA officials still refused to recognize the new breed of nitro-burning "outlaw" exhibition cars to run in their own class. Officials regulated them to run only in the B/FD class at all national events, where their unpredictable wheel-stands and burning up the tires promptly stole the show. Seeing how the NHRA refused to add Funny Cars, AHRA president Jim Tice welcomed the carnival-type atmosphere of colorful cars and drivers with open arms.

Instead of putting the cars in a regulated, obscure class, the AHRA turned them loose and offered increased cash payouts at all major events that included appearance, round advancement, and setting event low ETs and top speeds. Record cash purses were given to the event champion.

Not only did the drivers and owners reap the benefits but the AHRA facilities also heavily promoted the premier Funny Car events to gather up the top manufacturer's brand and bring in driver rivalries as announcers screamed over the public address system to fire up the crowds. AHRA drag strips realized that they could cater to the people and give them more than their money's worth. Soon, they were hosting huge giveaways and door

prizes, including color and black-and-white TVs, surfboards, radios, hair dryers, minibikes, concession food, and tickets for future events to the lucky ticket holders. You name it, they gave it away.

When the racing concluded, many AHRA tracks advertised top-named bands that performed on stages near the starting line. The psychedelic lights and sounds rapidly attracted the remaining spectators, who danced and partied into the early morning hours. The AHRA sold it, and the young people loved it.

New teams, drivers, and cars arrived on the scene, and Chrysler decided to build fewer of the factory full-size Dodge Cornets and Plymouth Belvederes A/FX match race bashers. The factory dropped its line, concentrating on a new compact line of the Plymouth Barracuda and

Doug Thorley's Chevy 2 Much Chevy II first hit the strip running an alcohol-injected 396-ci Chevrolet engine with Porcupine cylinder heads. The lightweight Chevy II tipped the scales at a racing weight of 2,100 pounds. Doug managed to lay down ETs in the high 9s with speeds above 150 mph, which at the time was believed to be the first car with a manual 4-speed to run higher than 150 mph in the quarter mile.

Emmet "Rattlesnake" Austin from Phenix City, Alabama, ran predominately in the NASCAR drag racing circuit, running an injected Thunderbolt. Austin's Ford *Little Rattler* was powered by a 427-ci Wedge that he ran on gas or fuel and a 4-speed transmission. The Fairlane was well traveled, and Austin used all the scratches and dented body parts to his psychological advantage by intimidating his opponent when he rolled up to the starting line. Austin made a rare West Coast appearance shown here at Fremont. (Photo Courtesy Paul Johnson)

Posting an impressive 67 wins out of the 90 total races, Ronnie Sox and Buddy Martin parked their record-setting A/FX Belvedere in favor of a newer lightweight ride. For the 1966 season, Sox & Martin campaigned this all-new production A-Body Barracuda, which was powered by a fuel-injected, nitro-fed 426 Plymouth Hemi and 4-speed transmission. Sox's fuel-injected fish dominated the 2,400-pound fuel class here at Lions Drag Strip. (Photo Courtesy Paul Johnson)

the Dodge Dart. These lightweights packed with a 426-ci Hemi had faster times and speeds, and the compact age was now in full mode.

Chrysler also reverted to race factory-backed Super Stock and Stocker versions, resembling models that the public could purchase off the showroom floor for street. Dodge and Plymouth teams continued to campaign their older 1965 cars without major changes to the already altered-wheelbase bodies. They concentrated more on updating mechanical developments to engines and chassis before the smaller compacts were available.

Kelly Chadwick was a pioneer drag racer whose passion was fast hot rods, especially for the Chevy-branded cars. His first altered-wheelbase racer was a 1964 Chevelle that he successfully campaigned match racing when he was not teaching school. His second masher was this 1966 Chevy II Wild Thing *prepped by Don Hardy with power from a fuel-injected 427-ci engine that ran on a 90-percent nitro mix.*

Cecil Yother lays down a holeshot against Pee Wee Wallace's Virginian *during eliminations at* Drag Racing *magazine's second annual East versus West Stocker Championships at Lions. Yother's* Melrose Missile VII *went on to capture the number-2 Eliminator title for the "heavier Funny Cars" against Roger Lindamood's* Color Me Gone *Dodge Charger. Yother's ET of 9.53 seconds was good enough to grab the gold when Lindamood shut off early.*

Funny Car drivers, as a group, were more approachable than the dragster racers. Drivers were readily available with the fans, using amusing antics and outrageous behavior to work up the crowds.

One such event, held at "The Giant of the West" Lions Drag Strip, was the first annual *Drag Racing* magazine's East meets West Top 10 Stocker Championships. More than 60 Funny Cars (national and local stars) assembled at one location for the "Super Car Circus."

The race attracted a record crowd of 24,000 fans for the two-day weekend that featured no-holds-barred round-robin match racing with added circus music from a steam-powered calliope. The Saturday afternoon and evening show opened with the East versus West competition. The stars from the East prevailed with five wins over the West's two, and each team split two ties.

A memorable Chevy-versus-Ford match race included Hubert "Huey-Baby" Platt in his *Georgia Shaker* and Dick Harrell in his 427 Chevy II. When they pulled up to the starting line, both drivers jumped out and switched cars. Platt handed Harrell a cigar, climbed up into the packed stands, and said, "This is going to be a great race. I want to watch it."

However, Harrell and Platt switched back to their original cars. Both cars made their burnouts through the rosin to make traction and rolled to the starting line. At the drop of the green, both cars leaped off the line, pulling the front ends 5 feet off the ground! The hysterical crowd went nuts!

Sunday's "Mr. Factory Stock" show featured the 2,500-pound-plus cars running both injectors and superchargers. Gas Ronda, Don Gay, Dick Landy, Roger

Dick Harrell lifts the wheels at Lions, competing at Drag Racing *magazine's Funny Car Championships. The Bill Thomas Race Cars/Nickey Chevrolet entry was one of the strongest Chevrolet-powered Funny Cars from the state of Missouri. (Photo Courtesy Paul Johnson)*

In November 1966, the nation's finest Funny Cars and drivers convened at Lions Drag Strip for the second annual Drag Racing Magazine East versus West Stocker Championships. The two-day event attracted 24,000 fans with more than 60 Funny Cars attempting to win large amounts of cash and trophies. The big winner from all the injected participants in this quarter-mile spectacular was Hayden Proffitt. Proffitt's Corvair posted two straight match race wins on Saturday and won rounds on Sunday that led up to the finals for the "Mr. Factory Stock" Eliminator title. Proffitt met Gas Ronda for the winner-take-all match, but the race did not go as planned when Ronda's SOHC Mustang would not fire. Proffitt did not deny the spectators the single run, so he closed out the meet with a humongous wheel-stand that brought all four wheels off the ground as he covered the quarter mile and waved to the crowd.

Funny Car legends Lew Arrington, Jim Liberman, Earl Wade, and "Dyno" Don Nicholson stand in the back and are focused on the performance of independent match racer Arnie Beswick at Lions Drag Strip. The Morrison, Illinois, resident proved he could compete against the top factory-backed cars, achieving maximum success with this 1966 blown GTO. Beswick has always been acknowledged as one of the top few Pontiac racers who ran several engine combinations that cashed in on the big payouts on the Factory Experimental circuit. Beswick squeezed out the power and torque from a stock bore and stroke 428-ci Pontiac engine.

Jim Liberman handled driving and tuning duties for both the Brutus GTO of Lew Arrington and his blown Chevy II Nova. Liberman recorded three consecutive wins driving his Chevy II over Clyde Morgan's Vicious Vette, the Hairy Canary, and Mac Young's Thweatt's Automotive Plymouth at the Cavalcade of Funny Cars round-robin extravaganza at Lions. (Photo Courtesy Paul Johnson)

Designed and built by the AMT Corporation's Custom Equipment and Speed Division in Phoenix, Arizona, the Piranha was one of the most unique Funny Cars of its time. Don Beebe, general manager of race car promotions for AMT, along with design director and custom car stylist Gene Winfield oversaw the operations. The two-piece body was molded from a new compact, lightweight, and rugged plastic material called Marbon Cycolac. Fred Smith, a former craftsman for Don Garlits and Dick Branstner, constructed the 4130 chrome-moly frame that had a 120-inch wheelbase. Joe Anahory built and maintained the 1958 Chrysler 392 Hemi with assistance from Jim Johnson. Top Gas star Walt Stevens compiled several ETs in the 8.20s and 8.30s with top speeds of more than 190 mph. When asked how the fish handled at speed, Stevens replied, "It drove and handled like a Cadillac." Stevens and Anahory toured the Piranha for six months before their contracts expired. The car ended up in the capable hands of Don Cook and Connie Swingle for a short period of time.

"Jungle" Jim Liberman cracks the throttle in the Brutus GTO before meeting Hubert Platt at the second annual Drag Racing Magazine Funny Car Fuel Fest at Lions. Modifications to the GTO involved moving the engine back to the firewall to gain better weight balance and increased traction and handling. Unfortunately for Liberman, Platt took down Brutus with a strong 8.69 to Liberman's losing 10.51.

Paul Perry made his maiden pass of the Perry Brothers' new altered wheelbase Ford Mustang that used an unusual combination of blown Pontiac power mated into the Mustang. The Mustang showed promise, but the new-car blues resulted in subpar performances for the Perry Brothers' Orion Ford. (Photo Courtesy Steve Reyes)

Wolford's *Secret Weapon* Jeep, Hayden Proffitt, "Jungle" Jim Liberman (driving both his Chevy II and Lew Arrington's *Brutus* GTO), Arnie "the Farmer" Beswick, the AMT *Piranha*, and dozens more kept the fans on their feet all day long.

The Flip Top Arrives

Many felt the A/FX stocker scene hit the stagnant stage on advancements to the car, so many looked to Michigan for new ideas and answers. Detroit had been well known all over the world throughout the 1960s for mass-producing cars, which now turned to mass producing a Funny Car with many new performance and safety changes for the new 1966 drag racing season.

Mercury once again took charge of what the future could hold for the Funny Car. During a directors meeting of the racing board, an engineer used a box of stick

Mercury and the Logghe Stamping Company introduced the lightweight tube-style chassis and one-piece fiberglass body to the Funny Car wars. "Dyno" Don Nicholson's tangerine-colored Eliminator I Comet was powered by a Mercury 427 SOHC-injected motor fitted with a Ford aluminum 4-speed transmission. Nicholson ran a time of 8.50 here at Irwindale during an AHRA meet, but when he entered the lights, the body blew off and exited the chassis. Nicholson got the car to stop without serious injuries, but the fiberglass body was damaged beyond repair and was quickly confiscated by the attending Mercury officials. The Mercury folks, not wanting to give away their secrets, broke up all of the body pieces, placed them in piles, set them all on fire, and burned them into mounds of melted fiberglass. (Photo Courtesy Paul Johnson)

matches and a plastic model car kit he brought to demonstrate the idea of a lightweight frame–style chassis with the model body resting over the entire wooden frame. The idea was unanimously approved for the Mercury Division to design and build a series of top-secret prototypes.

Logghe Chassis

Brothers Ron and Gene Logghe and Jay Howell, general manager of the Logghe Stamping Company of Fraser, Michigan, were commissioned by Lincoln-Mercury to build a fleet of three stock-appearing Comet Cyclones with a dragster-style, three-chrome-moly-tube-style chassis built with a looped-style roll cage that wrapped around the back behind the driver.

The combined weight of the chassis and engine was 1,380 pounds right out the door. When fully loaded, the scale tipped between 2,200 and 2,300 pounds. The one-piece fiberglass bodies were supported with five fiberglass plywood beams to strengthen the 250-pound body that arched back on the rear frame support rails, which allowed driver access in and out and maintenance on the engines. The bodies were anchored down in the front with a sliding rod through pins and were released by a lever. The Comet shells were also completely removable from the chassis in a matter of a few seconds.

The first two cars went to Mercury teammates "Dyno" Don Nicholson of Atlanta, Georgia, and "Fast" Eddie Schartman out of Ohio. Both ran fuel-injected, 427-ci SOHC engines. A third unit went to the first S/FX Californian exhibition driver Jack Chrisman, while the fourth Cyclone landed in the capable hands of Ron Leslie and Bill Kenz.

All four cars were identically built with four-wheel coilover shocks and oversized rear disc brakes. Each driver had the option to run an experimental 2-speed automatic, an aluminum BorgWarner T-10, or Ford 4-speed manual transmissions.

Only Jack Chrisman's car differed from the other three Comets. Chrisman's car was fitted with a topless Cyclone Comet body and ran a supercharged 427-ci Mercury Cammer engine. Chrisman's supercharged Comet ran the larger dragster-type drag slicks with relatively high tire pressure and wider rims. The car ran a high gear–only unit that relied on spinning the larger tires that maintained higher engine RPM off the starting line.

Chrisman was now a serious player in Funny Car, whereas the earlier Comet was just a loud exhibition vehicle that mutilated the rear tires, billowing smoke that drew the attention of spectators. In the early stages of testing, Mercury's captain "Dyno" Don ran nearly 1 second quicker and 15 mph faster than his previous 1965 Comet model! These were the men and cars that changed the face of drag racing.

The Funny Car Parade

With the introduction of the full-frame, tube-type chassis that created a bold new Funny Car breed, rival teams scrambled to bring out their own modern, lighter cars to keep up with the new technology. Tube frames for Funny Cars seemed to be the item of the day. When the Ramchargers ordered a new car, everyone else who raced a stock-bodied machine noticed and followed that route.

The major factors for the new style were safety and costs—along with the fact that they were comparatively easier to work on. Altering a standard production car was time-consuming and very expensive. There was so much that could be done with these modifications and not obtain satisfactory results.

The Logghe Stamping Company was now the leader in the industry for building cars, but the company was quickly overloaded. It wound up backlogged with countless orders and fell behind the demand. As with the California Gold Rush of 1847, new fabrication shops opened throughout the country to accommodate orders from the new wave of customers.

Dave Arlasky and Bob Chapman of Chapman Auto-motive in Chicago; Don Hardy in Floydada, Texas; Ron Scrima and Pat Foster of Exhibition Engineering; T-Bar Engineering; and Dick Fletcher Race Cars in Southern California were just a handful that jumped into the fire. They picked up the slack and produced high-quality products.

Fiberglass manufacturers and operators that were only producing individual body components were now building one-piece American production bodies. Along with the new pony cars built out of Detroit and hitting the showrooms, there were replica bodies of GM's Camaro, Corvairs, and Firebirds; Ford's Mustang; Mercury's Cougars; and AMC's Rebels!

The NHRA Finally Allows Funny Cars

During the time of radical changes in Funny Car, Wally Parks, the pioneering NHRA president, had heard enough of the "this is unfair to Funny Cars" cries and decided that it was time for a change. So, in the spring of 1966, he pushed through a plan for six Experimental Stock classes that would run at every NHRA event throughout the nation, including all four national events.

The breakdown for the new classes was simple. The top class S/XS was for blown cars. A/XS had a minimum weight requirement of 2,000 pounds, unlimited engine displacement, injectors but no blowers, and allowed any fuel use. The B/XS class had a minimum weight of 2,600 pounds, a maximum engine displacement 430 ci,

Jack Chrisman's topless Kendall GT-1 Mercury was the talk of the competition at the third annual Hot Rod Magazine Championships at Riverside. The factory-backed, Logghe-built 4130 chrome-moly tubular chassis roadster was well ahead of its time, being the only 1966 Funny Car running a one-piece fiberglass roofless body. Although two of his other Mercury teammates were already in action with their flip-top injected Funny Cars, the GT-1 Super Cyclone was the first to run a supercharger on top of the 427-ci SOHC Mercury engine prepped by fellow Mercury Funny Car owner/operator Dee Keaton. In Sunday's eliminations at Riverside, Chrisman rocketed to a 180-mph pass in the money run, defeating Jim Liberman's Brutus GTO in the Exhibition Stock class. A few months later at the prestigious Super Stock magazine Nationals at New York National Speedway, Chrisman was under full power when the engine exploded midtrack. The chute did not deploy, which caused brake failure and the car to run off track and catch fire. It stopped in a grove a trees. The car was destroyed.

"Fast" Eddie Schartman's factory-backed flip-top Mercury Comet dominated the match race trail and major NHRA National events. At the 1966 NHRA Nationals, Schartman, the hired gun for Mercury, defeated several blown Funny Cars in competition. Roy Steffey tuned the injected 427-ci SOHC engine to a low ET of 8.28 at 174 mph in the final round to put away teammate and rival "Dyno" Don Nicholson. The 1966 S/SX champion, Schartman, sports his bright yellow Automotive Research colors in the shutoff area at Irwindale.

injectors, and was gasoline only. The remaining classes were C/XS, D/SX, and E/SX, each of which used higher minimum weights but the same maximum 430-ci engine displacement and allowed carbs only. These new classes were received well by the racers and were quickly filled at every national event. Funny Cars finally got the recognition they deserved.

1966 US Nationals

The NHRA's most prestigious drag racing event of the year happens every Labor Day weekend in Indianapolis, Indiana. It is dubbed the US Nationals. At the 12th

Gary Dyer's racing career spanned more than 10 years before he climbed behind the wheel of a fuel Funny Car. His first driving venture was in a 1956 Chevy at his local track, and he made treks to Union Grove, Wisconsin; US 30 in Gary, Indiana; and Oswego, Illinois. Dyer continued climbing the ladder, driving a B/Gas Supercharged Chevy-powered Ford coupe he built to a 1964 427 high-riser Mercury Comet owned by Ed Rachanski, known as the **Marauders.** *This paved the way for Dyer to be a successful match racer. Dyer met Norm Kraus of Mr. Norm fame at the Summernationals and formed a new partnership with the Chicago magnate. Shown here at Lions Drag Strip, Norm primes the injectors as Dyer brings the Hemi Charger to life at* Drag Racing *magazine's Funny Car Championships. (Photo Courtesy Paul Johnson)*

George Weiler designed and fabricated one of the strongest Dodge Darts on the racing scene, The Honker, *for Bud Faubel. Faubel was not a skilled professional drag racer; he was the vice president of Shively Motors, a Dodge Dealership centered in Faubel's hometown of Chambersburg, Pennsylvania. The Honker was powered by a Hilborn fuel injected 426 Dodge Hemi with a Torque-Flite transmission sending power to the rear end. The Faubel-Weiler Dart stopped the speed traps, recording 8.70s/170-mph blasts. (Photo Courtesy Paul Johnson)*

The intense concentration on the Christmas tree seen in the eyes of Al Vanderwoude shows how match racing was a serious business. The Flying Dutchman *Dodge Dart* was one of the few roofless rides in Funny Cars where the early-type zoomie-style headers blasted nitro fumes next to the face of Vanderwoude.

The Charge-a-car IV *of John Flesher was the strongest A/FX Chevy II running out of the Pacific Northwest. It was powered by an injected Z11 409-ci Chevrolet linked up to a direct-drive unit. (Photo Courtesy Steve Reyes)*

Gene Loflin's injected A/FX Falcon unloads off the tarmac at Salinas Drag Strip, otherwise known as the Salinas Municipal Airport. The San Jose–based Ford was backed by Holiday Ford in Sunnyvale, California, and claimed the title of "The Greatest." (Photo Courtesy Steve Reyes)

The B/XS 466 Final Solution *Corvette Funny Car digs in at Puyallup International Dragway located in western Washington. The picturesque dragway attracted the big names of touring Funny Cars, including Roland Leong's* Hawaiian, *Don Prudhomme, Tom McEwen, Harry Schmidt, and a cast of others. Puyallup's stellar history ended when the track closed its gates for good in the fall of 1978. (Photo Courtesy Steve Reyes)*

GM A-Bodied Chevys and Pontiacs were common in the A/FX and early Funny Car classes, but to see either an Oldsmobile Cutlass or a Buick Skylark was a rare sight racing down the strip. Dick's Speed Center of Yreka, California, sponsored one of the coolest A/Factory Experimentals: a 1965 Buick Skylark running a massive 430-ci Buick. The Skylark raced throughout the Pacific Northwest, including this instance at Puyallup Dragway. (Photo Courtesy Steve Reyes)

annual NHRA Nationals, the new Funny Car Experimental classes debuted and were the "greatest show on earth" in drag racing. Although the AA/Fuelers satisfied the Indy diehards, it was those wild and furious Funny Cars that captured the multitudes of spectators. Fans stood and cheered loudly when they caught glimpses of the altered-wheelbase giants as they rolled out of the staging lanes.

Right out of the gate, the X/SX class stole the show during qualifying. The Logghe Mercury Comets of Nicholson, Schartman and Steffey, and Kenz and Leslie controlled the top spots when Atlanta's Don Nicholson ripped off an unreal ET of 8.31 at 174 mph to the crowd's delight. Entered in the S/XS class was every big-name supercharged Funny Car on the premises.

Sunday's S/FX class eliminations were one of the weekend meet's high points with both blown and injected cars running against each other for the title. When the smoke cleared, the last two cars remaining were the two Factory Comet rivals: "Fast" Eddie Schartman and "Dyno" Don Nicholson. When the cars cleared the top end, the win light went to Schartman and Steffey with low ET of the meet (8.28 at 174 mph). "Dyno" Don ran a slower ET of 9.29 at 112.50 mph due to two dead cylinders.

The A/XS class of the heavier unblown cars also captured the crowds with the likes of Charlie Allen, Bill Lawton, Hubert Platt, Sox & Martin, Hans Anderson, Preston Honea, Don Schumacher, Tommy Grove, Dave Strickler, and Gas Ronda.

In the trophy run, it was Bill Lawton versus Sox & Martin's Barracuda. Sox cut the tree a little too close and red-lighted, which gave Lawton's Tasca Ford Mustang the win.

Both Schartman and Lawton continued to compete in the Competition Eliminator bracket, where the other 15 class winners competed as well. At the end of the day, which was the final go in Competition Eliminator, it was the Funny Car of Gene Snow defeating Greg Gibson's B/Dragster. Snow's 2,180-pound, fuel-burning 426 Hemi Dodge Dart ran in the C/FD class, where he edged the D/D and C/A class winners.

Logghe Cars Are the Ones to Beat

The NHRA World Championship Series finale was at the Southwest Raceway in Tulsa, Oklahoma. This event was considered the highest point of 1966, and the NHRA allowed Funny Cars to run the S/XS runoffs, dubbed the Funny Car Finals.

No longer "funny" in appearance or performance, these Funny Cars laid down incredible numbers and impressive runs. They put together one of the most stellar shows during the event. Eddie Schartman (S/SX) and Hubert Platt (A/SX) both recorded national speed and ET records in a Comet and Mustang, respectively.

History repeated itself when both US Indy finalists met once again in the final round in S/XS Eliminator, and Eddie Schartman and Don Nicholson gave the fans quite a show. Both cars left evenly, but once again "Fast" Eddie stung "Dyno" Don with the win, turning an ET of 8.38 at 174.08 mph to an out-of-shape 10.60 at 80 mph. Funny Cars were the hot ticket and on the rise.

Fall West Coast Races

The largest one-day dragster event of the year took place on November 12, 1966, when Lions hosted Mickey Thompson's 200-mph dragster show with 48 dragsters running in the first round. On the same day, 35 miles north of Lions, Irwindale Raceway hosted the "All Funny

One of the strong runners from the Pacific Northwest was the candy apple Pagan Gold 1966 GTO sponsored by Dick Lewis Pontiac/Cadillac in Olympia, Washington. The massive 499-ci Pontiac mill was wrenched on by Bill Crow and featured Hilborn fuel injection, Vertex mags, and a TorqueFlite transmission. Weighing in at 2,500 pounds, the fiberglass GTO Tiger ran in the low 10s with speeds of 130 mph. (Photo Courtesy Steve Reyes)

Many relatively unknown cars showed up at the strip, made a few runs, and left, not to be seen or raced again. This could hold true with this steel-bodied Dodge Polara Funny Car that belonged to McCubbin and Guynn out of Northern California. They were a mystery of sorts, being unknowns who ran only a few races. Ace photographer and journalist Steve Reyes recalled seeing the Polara only once in this instance at Fremont. (Photo Courtesy Steve Reyes)

Pete Seaton's first Funny Car, a 1965 Chevy Chevelle, ran an injected 396-ci engine on a stout dosage of nitro. Delmar Heinelt handled the driving along with maintaining the tune-ups on the big-block Chevrolet. While the car had adequate power, the Chevelle produced excessive torque for the non-fortified stock chassis that would buckle under load, often lifting three of the four wheels off the ground.

Car Spectacular Meet." Irwindale outdrew the largest all-fuel dragster meet of the year with a record 11,000 people to the estimated Lions crowd of 8,000 spectators!

In the spring of 1967, several so-called experts wondered if the Funny Car honeymoon was through and the Funnies were falling their way out of favor at the strip. However, they soon realized how wrong their predictions were. Both local NHRA and AHRA tracks reaped rewards with record crowds returning to see their favorite Funny Cars from coast to coast.

Although everything looked great on paper, concerns mounted with safety and higher costs to race and maintain Funny Cars. The typical weekend Funny Car racer who punched the clock 40 hours a week working a full-time job and (if offered) grabbed as much overtime as possible was supporting the family. Whatever was left over went into his race car.

Working on the race car nightly often led to hours past the midnight hour with coworkers, old-school pals, and neighbors who shared the same interests. Many racers formed partnerships to offset the cost and

Money in exhibition racing was at an all-time high. Maynard Rupp jumped out of the Prussian *Top Fuel dragster and into the Gratiot Auto Supply* Chevoom *mid-engine Hemi-powered 1966 Chevelle. The tube chassis and suspension were more designed for an altered than a Funny Car with the rear end repositioned back nearly to the rear bumper. The front suspension was modified heavily by Logghe (not for performing wheel-stands). The 56 354-ci Chrysler Hemi was fitted with an Enderle "bug catcher" mounted atop a GMC 6-71 supercharger that was running a 27-percent overdrive. The engine was relocated behind the driver and mounted directly to a Mopar rear end. The* Car Craft *project car was sprayed with a striking yellow lacquer paint over the replica fiberglass SS 396.*

Originally built to compete in the A/Modified Sport (AMSP) class, Charlie Wilson stepped into the Funny Car class with driver Clyde Morgan in the Vicious Vette. Wilson purchased the brand-new 1960 Corvette off the showroom floor and tore it down. Then, he made extensive modifications and refinements to the frame and body. Chevrolet did not offer factory race-ready motors, so Wilson approached Bones Balogh of Isky Cams to build a stock bore and stroke 427 ci for the roadster. Right out of the gate, Morgan recorded 9.15-second ET at 158 mph in the quarter mile.

Service station owner Bill Taylor of Memphis, Tennessee, became fed up with his daily routine of tuning and servicing customers cars, so he visited the local drag strip to find out what all the noise was about in Funny Car racing. He liked it so much that he contacted Albright Chassis Shop to build him a tube chassis to fit with a 1966 steel-bodied Plymouth Barracuda body that was channeled 10 inches to lower wind resistance. The Kingfish was powered by a 426-ci Hemi engine that was built using the stock crankshaft and rods, Mickey Thompson pistons and intake manifold, a GMC 6-71 supercharger, and an Enderle injection system. Running on a 35-percent dose of nitro in both CCF/d and match racing, the Barracuda turned in an 8.90 ET and 163.74 mph top speed with driver Larry Reyes. (Photo Courtesy Paul Johnson)

Match racing was racing either with a handicap start or heads-up racing. It was exciting for the fans to watch a big-block blown nitro car square off with the lighter, fuel-injected Funny Car. No one could predict the outcome, but the blown big-block Blue Hell 1963 Corvette of Runyan and Grissom matched up well in a best-of-three encounter with the "All American Boy" Charlie Allen at Irwindale Raceway.

Arnie Beswick launches off the line at Irwindale Raceway in his infamous 1963 Pontiac LeMans, The Tameless Tiger. The Ford and Chrysler factory-backed Funny Car teams had unlimited cash and parts resources pouring into their programs. Independent racers, such as Beswick, spent their own money match racing with fabricated and out-dated parts. Several independents formed volunteer pickup crews on race day, which were paid with burgers, hot dogs, soda, and fries. Constant 9.20 passes at 140 mph thrilled the crowds, which was ideal for match race competition. When Beswick was not racing, he was back home in Morrison, Illinois, caring for his 200-acre farm and raising corn.

The heartbeat of Farmer's Tempest was a basic 1963 Pontiac Super Duty 421 Pontiac that was equipped with a 1963 Super Duty crankshaft, NASCAR racing heads, Mickey Thompson rods, Forged True reverse-deflector pistons, and a 6-71 blower that pulled a large amount of horsepower from an engine that was never designed to produce those high numbers.

ease tensions at home. It's not an exaggeration for these weekend warriors to spend $500 to $1,000 to make quality runs and make it into a show without serious breakage of parts and damage to the car in an attempt to collect a high-dollar payout.

Match Racing

The "battle of the stock-bodied cars," the "match race bashers," or the "run what you brung" stockers were the headliners at any drag strip. Compared to rival wrestlers on the TV, fierce competitors took their aggressions to the strip to kick their opponents' tails. Drivers often collaborated with each other to discuss the common problems or strategies that arose during their sets.

Ford versus Mopar alone made top billing at any track from early days in the A/FX and S/X classes. Local radio blasted over the airwaves, promoting the best of three or best of five match races with the likes of "Dandy" Dick Landy's fuel-burning, trick Hemi Dodge versus old time rival Gas Ronda in his super trick, lightweight Mustang. These jingles helped pack the stands with fans who supported their favorites by predicting a good beating and yelling, "He'll blow their doors off!"

Both drivers and their mechanics spread around powdered rosin to gain traction before each match. On one occasion, extreme rivals exchanged heated words, pointing fingers, accusing one another of cheating, which led to fisticuffs around the starting line. Even the fans in the stands backed their favorite driver and joined in

"The quickest gun in the West," Joe Davis, ran one of California's most resilient A/FX Funny Cars with his Colt 45 Mustang. Davis, from San Francisco, recorded numerous wins on the match race circuit throughout the West scene. He defeated some of the East's biggest guns, including Arnie Beswick, "Dyno" Don Nicholson, and "Fast" Eddie Schartman. (Photo Courtesy Steve Reyes)

Irwindale Raceway's creative advertising department provided some wild and luring handbills for upcoming racing, including this highlighted "Battle of the Stock-Bodied Cars" advertisement, which featured match races between Plymouth, Dodge, Pontiac, and Ford Funny Cars. It was a fan's paradise at Irwindale with additional fuel cars, stockers, and sporty cars running on the same card.

A/Gas Supercharged Italian legends Joe and Frankie Pisano made the switch to Funny Car. Joe Pisano, owner of the Venolia Piston Company and a seasoned Bonneville competitor, selected brother Frankie to pilot the 2,400-pound match racer powered by a supercharged Chevrolet 427-ci engine. Don Long built the frame with a dropped axle, while Fiberglass Trends added the nose and rear deck to the all-steel Fisher body. The Camaro recorded quarter-mile runs in the low 8-second, 170-mph range.

Ted DeTar and his Chrysler Hemi-powered Kansas Badman *Ford Falcon made a strong charge in the 2,400-pound Funny Car class at the 1966 AHRA Winternationals at Beeline. DeTar advanced to the semifinals where he lost to Charlie Allen's Dodge Dart.*

the melee, brawling in the stands before their first race. Reputations were made from these performances, and that's what made Funny Car match racing the top choice at the strip.

With many new teams, new drivers, and new cars arriving on the scene, Chrysler decided to ease back, building fewer FX-type match race cars for 1966. The Dodge and Plymouth teams continued to campaign their older 1965 cars with fewer changes to the already altered-wheelbase bodies. They concentrated more on updating mechanical developments to engines and chassis.

The match racing circuit continued to get hotter and wilder with more independent cars raising the levels in competition. During the long summer touring months, racers did not see their families for months. To keep up with the demand, teams hired agencies to handle booking the tracks and hotels, purchasing advertising, and making public appearances. Funny Car racing was a full-fledged business, as drivers and owners made decent livings with increased appearance and contingency awards along with higher cash payouts for winning the event. The life of a Funny Car racer was not extremely glamorous, and being out on the road during the hottest months of the year came at a steeper price as well.

West Coast racers zigzagged thousands of miles across the country, stopping at smaller venues to meet travel expenses just before getting to the meat of the bone of

Jim Hammons and his son Rich teamed with Don Williamson to create the Hairy Canary, which was a one-of-a-kind Chrysler-powered Valiant Funny Car. Goodies Speed Shop in San Jose sponsored the team. It took five months to build the car and cost of nearly $7,000. It produced runs in the 8.60-second, 170-mph range on a constant basis. Williamson was responsible for providing the power from the 1957 392-ci Hemi that featured Mondello heads, an Engle cam, and Venolia pistons and rings. An Art Carr Torque-Flite transmission transmitted power to the Oldsmobile rear end. The complete car weighed in at 2,250 pounds.

Don Kirby always held a special love for Corvettes, especially the topless models, including this 1967 roadster that was built at Exhibition Engineering by Ronnie Scrima, Pat Foster, and Kirby himself. Competition Fiberglass built the lightweight body, and Tom Hanna fabricated the aluminum work. Keeping the engine Funny-Car legal, Kirby used a stock-displacement 427-ci Chevy engine with Mickey Thompson rods and pistons, a 6-71 GMC supercharger, and a reworked B&M Hydro transmission. Driver Pat Foster put the Corvette through its paces, turning speeds around 200 mph.

Dee Keaton was a 10-year veteran in the stock car ranks with hands-on experience in the Funny Car field. Keaton spent time as a chief mechanic on Jack Chrisman's fuel 1965 Comet, partnered with Doug Thorley on the Chevy II Much Chevy II, did a stint behind the wheel of the Peanuts LTD Ford, and owned and drove a 1965 blown Wedge Comet. After Chrisman suffered a fire and chassis damage to the roadster, Keaton sold Chrisman back his Comet and built a new one-piece 1967 Comet body with the chassis built by Dick Fletcher. Keaton added an unblown and injected OHC Mercury 427 engine coupled to an Art Carr C-6 Merc-o-matic transmission. Don Kirby applied the colorful green and silver metalflake paint. Keaton racked up speeds of 170-plus with 8.70 ETs that outran the factory-backed racers.

Mercury standout Dee Keaton was a tough competitor from Southern California. He not only could squeeze the most power out of a SOHC Cammer but also drove the wheels off a fiberglass flier as well. Keaton purchased Don Nicholson's A/FX Comet and campaigned the Mercury on the match race circuit but later hired Dick Fletcher to build a series of lightweight Mercury Comets and Cougar floppers.

a grueling schedule. They were match racing five to six times during the week and on weekends at various tracks in various states (or crossing international borders), driving hundreds to thousands of miles to keep commitments and earn the big bucks.

Life on the road was not glamorous and often stressful. After a typical night of three rounds of match racing, these nomads quickly loaded the car on to the trailer, grabbed the toolboxes, and headed over to the office to collect the payout. Driving overnight was routine when heading to the next destination, pounding the interstate highways throughout several states with little or no time to pull off the road to stretch, eat nutritious meals, or sleep.

Free time included brief stops at gas stations to refuel the rig and grab snack food and then departing to meet their obligations for the next day of racing. Transporters occasionally broke down, causing a headliner or team to show up late or fail to appear. Then, the money was forfeited, and the threat of a possible riot from angry fans kept track operators on edge.

The touring season ran from April to September and concluded right after the NHRA Indy Nationals on Labor Day weekend. Many racers did not see their families for months at a time while out on the road and often missed birthdays, graduations, and anniversaries.

Al Vanderwoude was one of the most respected and toughest competitors who ran without any factory support. Ted Brown built Vanderwoude's match racer Flying Dutchman *Dodge Dart with a blown 1957 392 Hemi under the hood. The Art Carr TorqueFlite transmission transferred power to the rear wheels, which resulted in 8.00-second, 185-mph blasts against his opponents.*

Dave and Suzy Koffel's Flintstone Flyer *was the one to beat on the NASCAR Drag Racing circuit. The chassis and paint were done by Ron Tietze, and all the engineering was performed by Koffel, who was a metallurgist by trade. The* Flyer *ran a gas-burning late 426-ci Hemi with Hilborn injectors. Driver Gale Mortimer piloted the SUS1 Barracuda, where it turned out constant 9-second, 150-mph-plus runs on the injected circuit.*

Drag racing's great Gasser pioneers, Fred Stone, Tim Woods, and Doug Cook, parked their famous match racing A/Gas Supercharged 1940 Willys and entered into the Funny Car wars with their 1966 Dark Horse *Ford Mustang. Exhibition Engineering's Ronnie Scrima and Pat Foster built the lightweight tubular frame. A massive 448-ci 1958 Chrysler Hemi provided the horsepower. Cal Automotive provided the fiberglass components, including doors and the one-piece stretched front end, while Junior of Los Angeles applied the correct candy blue and gold colors of the fabled Willys Gasser. Late in 1967, while on tour in Alton, Illinois, the team attached an experimental rear spoiler that brought the nose up in the air at 180 mph and made the car flip several times, destroying it. Driver Doug Cook suffer multiple broken bones, which ended his driving career. Driver Ron O'Donnell is shown here in the* Dark Horse 2 *Hemi-powered Mustang.*

Misfit Oddballs of the Quarter Mile

When the new Funny Car procession marched down the nation's drag strips in record droves, only a few of the originals were still in contention, and those that did lagged to keep up with the modern scene. At the end of 1966 racing season and the years leading into the 1970s, Southern California became the pinnacle of the creative generation in Funny Cars.

Imaginations ramped up with some of the most unusual home and professionally built creations that ran down a drag strip. These contraptions ranged widely from military-themed Jeeps, Jaguar XKEs, a Ford Bronco truck, Volkswagen Bugs, several roofless models, exotic Gran Turismo Rallyes, and a steel-bodied flip-top Cadillac Eldorado. These were defined as being true misfit Funny Cars!

Jeeps Storm the Strip

The Jeeps were not close to resembling their stock counterparts off the assembly line. They were modified with stretched wheelbases, the driver's position was cen-tered in the back seat, and the motor sat repositioned through the dashboard.

Jeeps were highly unpredictable with the handling aspects of staying straight while powering down the track. One of the strongest running Jeeps, the *Secret Weapon,* belonged to both "Private" Ed Lenarth and driver "Five-Star General" Roger Wolford. A 392 Chrysler Hemi powered the 1,200-hp army-themed command car.

Another strong-running Jeep from Southern California belonged to Gene "Conway" Ciambella nicknamed the *Destroyer.* The body was narrowed, the driver and roll cage sat up higher in the body, and it had a front snow-plow-styled front spoiler and was a battleship gray color. Both cars put the fans in a frenzy watching how loose they could travel down the quarter mile.

Mustang Misfit

Junior Brogdon's *Phony Pony* was more of a sling-shot dragster than a member of the Funny Car group. The stretched, narrow body of a replica Mustang ran a

The US Army–themed Secret Weapon *Jeep of "Private" Ed Lenarth and driver "Five-Star General" Roger Wolford took no prisoners with the force from the 1,200-hp-plus 392 Chrysler Hemi.*

The US Navy's answer to the Lenarth and Wolford's Secret Weapon *was the battleship grey Jeep* Destroyer *owned and driven by "Admiral" Gene Conway Ciambella. Conway ran nearly the same components in the powertrain, but unlike the Army command car of Wolford, the Jeep featured more pronounced body modifications.*

The Super Mustang

When Mercury's top three match racers set many ET and top-speed records in the 1966 season, all indications pointed for a repeat performance for 1967. So, the top engineers at Ford brought a new idea to the quarter mile with a streamlined wedge Super Mustang. The futuristic Mustang was designed by the styling department at Ford as a concept car that crossbred dragster/Funny Car technology wrapped in a sleek fiberglass shell.

The Logghe Stamping Company built the frame that held the fuel-injected 427 SOHC motor. The engineers predicted speeds at or around the 200-mph range. However, disappointment set in after the top speed in the wind tunnel maxed out at 125 mph. The car was completed in late 1966 and trailered to Florida for testing by another Ford standout, Connie Kalitta, without the body. Tom McEwen was the selected driver, but the highly touted Mustang fulfilled its potential and quietly went away.

When Mercury debuted its trendsetting flip-top Comets in 1966, the top styling engineers at Ford went to the drawing board for a better idea to get higher speeds and lower times. It's how the concept of the Super Mustang *became a reality! Not fully classified as a Funny Car or a dragster, the innovative Mustang had a sleek fiberglass body attached to the Logghe-built frame that concealed a fuel-injected 427 SOHC motor. Driver Tom McEwen accelerates off the line at Pomona during initial shakedown runs under the watchful eyes of Ford's top racing executives. Although the concept behind the highly touted Mustang was to change drag racing, it never lived up to its potential and faded from public view. (Photo Courtesy Paul Johnson)*

Junior Brogdon's Phony Pony *was one of the wildest match racers that ever hit the strip. Speed Products Engineering built the digger-style chassis to fit either one (nitro supercharged) of two fuel-injected small-block Ford 289-ci engines. Cal Body designed and built the stretched and narrowed Mustang body.*

small-block 289-ci Ford engine, but on occasion, he doubled up with twin-injected 289s. Both engines mostly ran fuel injection, but at times, Junior switched out one 289 with either carbureted or blown.

Mopar Madness

Service station owner Pete Everett built an unusual but competitive Funny Car, the *Half Breed,* out of Southern California. The roofless half Dodge and half Plymouth creation ran a blown 426-ci Hemi and had Dr. Leroy Hales behind the wheel.

Cruisin' Caddy

The candidate for the most unusual and heaviest Funny Car ever built belonged to Dave Zachery. The "world's fastest" Cadillac Eldorado (shell) was all steel and ran a 500-ci injected Chevrolet engine. These unconventional and slightly strange cars ran mostly at the local tracks match racing but were rarely considered a competitive powerhouse.

Most of these cars were banned by the NHRA to complete in class eliminations at any national event. They could only make exhibition runs. Donnie Hampton's *Too Bad* Corvette ran a pair of side-by-side blown Chevy small-blocks mounted at 45-degree angles with one set forward and one set rearward. Hampton attached two 4-71 blowers with two-port Hilborn injectors.

Pete Everett eyes his driver, "Doc" Leroy Hale, heating up the big Goodyears on Everett's Half Breed *roadster at Irwindale Raceway. One of the most unique Funny Cars ever to hit on the strip was the combination of a Dodge front end mated to the back half of a 1962 Plymouth, running without a roof. Originally running as a B/Gasser with an injected Wedge engine, Everett swapped out the Wedge and replaced it with an early Hemi, added a blower, and switched over to fuel to compete in Funny Car.*

Heading the category of "one of one" Funny Cars was Dave Zachary with his stock-steel Cadillac Eldorado–bodied flopper. Zachary had a 500-ci injected Chevrolet engine bolted to a B&M Hydro transmission. The Caddy was never a competitive runner in the open fields, but it spent time match racing billed as the World's Fastest Eldorado. *Zachary lost his life when he lost control of the car, crashed into the guardrail, and flipped over, which separated the roll cage from the chassis.*

*The concept that "if one engine is good, two must be better," applies to this Funny Car. Donnie Hampton of Hampton Blowers ran with that idea for his **Too Bad Corvette**, which had with a pair of blown 350-ci small-block Chevrolet engines bored out to 368 ci of pure "Mouse" power. The side-by-side engines were mounted at slight angles with the right engine mounted in reverse so that both crankshafts rotated in the same direction while the power of the left engine was taken from the flywheel to a Crowerglide four-disc clutch setup.*

More Oddities

Hollywood stuntman Tex Collins ran a 1,710-ci, 12-cylinder, 3,500-hp, Allison-powered Mustang for exhibition runs only. Another Collins experiment that once belonged to Jim Lytle Jr. was the *Bad Brawma Bull*, which was a white 3,000 Tudor cab-over truck. Collins made only a few passes at the wheel of the Tudor and successfully made it pass the top end.

Two Were Mild but Three Were Wild

The award for being one of the most ingenious but unusual creations that spectators loved to watch was Tommy Stringfield's *Triple Trouble* all-steel Chevy II. Stringfield packed three potent 367-ci small-block Chevrolet engines that totaled 1,128 ci of pure chaos in the Chevy Nova. The front engine was nearly pure stock fueled with a single Holley carburetor, but the other two healthy fuel-injected motors sat side by side in the back seat behind the driver.

Stringfield crafted three side-by-side Pontiac differentials, and the center unit was used in a conventional way through a 3-speed manual transmission. The other units used a direct-drive unit that was linked through a clutch operative system. It was rumored that Stringfield was conducting test runs on a rural road, got out of shape, and drove the car straight into a ditch, which wrinkled the left front fender. Imagine the look on the towing operator's face when he winched the Nova out of the ditch.

"Hollywood Badman" and "Mr. Cal Automotive" Tex Collins invested $50,000 on one of the wildest Mustang Funny Cars that ever ran down the quarter mile. Without using the conventional power from an eight-piston motor, Collin, a movie stuntman, stuffed a 1,710-ci V-12 Allison engine from a vintage World War II P-51 Mustang into a chassis that he designed and built. Engine modifications included an injector and a supercharger from an Allison-powered P-38 that provided 9½ pounds of boost.

When major sanctioning bodies handed out their prestigious awards, including the one for best engineering, the title went to the all-steel Chevy II *Triple Trouble* of Tommy Stringfield. Stringfield implanted three 367-ci small-block Chevrolet engines into the Nova: one stock version under the front hood and a pair of fuel-injected mills sandwiched side by side behind the driver's bench seat. Handling the Chevy II was compared to controlling a pair of angry bulls!

Stringfield once encountered Eddie Schartman's flip-top Mercury in a best-of-three match race without knowing the outcome. Disappointing performance results of the 2-ton *Trouble* made Stringfield turn to an alternative approach. He pulled out the front engine and one from the back seat along with the multiple rear ends and installed a single differential.

Stringfield radically moved the rear wheels forward

Ford fanatic Doug Nash built one of the wildest match racing machines, the **Bronco Buster**. The Bronco truck was built with the help from the Ford Truck Division. Doug, with assistance from longtime friend Tom Smith, built the all-aluminum 112-inch wheelbase chassis with power by a small-block 289-ci Ford engine with Hilborn fuel injection that thrived on a healthy dose of nitro. The all-fiberglass, two-piece body was designed by Walt Phillips. The rootin' tootin' Bronco was a 1,400-pound lightweight pony that ran in the low 9.20s with speeds that averaged around the 150-mph bracket.

Fred "Shorty" Gendian laid down strong numbers driving his **Shorty Too!** chopped-top Mercury Comet at Irwindale. The A/FX Comet that was formerly "Dyno" Don Nicholson's then Pete Gates's was extensively modified in the interior, which allowed Gendian to drive the powerful Mercury. The Comet retained the injected 427 SOHC engine that was rebuilt by Dave Zeuschel of North Hollywood with both Mercury greats Don Nicholson and Earl Wade making the horsepower adjustments.

Advertising was huge. Promoting drag racing was important in the 1960s, as noted by Don Gay's blown fuel 1966 GTO that appeared on this advertisement for the Shamrock Oil Company in Amarillo, Texas. Shamrock's distributor, Ted Lokey, was a strong supporter from the 1960s at the historic Amarillo Dragway, providing fuel for the blown Funny Car and Dragster groups down to their patented "Cloud Master" gasoline for carbureted stockers.

just behind the front doors and transformed the car into one of the craziest wheel-standers that ever hit the strip. At Rockford/Byron Dragway, Thompson's converted wheel-stander sent the crowd into a frenzy when a lovely young lady was given the ride of her life as she sat calmly on the hood as a hood ornament, traveling down the strip on just the rear wheels!

When the NHRA finally pulled the plug in 1967 for experimental stock, it outlawed Jeeps and trucks from competing at any level in national competition, but they were still able to run at local sanctioned venues. Two West Coast entries (Roger Wolford and Ed Lenarth's *Secret Weapon* and Gene Ciambella's *Destroyer*) were nixed to run only at AHRA national events. Also removed from NHRA competition were cars built with all-aluminum chassis, including Doug Nash's *Bronco Buster*.

Cecil County Drag-O-Way, known as the

When Pete Gates from Wayne, Michigan, started his Funny Car career, he purchased "Dyno" Don Nicholson's 1965 A/FX Comet and converted it from a 4-speed manual transmission to an automatic transmission built by Art Carr. With only a few match races under his belt, Gates entered the 1966 Super Stock Nationals and took care of business by defeating some of the largest names in Funny Car and earning the win in his first major event. For the 1967 season, Pete ordered a new Mercury Comet Funny Car from Logghe that was fitted with a one-piece, all-fiberglass flip top. It was identical to the factory-backed Comets of Eddie Schartman and Don Nicholson. Ron and Gene Logghe built the 117-inch wheelbase chassis that utilized a straight axle with adjustable shocks. An Art Carr C-6 transmission transferred power to the Comet rear end. The SOHC Mercury retained stock displacement of 427 ci and ran on a 90-percent-plus nitro mixture.

Match racing was the bread and butter for both the factory and independents in the early Funny Car days. They drew large crowds and made money for both driver and owner. That money supported the independents, such as Pete Seaton, who took on the factory-backed hot rods, such as the Ramchargers Dodge. Seaton's driver, Delmar Heinelt, recorded low-10-second times in the fuel-burning Chevelle. Heinelt's counterpart, Jim Thornton, an F/X driver and president of the Ramchargers group, was rougher than ever, beating up on the match race competition.

There was little doubt that Fred Goeske could live up to his predecessor, Tom McEwen, in the Hemi 'Cuda. Goeske's first pass in the 'Cuda netted a top speed of 181.08 mph in defeating Dale Armstrong in this special match race at Irwindale. The Hemi 'Cuda was one of the earliest successful rear-engine Funny Cars that made frequent visits to the winner's circle.

Former go-kart champion Wendell Shipman was one of several low-buck racers who campaigned a Barracuda Funny Car in Southern California. Shipman was a regular at Lions Drag Strip, Irwindale, and Orange County International Raceway, where both Shipman and engine-builder Frank Pedregon took turns behind the wheel. Wendell eventually drove for "Big" John Mazmanian, Steve Plueger, and Nathan Valdez before hanging up his helmet.

*Gervase O'Neill and brother Johnny owned and operated an auto repair/tune-up shop during the week. However, on the weekends, the brothers were at the drag strip with their **King Rat Corvette**. Gervase drove the **Rat** while Johnny kept the big 427-ci engine in tune, turning low-7-second/170-mph blasts down the quarter mile.*

"Traction Capital of the World" held one of the largest races in the country: the *Super Stock & Drag Illlustrated* (SS&DI) Magazine Nationals. The *SS&DI* event was an independent outlaw event for any S/S through F/X, altered-wheelbase, injected, or blown car that ran on gas or fuel. It was defined as "run what you brung." Coined as the "Woodstock of Racing," future events took place at York US30 Dragway.

The 1967 AHRA Winternationals

The AHRA kicked off its largest winter event, the 1967 Winternationals, at Beeline Drag Strip in Phoenix with the nation's top names in Funny Cars competing in two separate divisions: Unlimited and FX/Fuel. The Unlimited Fuel class featured the new, tube-type lightweights running superchargers and nitro. Entries included Don Gay, Jack Chrisman, Arnie Beswick, and the *Bloomin Bullet* Camaro. Gas Ronda, Dick Loehr, Charlie Allen, Dick Harrell, Bill Lawton, and Ted DeTar were the 2,400-pound FX/Fuel-injected stars.

Jay Howell took on the task of building Pete Seaton's first Chevy Corvair Funny Car at Howells Automotive in Detroit, Michigan. After the competition of the Corvair, test runs were disappointing for the team, so when Delmar Heinelt left the team for other venues, the door opened for Howell to pilot the Corvair. With a few match races under Howells's belt, the Corvair was plagued with power issues and lagged behind the competition. Both Seaton and Howell searched for answers, and Howell made the decision to dump the injection system and add a blower to the engine, which immediately made the Corvair a strong runner.

Memories: Randy Walls

Owner and Driver of the **Super Nova** *Chevy II*

"Back in those days, the altered-wheelbase cars came out with all sorts of different looks. The rear ends were moved around, either forward several inches to a few feet up against the doors. The front axles were stretched out on the injected cars that mostly ran on alcohol.

"One day at the track, I remember some kid saying, 'That's a funny-looking car.' It really woke me up, as I wanted one of those cars, but I [had] never been around superchargers, fuel injection, alcohol, nitro, or any kind of that stuff—I went straight to carburetors. After learning all the ins and outs from San Diego gasser great Ben Travis, I went on to build my first blown car, the *Super Nova*."

Randy Walls's 1965 Chevy II Super Nova was the West Coast's fastest Chevy-powered Funny Car in the early years of Funny Cars. The stock steel-bodied Nova was completely stripped down and lightened to match race against the toughest Mopars and Fords that were backed by their factories. Walls built and maintained the blown 427-ci Rat motor that led to low-8-second times with speeds exceeding 165 mph.

Tom Strum progressed from a full-sized Super Stocker running a gasoline-powered 409-ci mill to a fuel-burning A/FX match racing Chevelle in 1965. Continuing the trend in 1966, Strum built a match basher Corvair, but a late summer crash in Lakeland, Tennessee, ended the Corvair's career. Noting the success and performances of the flip-top Mercurys, Strum decided to ditch construction of a new lightweight chassis and modify the older Chevelle model. He fitted it with a new one-piece Corvair body painted metal-flake rose pink. Strum stuck with the injected semi-hemi 427-ci Chevrolet rated at 800 hp.

Ted "the Kansas Badman" DeTar and his Chrysler Hemi–powered Ford Falcon made a strong charge in the 2,400-pound Funny Car class at the 1967 AHRA Winternationals at Beeline. DeTar advanced to the semifinals, where he lost to Charlie Allen's Dodge Dart.

The 1967 American Hot Rod Association Winternationals at Beeline Drag Strip in Phoenix featured the nation's top names in Funny Cars from nearly every state competing in two separate divisions: Unlimited and FX/Fuel. Battling in the Unlimited Fuel Class Title was "Dyno" Don Nicholson's Eliminator I against rival teammate Eddie Schartman for gold. The crafty Nicholson noticed an interesting fact while checking out the starting line. He raised his foot 1-1/2 inches in the far lane before tripping the staging beam. The near lane took only 1/4 inch to activate, so Nicholson was hoping to be in the far lane. Nicholson got his wish. At the green, both cars left together, but at the eighth mile, Dyno was out in front and crossed the finish line. Nicholson recorded the win (8.26 at 171.00 mph) to Schartman's ET of 8.48 at 167 mph.

Memories: Bruce Larson   *Owner and Driver of the USA-1 Chevelle*

"My first experience in drag racing was with a 1962 Ford Galaxie lightweight running out of a dealership where I worked. I soon became involved with Jim Coslo on a Shelby Cobra that we did well with.

"I then went to work at a Chevy dealer, where I installed a dynamometer and performed tune-ups. One day, I was tuning a Cobra on the Chevy dealer's dyno when the owner of the dealership, Craig Sutcliffe, approached me and mentioned that since we were doing very well with a Ford car, maybe we should be running a Chevrolet. This was my first involvement with Chevrolet: an all fiberglass 1966 Chevelle *USA-1*."

Bruce Larson's USA-1 Chevelle was built to go match racing with the identification of a factory stock muscle car. Larson used a 115-inch wheelbase box-tube frame that was shortened to 109 inches and built with CAE-dragster-type one leaf spring front end. The engine was a 1967 427-ci Chevrolet semi-Wedge with Hilborn port injection system with the curved ram air tubes running a 70-percent nitro and alcohol mixture. (Photo Courtesy Lloyd Wolfe)

Jim St. Clair and Clare Sanders had been racing together since their A/Street Roadster days of 1963, and along with retired defense contractor Jack Groner, they formed J & J Enterprises to promote their product Boss Bite liquid traction compound. The trio, from Felton, California, invested a sum above $20,000 and approximately four months of their lives to build the Lime Fire Plymouth Barracuda match racer. Powered by a 400-ci Chrysler, Sanders often landed the fish into the winner's circle with constant runs of 8.40 at 180 mph.

East Coast racer Jerry Caminito purchased his 1967 Logghe flip-top Mercury Comet injected SOHC Funny Car from Howard Neil and renamed it Holeshot. Caminito ran the car for a few seasons before updating the Comet with a new 1969 Mustang body.

Ray Alley built and drove this blown tubed-chassis Dodge Charger for the match-race circuit. Fiberglass Limited in Stone Park, Illinois, manufactured the two-piece Dodge shell. Alley set the crowd a buzz at Irwindale when the three-week-old Charger equipped with a 345 Dodge Hemi stopped the clocks with an ET of 8.19 at 185 mph, which was the quickest ever for a Funny Car that qualified his Engine Masters Dodge Charger in the number-one position.

When Ray Alley qualified his **Engine Masters** *Dodge Charger* number one, running an unheard of 8.19 ET, he never realized that he would experience one of the wildest rides in his racing career. The Charger traveled nearly another eighth mile with the throttle wide open, but before the engine shut off, the excessive speed ripped off the entire roof! Taking the spoils with the victors, Alley received an ovation from the crowd when he brought the Charger back up to line for the first round of eliminations against Steve Bovan. Both cars experienced traction problems going up in smoke, but Alley crossed the finish line ahead of Bovan.

Starter Larry Sutton reacts as "Flash" Gordon Mineo goes full throttle off the line at Lions Drag Strip. Mineo was born in Detroit, Michigan, and relocated to Southern California. He was a regular on the southern Funny Car scene and a favorite of the fans. Teamed with fellow Funny Car owner and driver Tom Sturm, both enjoyed a successful campaign running top numbers.

Bob Davis's Jolly Green Giant II *Corvette* Funny Car was the predecessor to the Jolly Green *Chevy Impala* that competed in the early Funny Car wars. In the driver's seat was Denny Savage. Savage spent time in several other Funny Cars through the 1960s and 1970s, including the **Panic** *Vega*, the **Power Steel** *Camaro*, and the infamous Chi-Town Hustler.

Mike Thermos pushes the butterflies wide open as the California Camaro of Stuart-Maggio-Thermos grabs some asphalt coming off the line at Lions Drag Strip. Thermos owned and tuned the blown Camaro with power from the Paul Gommi–built 354 Chrysler Hemi.

The Tack Chevy Corvair of Lee Jones, shown here at Irwindale, created havoc in the match race circuit on the West Coast. Jones later campaigned a Pontiac Firebird with backing from McFadden Pontiac and later teamed with the "D.C. Dip" Malcolm Durham to run a West Coast version of Durham's Strip Blazer Camaro.

Bill Nash and George Brown from Wilmington, California, were huge Funny Car fans, so they pooled their money and talents and built this fuel-burning Chevy Camaro named Insanity. After the red and gold Chevy experienced early engine failures, Brown worked out the kinks of the injected 427-ci Rat engine, which built a reputation of performance and consistency. Nash piloted the Camaro in the low-9-second bracket and speeds in the excess of 160 mph.

Kip Brundage jumped out of a fuel-burning flathead dragster and got behind the wheel of the Parts Mart Speed Shop match racing Chevy Camaro. Brundage was from Campbell, California, and traveled up and down the golden state to race, but business and family commitments kept him only on the West Coast.

Bob Blinn's Contemporary Fiberglas Mustang with Bud Fazone at the controls rips off a an ET of 8.52 at 168 mph at Irwindale. The Azusa, California, Mustang featured a Sammy Vildo chassis and an Art Carr TorqueFlite transmission. The OHC ran injectors but later switched to a huffer.

The original Chevy exhibition car that challenged Jack Chrisman's Sachs & Sons Comet was sold off by Steve Bovan and bought by Ed Carter and Bob Little from Fremont, California. Carter and Little's Chevy II Heavy kept the original powertrain combination (the blown 396-ci Chevrolet with a 3-speed transmission), which surprisingly drove Carter and the old Chevy II into the winner's circle at the ninth annual Fuel and Gas Championships at Bakersfield. Carter unleashed his quickest-ever 9.25 ET for the Chevy, which upset favorite Bruce Larson in the final round of the 2,600-pound class.

Steve Garcia drives the Garcia Brothers' Out of Sight Camaro at Lions. Steve and Joe were out of Sacramento, California, and raced up and down the state of California. The Camaro ran a blown 392-ci Chrysler that powered mid-8-second ETs at 170 mph.

Jess Tyree was the West Coast's "Mr. Pontiac." He ran successfully in his early days with several A/Stock and A/FX Pontiacs, which enabled him to obtain one of the few factory-built S/S Catalinas from Mickey Thompson. Tyree also owned and operated his header business, Tyree Headers, which helped him cover his racing expenses. Tyree's first Funny Car was a 1967 Firebird, which is shown at Lions. It was powered by a blown 421-ci Super Duty Pontiac engine built with 1963 73-cc heads with a compression ratio of 6.5:1. Running on pure Pontiac power, Jess averaged 8.32 ETs with top speeds of 169.70 mph.

Johnny Wright deploys the laundry at the top end in the Wright Brothers' 1965 Topless II Chevy II roadster at Irwindale. The brothers were low-budget weekend racers running mostly in the Southern California area, but Johnny made the injected Chevy II extremely competitive with his lightning-quick reactions coming off the starting line.

One of the first female pioneers to drive a fuel-burning Funny Car was Paula Murphy, who started her driving career racing a MG in the Women's Sports Car Association. Murphy also spent time with legendary Andy Granatelli, driving several of his vehicles, including at the Bonneville Salt Flats and at Indy time trials in 1963 driving one of Granatelli's Novi Indy cars. Ms. Murphy made the jump into Funny Car in 1967 with this 1966 blown Mustang fastback on nitro when "Fat Jack" Bynum and Murphy teamed up to build the 8-second Mustang Funny Car, Miss STP. Speed Products Engineering designed the chassis, which Bynum constructed, and the build ran a Dave Zeuschel–built, early 392-ci Chrysler Hemi tuned by Bynum. Cal Automotive built the two-piece, all-fiberglass 1966 Mustang body with a removable front clip that was easily unfastened for engine repairs and maintenance. The diamond red paint was the work of Gil's Auto Body. The appearance of Murphy at the strip was popular for spectators, who saw her take her male counterparts to the woodshed.

American Motors entered the flip-top wars when Carl Chamakian (front of car in suit and tie), the performance activities director for AMC, collaborated with Grant McCoon, owner and CEO of Grant Industries, the automotive aftermarket giant. They built the Grant Rebel SST driven by "Bonzi" Bill Hayes, which is shown in the pits at Irwindale.

There are only a few examples in drag racing when a Fuel Altered could be quickly converted over to race in a Funny Car show. One of them was the Psycho Mustang, which was the AFX/FX Mustang/Altered of Ron Pelligrini of Dennison, Arlaskey, and Knox of Cicero, Illinois.

The **New Breed** *Pontiac Firebird of Montrelli, Williams, and Barrett ran an early Chrysler Hemi that was bored out to 424 inches. Steve Montrelli owned and maintained the popular Pontiac with Steve Barrett behind the steering wheel. The TorqueFlite transmission transferred power to the rear wheels.*

Fiberglass Trends' Marv Eldridge powers his week-old topless Corvette roadster to a qualifying ET of 8.86 at 175.45 mph at Irwindale. The new lightweight blown Hemi roadster logged its first win, dumping the injected flip-top Comet of Dee Keaton when he ran an ET of 8.46 at 176.88 mph to a losing 8.80 at 166.66.

Memories: Randy Walls

Owner and Driver of the *Super Spyder* Chevy Corvair

"I was getting more serious in racing and stepped up when I purchased [Hayden] Proffitt's Corvair and installed my engine and transmission. It was a complete steel car and was not that light. Even with fiberglass doors, trunk lid, and front end, it topped the scales around 2,500 pounds. It already had the Shelby 2/3 steel tubing frame, so I made slight modifications, but all I really did was super tune the engine."

Randy Walls purchased the topless Corvair of Hayden Proffitt, installed the blown 427-ci Chevy and driveline from his Super Nova, and continued where Proffitt left off with the West Coast's fastest match racing Chevy Corvair. Randy campaigned the stock-steel bodied Corvair until a finish-line collision at Irwindale with Frank Pisano driving the Pisano Brothers' Corvair totaled both cars.

The Trojan Horse *Mustang of Fullerton and Solarie was one of the strongest injected SOHC-powered Funny Cars from the West Coast. The Logghe-built Mustang with driver Larry Fullerton drops the laundry here at Irwindale.*

The Blue Hell *Corvette of Glen Grissom and "Rapid Ronnie" Runyon was one of the top Corvette performers that eluded the fabled Corvette curse for Funny Cars. The J&D Corvette entry ran a blown 427-ci Chevrolet under the hood bolted to an automatic transmission. Runyon, from Raytown, Missouri, pocketed the top prize of $1,000 cash when he survived three rounds of eliminations here at Irwindale.*

Bob Sullivan learned from his outstanding dragster career that the winning formula started with a solid chassis, driving abilities, and power from a durable Hemi engine. Sullivan put all these winning ingredients together and built his Pandemonium VI *topless Camaro. Lakewood Chassis in Cleveland, Ohio, constructed the frame, and it was powered by a reliable 1958 392 Chrysler Hemi that was connected to a direct-drive unit aided with a Donovan flywheel, Schiefer clutch disc, and pressure plate. During one of the earliest tests runs in Texas, the body became dislodged from the mounts and flew, destroying the body. When the new fiberglass Camaro body was fitted to the chassis, Sullivan did not like how the body looked on the car, so he and the crew (Butch Smith and Ralph Suman) created the roadster design.*

Gene Ciambella was one of top runners in the gasser wars on the West Coast running his MGM C&O Automotive Austin truck. Since the Funny Cars were earning the bigger bucks, Ciambella jumped over to run a series of Funny Jeeps and Pontiac-bodied Firebirds. He changed his last name from Ciambella after the gasser era and took the Conway name, while being nicknamed "Cinderella." Conway's Proud Bird *multicolored, Hemi-powered Firebird was his nicest yet with driver Gene Modlin behind the wheel pounding the strip at Lions Drag Strip.*

Cecil Yother's latest entry in the Funny Car wars was this ultra-light 1,600-pound edition of the Melrose Missile *Barracuda that replaced the older roadster. The new Barracuda gelcoat glass body was molded by a Florida boat manufacturer with blue metal-flake fragments throughout the body. A late-model 426 injected Hemi with Hilborns fed the Oakland, California–based "muscle missile" to constant ETs of 8.20 at 170-mph.*

Gas Ronda heats the hides through the water box at Irwindale. The Exhibition Engineering–built Mustang had an Ed Pink 427-ci SOHC engine under the hood; Ed called the tune-up shots with Randy Richie and Charlie Gray assisting with the Russ Davis Ford Mustang. (Photo Courtesy Tim Pearl Archives)

Butch Leal's newest entry in the Funny Car wars was a real face saver for Mopar, as the Mercury Comets pretty much had the run of the land. Leal was on a mission to squash the Cyclones at their own game. His arsenal of the **California Flash** included a late 426 Hilborn-injected Hemi with an Art Carr TorqueFlite transmission. The orange and white Barracuda body was supplied by B&N fiberglass and when tilted upward, it exposed the Logghe tube-type chassis. Lions Drag Strip became muscle beach at the second annual Funny Car Factory Showdown when Leal's **California Flash** overpowered the opposition when he averaged three consecutive 8.03 ETs, which were the best for the Mopar!

These negatives show the construction of drag racing's newest super track: Orange County International Raceway in East Irvine, California. The images reveal detailed progression of the tower, permanent grandstands, restrooms, starting line, pit area, strip, and concessions.

The frame of the newest jewel on the West Coast, Orange County International Raceway's four-story tower, was a spectacle of modern design and technology. Orange County International Raceway hosted several top-billed Funny Car events, including the Hang Ten Funny Car Championships, the Eastern Funny Championships, and the greatest Team Funny Car Manufacturer's All-Star race held on the West Coast.

This is Orange County International Raceway's famous logo. The multifunctional track hosted many racing events, but drag racing was its forte.

"Dyno" Don Nicholson had the crowd buzzing when he drove his *Eliminator I* factory-backed Comet through a strong eight-car field to defeat his factory team rival, Eddie Schartman, for the Unlimited Fuel trophy and gold.

Orange County International Raceway

Founding vice president and general manager Mike Jones was the force behind California's first super track, which was named Orange County International Raceway (OCIR). It opened for business in August 1967 in East Irvine. Architect William T. White, Business Manager Larry Vaughn, Public Relations Manager Mike McKenna, and Jones were the men associated in the planning and development of the $5,000,000 120-acre facility.

Built adjacent to El Toro Marine Air Corps base, the state-of-the-art facility featured a modern four-story timing tower, an electric scoreboard illuminating times and speeds, permanent grandstands, restroom facilities, a playground for children, and concession stands. The area was complete with tree-shaded picnic areas and a paved pit and parking lots. OCIR gained the reputation of presenting original shows and had a professional atmosphere.

The multi-purpose facility listed professional drag racing as the top billing. Other organized events included motorcycle, sports car, and codriver racing, and Bob Bondurant's driving school was mapped out in the tower-side parking lot. Airplane races along with daredevil shows were fan favorites, and through the years, a dirt track was built on the grounds for both off-road trucks and motocross riders.

OCIR hosted several of the country's top annual drag racing events, including the Funny Car Team Championships, Funny Car Hang Ten 500, US Super Stock Championship, the All-Pro Series, and the Jewel west of the Mississippi, the Manufacturer's Funny Car Championships. The Manufacturer's Funny Car Championships included all of the pomp and circumstances with driver and team introductions, marching bands, and fireworks. Even the unscheduled flybys by the El Toro–based A-4 Marine fighters were spectacular.

New to the non–drag racing scene was OCIR's concessions. A complete luncheon menu was offered and was open weekdays for the area residents and people to discover the raceway.

The Manufacturer's Funny Car Championships

With the fate of the unproven and somewhat erratic Factory Experimental Funny Cars, some had their doubts. Add in a brand-new facility, and both were given very little chance for survival. With a roll of the dice on November 25, 1967, the largest one-day Funny Car Team Championship in the western United States took place at OCIR in Irvine, California.

More than 12,000 frenzied fans witnessed OCIR's inaugural season event. There were 47 of the nation's top Funny Cars in attendance, representing 14 states with 27 cars from California alone.

Each team of six carried five seeded cars. The representatives for the Plymouth team included Butch Leal, J&J Enterprises (*Lime Fire*), "Fearless" Fred Goeske, Cecil Yother, and Larry Reyes. The Dodge team consisted of Al Vanderwoude, Charlie Allen, the *Samson* Dart, Roger Lindamood, and Gary Dyer in Mr. Norm's new Charger. Representing Ford's team were Tommy Grove, "Psycho" Dick Loehr, Larry Fullerton's *Trojan Horse,* and the Mustangs of Gas Ronda. Chevrolet's team included the Corvairs of Doug Thorley, Seaton's *Super Shaker*, the Camaros of Kelly Chadwick, and Dick Harrell and Ron O'Donnell driving the Chapman entry. Topping Pontiac's seeded entries were the Firebirds of Don and Roy Gay, Don Sappington, the *New Breed,* and both of Lew Arrington's entries: the all-new *Brutus* Firebird and the tried-and-true *Brutus* GTO. Running under the Mercury banner were "Fast" Eddie Schartman, "Dyno" Don Nicholson, Dee Keaton, Pete Gates, and Funny Car pioneer Jack Chrisman.

Along with the 30 team cars were an additional 15 standby cars in case a team member broke down and could not make a run. Each car matched up against other squads, racing tag-team style in competition for three rounds. One point was awarded when an original team car outran its opponent, but if an alternate filled in for a broken car and won the round, a half point was awarded to the team it filled in for. Teams could earn a maximum of six points per round, as low ET of the round received the extra point.

The overall champion was determined at the end of the night, with the two lowest ET cars returning for a sud-

Cleveland's Eddie Schartman brought more than 12,000 screaming fans to their feet when his Air Lift Rattler *Comet crossed the finish line ahead of "Texas Teenager" Roy Gay, driving his blown Pontiac Firebird in the final round at the inaugural Orange County International Raceway Manufacturer's Meet. Both drivers ran their quickest ETs (Schartman 7.85 and Gay 7.90) during the round-robin meet that started the day with 42 of the country's finest Funny Cars. Engine master "Famous" Amos Satterlee was the force behind Schartman's success, keeping the blown 427 SOHC in front of the competition. (Photo Courtesy Paul Johnson)*

Eighteen-year-old Roy Gay found the Thanksgiving holiday break to his liking in East Irvine, California, when he drove the family Funny Car to the runner-up spot at Orange County International Raceway's Inaugural Manufacturer's Funny Car Team Championships. Gay's Pontiac-powered Firebird lost to the Mercury Comet Air Lift Rattler *of Eddie Schartman in the finals. Roy took care of business in his three rounds of round-robin match racing when he defeated Gas Ronda, Ron Roseberry in the Von Fritch Automotive Dodge, and Kelly Chadwick before meeting Schartman in the final pairing of the night for the cash, champagne, and gold! (Photo Courtesy Steve Reyes)*

Northern California was well represented by the huge contingent of independent Funny Car racers in the early years, including Ron Rinauro's steel-bodied 1955 Chevy Blown Hell altered-wheelbase Funny Car. Under the hood was a supercharged 392 Hemi built by South San Francisco's Ted Gotelli. The high-horsepower Top Fuel nitro motor was dropped into the modified 1955 sedan and stressed out the drivetrain, which suffered from severe transmission failures. (Photo Courtesy Steve Reyes)

The crew of the Watts Riot blown Camaro of Smith & Watts assist the driver suiting up for his first encounter at Fremont. The debut of the new Camaro did not go as well as expected for the young team. The Chevy met its demise when it crashed after the throttle hung up on the initial burnout. (Photo Courtesy Steve Reyes)

The moment master photographer Steve Reyes snapped this photo of the Watts Riot, the car took off on one of the wildest rides ever at a drag strip! On the burnout, the Camaro lost control when the throttle stuck wide open in reverse, running over the staging lane officer and into the spectators and racers around the area, who dove away from the car. The Camaro climbed up the wood boards, still running, before running out of fuel. The driver and car were not badly hurt or damaged, but the lane officer was sent to the hospital with two broken legs. The car and Smith & Watts team were never seen again. (Photo Courtesy Steve Reyes)

Ed Carter's Color Kart 1965 Chevy II was once the scourge of Blairs Speed Shop. It was formerly owned and driven by Steve Bovan. Ed Carter and Bob Little bought the car and campaigned it as the Chevy 2 Heavy Chevy II. Ed won class honors with the car at the March Meet in Bakersfield. To be more competitive, the car was revamped and renamed the Color Kart. It was refitted with a longer nose, the front end dropped down, and awful paint. Ed and Bob were neighbors in the town of Newark, a small suburb of the Fremont area. The two competed in the sport for fun, and both had day jobs, so they could not take off time to race. (Photo Courtesy Steve Reyes)

den-death, winner-take-all race. Only Terry Hedrick and Roy Gay had the honors to win all three of their races.

Mercury's "Fast" Eddie Schartman and the "Texas teenager" 18-year-old Roy Gay from the Pontiac team met for the individual honors. When the dust settled, the win light went to Schartman's ET of 7.86 at 184.42 to Gay's 8.10 at 175.09 mph.

In addition to Schartman's and Gay's awesome performances, Doug Thorley piloted his Chevy-powered Corvair to top-speed honors, hitting 191 mph on the clocks. Mr. Norm's *Supercharger* Dodge Charger and "Dyno" Don were huge thunder makers for their respected teams. The event also included the unexpected debut of a young driver from San Jose, California, whose blue Chevy II Nova carried the name "Jungle" Jim Liberman.

The overall points tallied at the first Manufacturer's Funny Car Team Championship ended in a tie. Both Chevy and Ford earned nine points, but Chevy broke the tie and enjoyed the champagne based on recording lower elapsed times.

Bay Area Brawlers

Match racing was on fire up in Northern California at Fremont, Half Moon Bay, Sacramento, Fresno, Ballico, Lodi, Kindon, Inyokern, Redding, and Madera. Some of the biggest names came out the bay area including Lew Arrington, Tommy Grove, and "Jungle" Jim Liberman.

One local fan favorite was Ron Rinauro, who owned and drove the *Blown Hell*, a 1955 Chevy hardtop that wasn't your average Funny Car but ran hard and the crowd dug it. The steel-bodied Tri-Five was one of many stars that ran only in the northwest but made an impact on Funny Cars.

Several "unknowns" showed off some of the widest Funny Cars that were infrequently seen at the strip. Some enjoyed success but there were a few that didn't fare so well.

One memorable incident that unfolded at Fremont was witnessed by photographer Steve Reyes during the debut of the brand-new Smith & Watts fuel Camaro Funny Car fresh out of Fresno. Steve Reyes said the following about the *Watts Riot* blown Chevy Camaro:

"This was toward the end of '67 and the first time out for the car. It was sitting in the staging lanes in Fremont when the command was given to fire up the car. The roar of the blown fuel engine came to life, and then I realized people were diving out of the way of this wayward Camaro, boiling the rear tires with the engine screaming! The cop, who handled the crowd control in the staging lanes, did not move quickly enough to get out of the way, was hit by the car, and flew several feet in the air and landed hard, receiving two broken legs. Exiting the staging lanes, the Camaro was now spinning out of control and drove between that evening's entertainment, the *Little Red Wagon* and the *Hemi Under Glass* wheel-standers

The Souza Brothers and Dad team based in Hayward, California, raced a 1933 supercharged A/G Willys in 1965 and 1966 before turning to Funny Cars with a Ford Mustang. The all-steel fastback Mustang first appeared in 1967, running a fuel-injected big-block Ford Wedge engine with lightweight fiberglass doors and a one-piece glass front clip. Dave Souza drove while brother Harold made the horsepower from the 427-ci injected Wedge. Dave filled out the driver's compartment with his 300-pound frame but had cat-like reflexes against his competition. In early 1968, they added a blower to the Wedge and later stepped up with a blown SOHC Ford Cammer. (Photo Courtesy Steve Reyes)

and ended up hitting and running up the large sign boards behind the starting line.

"With the nose first and rear tires still smoking, the car started to climb up the sign boards, ending up vertical against the boards. The car starved out of fuel and shut off because of the angle that it was in. I was told that the car was built with the brake and throttle pedals reversed so when the throttle stuck wide-open, the driver stepped on the throttle instead of the brake in trying to stop. That was the last time I saw those guys!"

The Challenger Mustang was one of those Funny Cars that was basically unknown. Not much information was written about the driver, car, team, or overall performance and numbers. The team had a core of passionate racers who would show up on the weekends and make a few runs regardless of budget or the quality of parts. The goal was to have some fun racing. If lucky, a scheduled car wouldn't show up, and the Challenger would fill in to earn a few bucks. (Photo Courtesy Steve Reyes)

Cutting his teeth in the seat of Skip Johnson's nitro Junior Fuel dragster, Dale Pulde earned his competition license driving Charlie Wilson's Vicious Vette Funny Car. He remained Charlie's driver for the Corvette and the Vicious Too Camaro for several seasons.

Steve Bovan stepped up in 1967 with a blown 427-ci Chevy Rat-powered Camaro. Mike Hoag built the 125-inch chrome-moly tube chassis while Antique Fiberglass provided the stretched body. Blair's Speed Shop in Pasadena continued to sponsor the 1,900-pound Camaro.

The Precision Speed Shop of Buena Park, California, was one of the local independents that ran mostly in the injected Funny Car group but occasionally would bolt on a blower and tip a healthy dose of nitro into the fuel tank to fill out a blown fuel Funny Car card. The steel-bodied Chevy Corvair was not a top performer, but it was a sight to see the driver hang on as if he was riding a raging bull with a bad temper.

Jack Chrisman was one of drag racing's first trailblazers. He was a predominant figure with the inception of the blown fuel Funny Car. Hired by the Lincoln-Mercury Division of Ford, Chrisman drove the first steel-body Funny Car on nitro in the exhibition class. He went on to be one of the heavyweights out of the Mercury camp and was one of the most recognized figures in all of drag racing. Chrisman raced Funny Cars for nearly a decade and was one of the founding members of the Coca-Cola Cavalcade of Stars in 1969.

The Manufacturer's Meet was expanded to two full days. Friday was limited for qualifying only, while team challenges took place on Saturday night. The team field now included the "wacky racers," which featured various engine-to-body configurations, such as a Chrysler Hemi engine in a Chevrolet Camaro. Both the Chevrolet and Plymouth/Dodge teams are shown. Included in the mix were drivers Kelly Chadwick, "Big" Mike Burkhart, Charlie Allen, and Terry Hendrick.

Chapter Three

The Magical Realm of Funny Cars

Funny Cars were still in their adolescent years and had progressed a long way in the four years since the debut of Jack Chrisman's blown Sachs & Sons Mercury Comet. Funny Cars began cresting into the magical 200-mph barrier, although many of the times may have been bogus since the calibration of some clocks was performed incorrectly.

Don Nicholson reigned terror throughout the match race circuit in 1966. When the new season arrived, he picked up where he left off by keeping the pressure on with his new Logghe Stage-I Eliminator II 1967 Comet. The new car was nearly an exact copy of the previous year's model but built with more chassis and weight refinements and safety measures. The 427 SOHC-injected engine was set back 5 inches for better traction, and the Mercury C-6 3-speed transmission was geared out with the stall speed set at 3,000 rpm. Crew chief Earl Wade was once quoted as saying Don was "the number one driver in drag racing."

The first three unofficial speeds seemed unreal because all three were identical. First, Tommy Grove ran an ET of 7.57 at 202.24 mph at Capital Raceway in Maryland. Then, an Iskenderian cam advertisement listed that Northern California's Steve Garcia wheeled the *Out of Sight* Camaro to 202.24 mph and backed it up with a 198-mph pass on July 13, 1968, at Rockford, Illinois. Finally, Gene Snow ran 202.24 mph at Houston on August 18.

The motto in the early years was "run what you brung." If you were lucky enough to run, especially on a Sunday afternoon, you could wind up in the winner's circle collecting a trophy, a case or two of oil, or possibly a savings bond for a few bucks. Oh yes, don't forget the congratulatory kiss from the trophy queen; it was fun times back then.

Factory participation by Chrysler and Ford had pulled back considerably, as Detroit was going back to its roots in the Super Stock classes, where the cars resembled what could be purchased from the showroom floor. The playing fields were considerably leveled, which opened the door to the non-Hemi and SOHC high-dollar powered haulers.

The Logghe dominancy continued into the 1968 season with the most-feared competitor, "Dyno" Don Nicholson, and his *Eliminator II*. Nicholson made easy work of the competition at the $10,000 Funny Car Showdown at Fontana International Raceway, earning $2,000 for winning the title. With 42 cars on the premises, his Stage-II Logghe chassis Cyclone ran away from everyone, turning an amazing 8.01 for low ET of the event on a track with cold asphalt.

The 13th AHRA Winternationals at Lions attracted nearly 100 Funny Cars competing for the FX-Fuel title.

Not surprisingly, another Logghe found its way into the winner's circle, this time by "Jungle" Jim Liberman. The mainstream of Funny Cars were now built with chrome-moly tubing with the average length of 118 inches. Fitted with one-piece, lightweight fiberglass bodies that were built near factory production specs, they were now the big deal in the quarter mile!

Funny Cars set numerous world speed and ET records throughout the season, hitting speeds of more than 205 mph and stopping the clocks in mid-7.40 range. Many Top Fuel drivers were now making the transition to the

*"Rapid" Ronnie Runyon hits the pedal in front of 12,225 fans at Lions Unlimited Funny Car Spectacular. With more than 50 Funny Cars in attendance to vie for a spot in the 32-car field, Runyan drew low-qualifier Bob Sullivan (at the helm of the **Pandemonium** Camaro roadster) in the first round. Unfortunately for the **Blue Hell,** new car bugs kept the Corvair from advancing. Sullivan skated through the traps with an ET of 8.14 at 180.72 mph.*

Teenager Dale Pulde drives Charlie Wilson's **Vicious Too** *Camaro at Riverside Raceway. The 2,220-pound Camaro ran a blown 427-ci Chevrolet on a 50-percent dose of nitro. Transferring the horsepower and torque to the rear wheels was an automatic transmission. The Camaro was the second Funny Car Pulde drove for Wilson, and he posted his best ET of 7.92 at 182 mph.*

Oklahoma cattle rancher Nelson Carter built an impressive Funny Car that hit the scene in 1968. Nelson ordered a 120-inch steel-tubed chassis from the Logghe Stamping Company and contacted Ron Perau, owner and operator of Imperial Customs, to drive the lightweight 1968 Dodge Charger. Keith Black Racing Engines installed the blown Black Marine 426 Hemi to the B&M-modified Torque-Flite transmission.

Doug Thorley added another weapon to his arsenal with the **Doug's Headers** *Corvair campaigned by Dick Bourgeois and Earl Wade Racing Enterprises. Doug ordered the chassis from Logghe with a Fiberglass Trends one-piece fiberglass body covering the pipes. Earl Wade built the 427-ci Chevrolet engine with a modified Hydra-Motive transmission putting power to the rear wheels.*

Maynard Rupp and Roy Steffey campaigned the STP Cougar Country S/XS Funny Car. When Rupp and Steffey parted ways, Gerry Schwartz from Fort Wayne, Indiana, purchased the car from the Logghe Stamping Company with the Steffey-built 427-ci SOHC engine included. Schwartz ran the 427 SOHC for a season, replaced the Cammer with a blown Chevy 427-ci Rat engine, and named the car the Ratty Cat Cougar. On October 12, 1968, John "the Zookeeper" Mulligan of the Beebe & Mulligan AA/FD fame made his Funny Car driver's license passes in Schwartz's Cougar here at Lions Drag Strip. Mulligan turned a credible ET of 8.91 at 184.04 mph for his first time behind the wheel of a Funny Car. Mulligan hung up his gloves for the day after making two licensing passes.

Larry Arnold cracks the butterflies in T.B. Smallwood's King Fish Barracuda from Memphis, Tennessee. Ed Pink built the Chrysler Hemi that produced 7.30 ETs with speeds above 205 mph.

Bill McDuell of Newark, Delaware, owned and drove the She-Devil II Barracuda. It was powered by a nitro-injected 426 Chrysler Hemi bolted to a 3-speed automatic transmission. Crew chief Terry Heckman provided the tune-up on the popular East Coast match basher, running a consistent ET of 8.80 at 158 mph.

Lew Arrington had always been a Pontiac man. He began his drag racing career with a B/MP Studebaker powered with a Pontiac engine. Just when Funny Cars were coming on the scene, Arrington and Jim Liberman formed a partnership with the Brutus *GTO*, which featured Liberman doing most of the driving. Both partners gained notoriety in the match racing wars, and the GTO saw action in its day. It raced in 1966 and all through the 1967 season, but the old car was simply too outdated to keep up with the newer, modern machines. While on out on tour, Arrington and Liberman knew they were going in different directions, so the two ventured out on their own. Liberman began driving his Chevy II Funny Car and Arrington ran in his latest version of the *Brutus*, a Logghe-prepped 1968 Pontiac Firebird. The one-piece body was built at Fiberglass Trends, Al Bergler hand-formed the tin work, Mel George built an early 392 Chrysler Hemi, and in the drivetrain was an Art Carr TorqueFlite transmission with a mechanical shifter to change gears.

Ted McOsker's King Rebel *AMC Rebel* was one of the AMC's top performers that relied on a blown fuel Chrysler Hemi for power. McOsker debuted his *Rebel* Darn Tootin', I'm a Rebel with Gary Gabelich at the wheel at Lions Drag Strip on August 18, 1968. Soon after, Ron Roseberry climbed behind wheel of the hybrid to post a best ET of 9.58 at 148.02 mph.

Pete Seaton competed in various classes in drag racing, driving several different Pontiacs and a Corvette. GM cars were always in his blood, since his dad was a vice president with General Motors. When Funny Cars grew in popularity, Seaton built his first match-racer Funny Car: a Chevelle using a big-block 396 Porcupine injected engine with capable driver Delmar Heinelt behind the wheel. While the performance was way off the mark of a competitive car (consistent runs were in the 9-second range), Seaton wanted to run faster. Jay Howell built a new steel-bodied Corvair that ran in the 8-second range, but soon the competition caught up and surpassed it. To run a successful business, Seaton Enterprises, Seaton went all in and spared no expense, contacting the nation's top chassis builders, Ron and Gene Logghe. Fiberglass Trends lengthened the Corvair body 8 inches with Al Berger installing the aluminum sheet metal. Seaton increased the power by adding a supercharger to the 427-ci Chevy bullet and hired the capable Terry Hendrick to drive. John Ylitalo was retained as mechanic and crew chief. Berger Chevrolet in Grand Rapids, Michigan, was the main backer of the "East's quickest Corvair." (Photo Courtesy Steve Reyes)

The Infinity *Pontiac Firebird* by way of Dickinson, Texas, was the top-running Pontiac of its time. Don and Roy Gay campaigned their "psychedelic warrior" with a supercharged 428-ci Pontiac engine tuned by mechanic James Olsen. During the AHRA Winternationals hosted at Lions Drag Strip, Roy Gay drew fellow Texan Gene Snow in the first round in F/X Fuel. Gay thundered past Snow with an ET of 8.04 at 180 mph. (Photo Courtesy Steve Reyes)

Gene Snow waded through a stout 32-car Funny Car field with his blown 1968 *Rambunctious F/X Fuel* Dodge Dart at the 1968 AHRA Winternationals only to lose to "Jungle" Jim Liberman in the semifinals. Liberman advanced to the finals against "Dyno" Don Nicholson, but Nicholson blew a transmission and Snow was back in via the break rule for a second encounter. The results were repeated when Liberman ripped off an ET of 7.84 at 181.08 mph to Snow's off-pace 10.06 at 120 mph in the final round for the money.

Two legendary Funny Cars from the Midwest were Pete Seaton's *Seaton's Super Shaker* Corvair from Michigan and the Windy City's *Chi-Town Hustler* Dodge Charger of John Farkonas, Austin Coil, and Pat Minnick. They shared pit and trailer space in Fremont. Many of the Eastern stars invaded the West Coast for the warmer weather during the winter months, making money match racing at Funny Car meets while testing new power and suspension combinations. (Photo Courtesy Steve Reyes)

Funny Cars, including John "the Zookeeper" Mulligan, making his driver's license runs in Gerry Schwartz's *Ratty Cat* Cougar.

Dragsters versus Funny Cars

Well, it had to happen sooner or later, and on April 27, 1968, Irwindale billed the first-ever meeting between four 225-mph Top Fuel Dragsters versus four 7-second Funny Cars. A 1-second handicap round-robin match race series gave fans three full rounds of some of the wildest racing.

The four top-caliber Fuelers were Roland Leong's *Hawaiian* driven by Mike Snivley, Winternationals champs Warren-Colburn-Miller of the Ridge Route Terrors, the Fighting Irish of Beebe and Mulligan, and Irwindale Grand Prix champs Stellings and Tapia with Butch Mass behind the wheel.

Representing the "Plastic Fanatics" were the two SOHC Ford Mustangs of Dick Loehr and local favorite Gas Ronda. Steve Bovan pulled double duty, driving his Blairs Speed Shop 7-second Camaro and jumping over into the seat of Nelson Carter's Imperial Customs Dodge Charger from Oklahoma. Also in attendance were the engine masterminds Ed Pink and Keith Black, keeping tabs on both their digger and flopper entries.

The 7,500 ardent and rowdy fans cheered for their favorite type of car (Top Fueler or Fuel Funny) for the full three rounds of head-to-head racing. Out of the gate, the

Dick Loehr loud pedals off the line in his new blown flip-top 1968 Ford Mustang. Loehr, from Lansing, Michigan, was an independent racer who won several major events driving Ford products. Ford's top brass took notice of Loehr's success, and soon he took delivery of a new Mustang Funny Car with the cooperation of Ford. Race Car Specialists fabricated the 124-inch tube chassis that carried the Cal-Automotive all-fiberglass Mustang to lengthen body to the total of 21 feet. Mechanic John Skiba tuned and maintained the 427-ci SOHC Cammer, which was fed by an 85-percent nitro mixture. Loehr's Max Curtis Ford–sponsored Stampede competed in the 2,400-pound fuel class that recorded 8.80 ETs with speeds of more than 165 mph.

Gas Ronda dumped the Hilborn injectors in favor of a new blower setup on the top of his 427 SOHC engine. The combination made him one of the toughest to beat out on the West Coast. The new supercharger unit was prepped by Ed Pink, who also called the tune-up shots on the Mustang that led Ronda to low-8-second times with speeds in excess of 180 mph.

Ray Alley swapped out his roofless Charger body for a new Barracuda one-piece fiberglass model with positive results. The Engine Masters entry won the Funny Car Round Robin Invitational at Orange County International Raceway. Ray blasted to an ET of 7.86 at 186.32 mph in the final round when he outran Charlie Allen.

Investing more than $8,000 to build a competitive race car, Al Vanderwoude's Flying Dutchman *Dodge Charger was a fine example that an independent racer could run with the high-dollar factory-backed teams. Ron Pellegrini's Fiberglass Limited of Chicago prepped the 1968 Charger body that sat on a 120-inch wheelbase chrome-moly chassis that Vanderwoude built himself. The functional aluminum interior was fabricated by Dee Keaton, and Dennis Richlef sprayed the candy green over pearl white paint. Vanderwoude's 400-ci Dodge Hemi had 1,500 hp and ran a mixture of 80-percent nitro. It produced quarter-mile ETs in the 7s at 190 mph.*

The somewhat bewildered look on the face of starter Larry Sutton was a reaction to Dee Keaton completing one of his dry-hop burnouts without his flame mask. Keaton's newest entry into the Funny Car wars was this flip-top Mercury Cougar that reeled out constant 7.90s with speeds above 185 mph. Dick Fletcher constructed the rail chassis that supported the Fiberglass Trends body, and the tin work was crafted by Keaton himself.

Funny Car hopes looked dim after losing the first three matchups of the first round. The second round was completely dominated by the Funny Cars, shutting out the rails 4-0. When the dragsters experienced traction woes from the slick surface in the second round, the handicap was lowered to 0.65 for the third and last round of racing.

When the smoke cleared and votes were tallied at the end of the night, the experimental stock team capitalized with 1-second head starts to pull out a 7 to 5 win against the "Kings of the 1320."

Gas Ronda's SOHC led the charge with three round wins while Bovan in the Imperial Customs Charger ripped off impressive top speeds of 193.48 and 191.52 mph only to back it up in the third round, running a slower 188.66 mph with a 7.95 ET.

Big Three Battle Sweeps Lions

On the same night, just down the I-405 in Wilmington, Lions hosted its first Big Three Battle Factory Showdown Tournament. More than 30 cars participated. The crowd of 8,000-plus jammed the stands, taking in some high-quality racing that proved Funny Cars were becoming the crowd favorites at any track.

Hayden Proffitt is nearly even off the line against Gene Snow's Rambunctious *Dodge Dart. Proffitt gave the AMC fans something to smile for with strong performances for a true American Motors–powered blown nitro Funny Car. (Photo Courtesy Jake Johnston)*

It was a blast when a drag strip booked large Funny Car meets that featured some of the area's top-notch talent, which allowed the fans to follow their favorite heroes. It seemed like every week, new cars, drivers, and teams debuted new iron in hopes of being productive, racing safely, and just having a great time. One might remember a certain race, winner, or speeds or times, but one never forgets who made that impression. "Jungle" Jim Liberman, the *Chi-Town Hustler*, "Dyno" Don Nicholson, and Arnie Beswick fit that bill.

"Dyno" Don Nicholson's **Eliminator Cougar was his newest entry in the Funny Car wars in 1968. The Mercury Cougar was his strongest running, best-looking car to date. It ran the new Stage-II Logghe-built chassis with a blown supercharged 427 SOHC engine that Nicholson successfully ran from the previous years. Nicholson hired mechanics Pete Williams and Jim Campbell to handle the wrenching chores. With the increase of engine fires and blower explosions, Nicholson became more concerned about injuries and car damage, so he decided in late 1968 to leave Funny Cars and return to Super Stock racing for 1969. Keeping booking dates throughout 1968, Nicholson turned the driving over to Frank Oglesby.**

Some paint schemes from the late 1960s featured psychedelic art and bright colors, which were sprayed onto several Funny Cars, including Kip Brundage's latest edition of the Parts Mart Speed Shop flip-top Camaro. Brundage, from Northern California, was known as a tough contender who ran a blown Chevy L88 427-ci Rat engine between the pipes. Brundage's best performance was at Sacramento Dragway, where he took the runner-up spot to Don Prudhomme at the 1970 Governor's Cup Meet.

Fred Goeske rattles the bleachers, posting an ET of 7.86 at the Lions Unlimited Funny Car Spectacular in the Plymouth Dealers Association of Southern California Hemi Cuda II. With more than 12,225 ardent Funny Car fans in attendance for the Fiberglass Underground extravaganza, Goeske met the Blair Speed Shop entry of Steve Bovan. Goeske prevailed and grabbed the $2,000 cash when Bovan's Camaro blew the transmission. Overall, the Funny Car Spectacular was an enormous success, and all spectators received the reward of knowing that every cent of their admission went to charity.

The OCIR Inaugural All-Star Festival

The OCIR promoters organized the first of what was likely the beginning of the Funny Car Manufacturer's Meet with the 1968-1/2 Funny Car All-Star Race. There were five star-filled teams. The manufacturers represented were Dodge, Ford/Mercury, Plymouth, Pontiac, Chevrolet, and a group of alternates.

Most entrants were from the West Coast with a mix also from Michigan, Missouri, Colorado, and Texas. This was the first race that a team car collected a full point from a win down to a half a point for an alternate subbing for a team car, and a point was awarded for running low ET and top speed of the meet.

More than 10,000 fans were on their feet when the

The Mr. Pickett Corvette roadster owned and driven by Bob Pickett drove through a field of 35 Funny Cars, including Gerry Schwartz's Ratty Cat Chevy-powered Cougar and the Doug's Headers Corvair of Bourgeois and Wade. Pickett met with Dee Keaton for the $1,000 in the final round at Lions. The 7,232 fans in attendance were treated to one heck of a final, as the Corvette gave its all, running an ET of 8.35 at 174.08 mph in a losing effort to Keaton's 8.16 at 174.75 mph.

"General" Roger Wolford hammers down on the pedal in the Secret Weapon Jeep at Carlsbad Raceway. Jeeps hit the drag strips in 1966 and were welcomed by the fans but outlawed by the NHRA. They were not allowed to compete at all national events. In contrast, the AHRA welcomed the unique machines. During an eastern tour, the Jeep experienced misfortunes with engine and driveline parts failures and even hit the guardrail on occasion. All was not lost though when the Weapon pulled off an upset win at the Cars Illustrated Magazine Funny Car Nationals. "One-Star" General Wolford and "Sargent" Kelly soon parked the camouflaged wonder, as the team split up for other ventures.

More than 50 fiberglass flip-top Funny Cars covered the grounds at the Lions Unlimited Funny Car Spectacular. The 32 quickest cars formed two brackets, including the Funny Bunch Chevy Corvair of Campbell and Moore. After qualifying eighth with a 9.11 ET, the injected Chevrolet's hopes ended in the third round when the Flying Dutchman of Al Vander-woude defeated the Corvair.

East versus West Boycott

One infamous incident occurred at Lions Drags Strip that left a bad taste with the top touring pros. They were booked in an invited-only race with guaranteed money. However, the management at Lions rescinded the 16-car "invitational" Funny Car East versus West race with little to no notice to the racers involved. The meet was abruptly changed to a "John Doe" 32-car open competition with all cars needing to qualify. This was considered a breach of contract to the top cars and drivers. A war of words ensued with both sides, including drag strips, expressing heated feelings.

Lions readvertised its "East vs. West" Funny Car Open for November 2 in *Drag News* and challenged the original group of "fraidy" car owners, drivers, and sponsors. Irwindale, on the other hand, brought back the East–West stars from its prior event two weeks before and promoted it with the "East re-challenging the West." All those concerned accepted. The rematch ran on the same day as Lions' John Doe Open. Lions reported a crowd of 8,840 happy fans in attendance, which was fewer fans than at the Irwindale track.

A letter by the original 16 cars and teams was printed in the November 16 issue of *Drag News*:

"ATTENTION FUNNY CAR FANS NATION WIDE. THE FOLLOWING IS THE REACTION TO RECENT ACTION AT LIONS DRAG STRIP BY 16 TOP FUNNY CAR OWNERS:

"Since there are undoubtedly many fans and strip operators nationally who were wondering about the recent advertisements and stories regarding East versus West Meets at both Lions Drag Strip and Irwindale Raceway, the Racers hereby state their story.

"Lions Drag Strip contracted several top professionals to compete in their annual East versus West Funny Car Championships from both the east and west. However, at a time when several of these cars were either en route to California or in California, notice was given that ALL contracts were cancelled. The meet was changed to open competition only! This, in effect, gave the racers every right to run anywhere they chose to.

"Several of these professionals have week-to-week contracts to run in California from October through November. The cancellation gave the racers open dates in the middle of their California schedule. Nearly all the racers felt they had been slighted by this action; they contacted Irwindale Raceway, who had a limited schedule for that week. Irwindale expanded its program to add a top-flight Funny Car show that featured both the elite group of cars from both the east and west. The results are history now, but the competition was at Irwindale! During competition, there were a total of 21 runs that were less than 8 seconds and 13 top speeds above 190 mph. We'll let you judge where the real competition was!

"Who is afraid of the competition? We were unjustly afraid of the competition. How about a 16-car winning team take all at Lions for $16,000?

"P.S. Why was the attendance at this year's Lions Drag Race East–West meet down from last year? The fans can answer that question!

Signed,
Larry Reyes, Tenn. 7.70/192
Lew Arrington, Calif. 7.60/193
Gene Snow, Texas 7.68/205
Tommy Grove, Calif. 7.50/200
Eddie Schartman, Ohio 7.58/195
Bourgeois & Wade, Calif. 7.58/195
Don Schumacher, Ill. 7.38/202
John Mazmanian, Calif. 7.65/195
Kelly Chadwick, Texas 7.64/193
Fred Goeske, Calif. 7.69/195
Dick Loehr, Mich. 7.60/194
Gas Ronda, Calif. 7.80/185
Nelson Carter, Okla. 7.63/197
Charlie Allen, Calif. 7.60/193
Mike Burkhart, Texas 7.70/192
Jim Liberman, Calif. 7.60/192"

Although it was a war of words and actions, the winners were the combined crowds of nearly 19,000 fans at both venues on one Southern California evening! Soon after the boycott, both parties agreed to settle and mend their differences.

The Speed Sport *Barracuda of Gary "Red" Greth and Lyle Fisher hailed from Tucson, Arizona. Red, Lyle, and Don Maynard campaigned their successful rear-engine A/M fuel roadster in the earlier days of drag racing.*

first pair rolled up to the starting line to kick off the event. The rainbow Firebird of "Texas Teenager" Don Gay met with Fred "Go-Go" Goeske's *Hemi Cuda II*, and Goeske took the win.

At the conclusion of all three rounds, the Ford/Mercury Team was crowned the team champion, as it collected most wins and team points. There was still some unfinished business with the two quickest cars remaining facing off for the $1,500 grand prize.

Charlie Allen (7.84 ET) and Dick Loehr (7.86) met in the final run. The cars left evenly, but the Mustang of Loehr forged ahead by four car lengths before his goggles fogged over and he couldn't see. He pulled the chute,

coasting through the lights. Unknown to Loehr, Allen's Dart locked up the rear end, causing extensive damage to the driveline. For his efforts, Loehr walked away with more than $3,000.

The Life of a Funny Car Driver

A decent living could now be made as a professional touring racer, but it was brutal, especially being away from family for months at a time. Many downsides to the business affected several East Coast Funny Car professionals, who went out to the West Coast in the fall and

Southern California had a strong contingency of the wildest injected Funny Car group that competed hard, were fun to watch, and flat-out raced! Occasionally, the word got out about needing to fill up nitro Funny Car shows, and then the Hilborns were swapped to 6-71 superchargers with a healthy dose of nitro in the tank. One of the more successful teams that took on the challenge was the Gage and Barnes Raunchy *Corvette roadster.*

Jay Gage replaced the Hilborn tubes, bolted a blower to the top of the motor, tipped a mixture of nitro into the fuel tank, and went racing at the Lions Drag Strip's 35-plus Funny Car show. Gage qualified the Corvette fifth with the hot setup and defeated his first-round counterpart King Rebel *with an ET of 8.38 at 171.10 mph to the AMC's 9.58 at 148.02 mph.* Raunchy *was the surprise car at Lions, but in round two, Gage freewheeled against Dale Pulde and went out of contention. Overall, the performance of the injected car was outstanding.*

Header pioneer and longtime Chevy star Doug Thorley made the jump to AMC with this sophisticated mid-engine Javelin Funny Car. The underdog Rambler ran a 390–401-ci AMC motor (punched out to 499 ci) that was connected to a B&M Tork Master with a custom-built in-and-out box that eliminated the need of a driveshaft. Mechanic Gary Slusser handled the wrenching duties on the 1968-1/2 Javelin 1 that weighed in at 1,665 pounds in full race trim. On its first full pass, the Javelin ran an ET of 8.53 at 182.54 mph at Orange County International Raceway. After the run, Thorley was asked, "How did it compare with driving the front motor setup cars?" Thorley replied, "I got more whistle noise from the blower and less exhaust noise." On Thorley's second full pass in the car, he was within 100 feet of the speed traps when the windshield disintegrated, blew off the car, and ripped off his goggles!

Another participant at the Unlimited Funny Car Spectacular at Lions Drag Strip was the Corvette roadster Little Jon, *which was driven by Rusty Dellings. Dellings put the Corvette into the second part of the program, running an ET of 9.77 for the 15th slot but could not get past the* Funny Bunch *Corvair in the first round.*

Illustrator Tom West pinpoints the detail of the tubular chassis, looped roll cage, and the 427-ci Rat engine in one of his BBC number-1 "X-ray" drawings of Don Kirby's Beach City Chevrolet *Corvette. The car was driven by the versatile driver Gary Gabelich.*

Nothing drew the attention at the local Rambler dealership like seeing Doug Thorley's Javelin 1 AMC Funny Car in the middle of the showroom floor. Woody Gilmore built the 120-inch custom chassis to Thorley's safety and weight specifications. The original 390-401-ci AMC engine was built by Gary Slusser. The block was bored out to 499 inches and assembled with all the goodies, including a Joe Reath crankshaft, Mondello heads, Venolia pistons, and a Sig Erson cam. The fiberglass Javelin body was from Randall Rambler in Mesa, Arizona, which incorporated a swingout front windshield, allowing Thorley to enter and exit the car. Later in its life, he replaced the AMC engine with a 426 Chrysler Hemi. Under full throttle with driver Bob Hightower behind the wheel at Irwindale, the Javelin stood up on the rear wheels and flipped completely, which destroyed the car.

Don Schumacher's number-two Barracuda with driver Ron O'Donnell lost to "Mighty" Mike Van Sant driving the Invader Corvette at Lions Drag Strip. O'Donnell took home the $750 runner-up cash to his boss, as Schumacher was taking delivery of his new Ed Pink "Elephant" Hemi for his Stardust Barracuda.

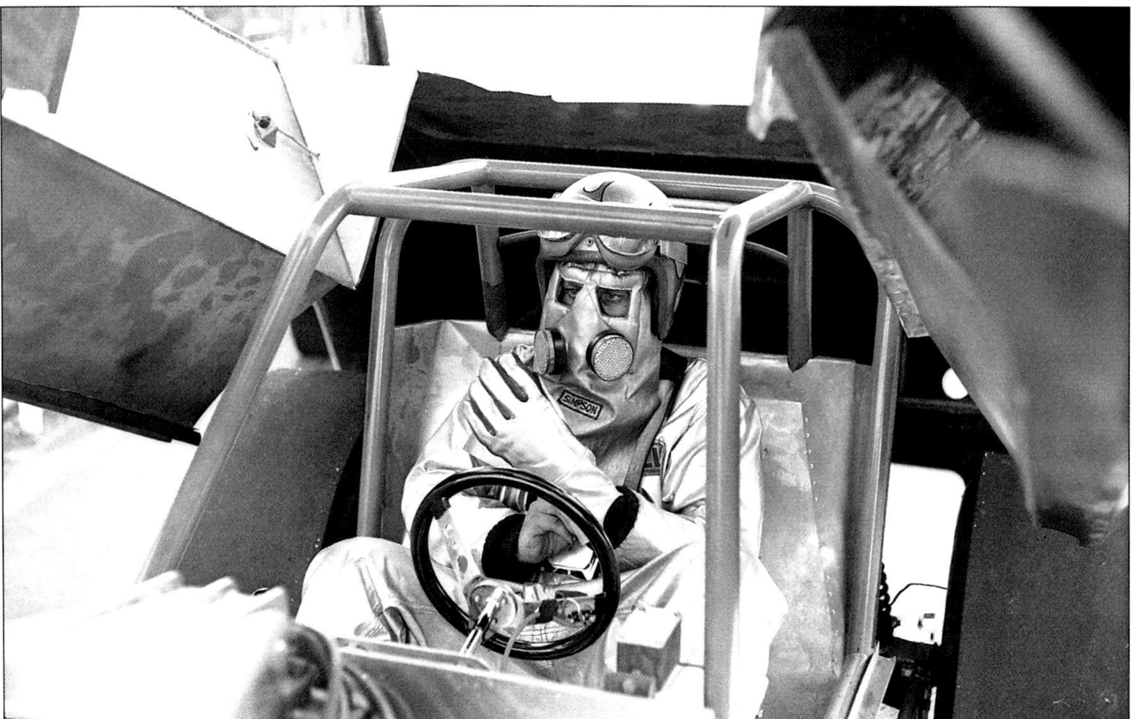

Ronnie Runyan gets into the zone in the Blue Hell Chevy Corvair at Irwindale Raceway. Runyan was one of the top Chevy drivers and was available for autographs and fan questions.

With 300 names submitted by spectators at Orange County International Raceway to rename the Imperial Customs Dodge Charger, it came down to two names for owner Nelson Carter: the **Super Chief** *or the* **Cherokee Stripper.** *Both names were based on Carter's family heritage.* **Super Chief** *was chosen for his Osage (Native American) background with veteran driver Steve Bovan at the wheel. Dave Beebe soon came aboard to take the controls.*

winter months to test new equipment, new combination setups, or new parts or just went match racing. It was a constant grind.

Most racers either had a signed or verbal contract to make appearances at certain tracks with the assurance of guaranteed prize money. In most cases, these contracts ran month to month, mainly in October and November when the weather was ideal. The drag strips often highlighted the professionals from both the eastern and western states competing head-to-head.

The Second Annual Manufacturer's Meet

The second annual Manufacturer's Meet was halted due to inclement weather and then took eight days to complete. The first attempt to get racing underway was on the scheduled race day, when a massive blanket of dense fog rolled into the facility. It stuck around overnight and halted racing.

The following weekend on Saturday, the dark skies opened one hour before the second attempt to race, which was to commence at 6:00 p.m. The rain washed out the festivities. The third attempt was Sunday morning. The skies cleared, and the sun dried the track and pits. The race went on successfully without any major glitches.

Racing began in the morning, but the results weren't determined untill later in the evening under the lights. The longshot, a young Richard Siroonian, piloted the Plymouth Barracuda of John Mazmanian (his uncle) to victory over the "Chicago Kid" Don Schumacher. Siroonian, the ex-Gasser ace now a rookie in the Funny Cars ranks, outdrove the veteran Schumacher in the final round when he laid down an ET of 7.61 to the Shumacher's 7.93.

Jim "the Wrench" Wetton and "Dapper" Don Cullinan's Mako Shark *Corvette was a product out of Jack Head Chevrolet's high-performance department in Pasadena, California. The Chevy 427-ci Chevrolet Rat mill was mounted into an Exhibition Engineering Chassis built by Ronnie Scrima. While at the 1968 Manufacturer's Meet, the team was testing an early supercharger/injector shield fixed to the top of the Funny Car engine to help prevent damage to the body if the blower backfired.*

Terry Ivey brought Ted DeTar's Kansas Badman *to Orange County International Raceway's second annual Manufacturer's Meet and was working out the new car bugs. Ivey's first-round encounter with Gordon Mineo's hard-charging Firebird resulted in a win for Mineo. He drove past the lagging Torino with an ET of 8.53 at 166.66 mph to a losing 8.84 at 166.35 mph.*

A crossed-up Larry Reyes in the Super Cuda *had his hands full when he experienced a 4-foot-high wheel-stand that carried the 'Cuda across the centerline, giving the automatic win and a point to Larry Coleman's* Super Ford *Torino at the 1968 Orange County International Raceway Manufacturer's Funny Car Championships.*

Memphis, Tennessee, which is known as the "birthplace of rock 'n' roll" and the "home of the blues," could now add one of the strongest Funny Cars, the **Super Ford** *Torino* of Larry Coleman, Larry Graces, and driver Sidney Foster, to the list. Coleman's entry was the first Torino flip-top Ford-powered flopper in drag racing that broke the 200-mph barrier with ETs in the mid-7 range.

Gene Snow, a used car salesman from Fort Worth, Texas, invested $13,000 and wound up with one of the fastest Funny Cars in 1969. Snow's Rambunctious *Dodge Charger* had all the best equipment available that included a low-profile 118-inch tubular chassis from Logghe, one of Keith Black's blown Hemis that was maintained and tuned by ace mechanic Jake Johnston, and a narrowed and chopped Fiberglass Limited body. Snow ran a direct-drive transmission with a triple disc drive clutch by way of a dragster. Snow broke the 200-mph barrier with legitimate numbers at Wichita (202.70 mph) and Houston (202.56 mph) in the car's early outings.

The team of Bill Kenz and Ron Leslie was contacted in mid-1966 by the Mercury Performance Project to receive one of four Logghe-built tubular chassis that changed the history and safety in Funny Cars forever. The team was successful in Funny Car with its 427 SOHC-powered High Country Cougar and set the NHRA national top speed record that earned the car the title of "World's Fastest Cougar."

Roger Lindamood was one of the early founders in drag racing from the early factory altered-wheelbase days to the modern fiberglass fuelers. Lindamood's newest entry, the Color Me Gone *Dodge Charger, is shown at Orange County International Raceway's Manufacturer's Funny Car Championships.*

Chevrolet stalwart Bruce Larson was one of the most recognizable personalities in Funny Car with his patented red, white, and blue USA-1 Chevrolet Chevelle-, Camaro-, Monza-, and Corvette-bodied Funny Cars. Larson depended on the power of a 427 Chevrolet Rat engine in the earlier years.

Eddie Schartman was a hired gun by Mercury to drive one of the first factory-backed Comets in 1966 that revolutionized the Funny Car industry. Logghe built the first ultra-modern tubular chassis fitted with Comet bodies for Don Nicholson, Jack Chrisman, Kenz and Leslie, and Steffey and Schartman that were ahead of the times and nearly untouchable. By 1968, the original tube frames were now too heavy and outdated to be competitive. So, Schartman ordered a new lightweight 120-inch sculpted, tubular frame from Ron and Gene Logghe, complete with a supercharged 427 SOHC lurking under the new fiberglass Cougar shell. Schartman and crew chief Arnie Behling developed a chain and sprocket drive unit for the cams and magneto and installed a new Schiefer triple-disc clutch and direct drive.

Leonard Hughes kept the pressure off the Plymouth team at the 1968 Orange County International Raceway Manufacturer's Funny Car Championships when he drove the Candies and Hughes *Barracuda to two round wins. Hughes won over a red-lighting Steve Bovan and Gas Ronda, who swerved out of control and smacked the guardrail with a broken steering box.*

Randy Walls calmly waits in his new Super Nova II *with his crew and family members, including his wife, Cheri, at Lions Drag Strip for starter Larry Sutton to say, "Fire up the next pair!" Walls, an independent racer, was one of the few Funny Car owners/drivers who built his own fiberglass bodies by making his own molds with a weekend rental from the local Avis Center. Walls and his crew would strip the trim and moldings from the car; apply body putty to fill the door, hood, and trunk seams; and apply fabric soaked in fiberglass. Walls confessed that it was hard to explain the dried green putty and stains throughout the body to the Avis manager when the car was returned on Monday morning.*

When the smoke cleared at the second annual Manufacturer's Funny Car at Orange County International Raceway, it boiled down to a pair of Plymouth Barracudas. The "Chicago Kid" Don Schumacher raced against "Big" John Mazmanian with underdog Richard Siroonian between the pipes. Both cars fired up simultaneously, completed their burnouts, and staged. Both cars left at the green, and Schumacher's Stardust *released a massive cloud of smoke when the front seal blew out of the engine and threw down oil on the track. Siroonian powered to a winning ET of 7.61 at 191.82 mph to a slowing 7.93 at 183.28 mph for the wounded fish.*

The Mako Shark *Corvette of Jim Wetton and Don Cullinan was backed by Jack Head Chevrolet in Pasadena, California. Wetton and Cullinan co-managed the high-performance department at the dealership and decided to merge their past Funny Car experiences. They went to Exhibition Engineering's Ronnie Scrima to construct a 120-inch wheelbase chassis. Originally fitted with a factory Corvette fiberglass body that was pieced together by hand, the crafted body was too heavy, so a replica one-piece lightweight J&D body was lengthened 20 inches. Under the shell was a supercharged stroked 427-ci Chevrolet engine. (Photo Courtesy Tim Pearl Archives)*

With 45 Funny Cars vying for a guaranteed $22,000 cash purse, it was three rounds of non-stop racing with fans holding on to the edge of their seats and rooting for their preferred brand of cars. This was becoming a familiar sight every fall at the OCIR, but this time, the Dodge team outscored the competition and took home top honors and its share of the loot!

Primetime for Funny Cars in 1969

For 1969, New Year's ay in Southern California was greeted with a warm, sunny day with many watching the Rose Parade, tailgating at the Rose Bowl, or watching Funny Cars at Irwindale. It was also the time when many Midwest and Eastern stars stayed out West to stay away from the frigid tundra at home and to race and test new parts combinations and techniques for the upcoming year. It also allowed the few new multi-car teams to exchange data for the new year, including Clare Sanders driving for "Jungle" Jim and Lee Jones driving for Malcolm Durham.

The third annual Funny Car Championships at Irwindale welcomed in the new year with 8,000 ecstatic fans basking in 80-degree weather under cloudless skies! With a $2,000 cash purse up for grabs, a record entry of 40 cars were out in force to earn a berth in the elimina-

tor field of 16 to see who would start out the year on a positive note.

When it was all said and done, Southern California's All-American Boy, Charlie Allen, took home top honors, defeating Don Schumacher's *Stardust* Barracuda.

"Jungle" Jim Liberman is fixed on teammate Clare Sanders, as he qualified the number-2 "Jungle" Jim Chevrolet into the 16-car car field with an 8.13 ET at Irwindale's New Year Championships. Both Sanders and Liberman made the show, running out of 13th and 14th spots, with more than 8,000-plus spectators witnessing the first event of the year.

Dick Harrell was one of the mild-mannered Funny Car stars that made his presence known when he hit the pedal with his Chevy-powered Camaro Funny Car. Dick ran his share on the match race circuits at both NHRA- and AHRA-sanctioned tracks. In national competition, Dick mostly ran at all AHRA events. Mr. Chevrolet took home the Funny Car title crown at the 1969 AHRA Winternationals at Beeline.

Charlie Allen began January 1, 1969, winning $2,000 by defeating Don Schumacher in a classic East versus West battle in the final round at Irwindale's third annual New Year's Day Funny Car Championships. Allen outdistanced the record field of 40 Funny Cars entered for the 16-car field. The "All-American Boy" from the Dodge Rebellion ran a best 7.56 ET during eliminations.

Don Schumacher took runner-up honors at Irwindale's third annual Funny Car Championships when the transmission failed to shift and the car swerved as fluid got under the rear wheels. All was not lost for Schumacher's Illinois-based Stardust Barracuda, as Don set the ET track record with a 7.44, steamrolling his way to meeting Allen in the finals.

Going Pro or Staying Home

This was the $60,000 question for the serious racer: "What should I build as a full-time, top-touring machine to race week in and week out that will keep up with the grueling schedule from one race to another?"

As the old cliché says, "You need to spend money to make money."

Beginning with a strong budget, one would need a top-rated chassis manufacturer, engine supplier, and builder with an inventory of both engine and transmission driveline components, spare parts, a high volume of routine parts (spark plugs, oil, automatic transmission fluid, nitromethane, slicks and tires, etc.), and a dependable transporter. One cannot overlook the fiberglass body and tin work, custom paint and lettering, and a full-time working crew of a minimum of three multitasking crewmembers just to keep actively campaigning the car. The amount of $25,000 to $35,000 was not out of the question before the car ever even rolled onto the track!

A major game changer for the Funny Cars was in 1969, when they were finally recognized and awarded their own 16-car Funny Car Eliminator bracket at all four NHRA National events starting with the ninth annual Winternationals at Pomona. Forty-five fuel-burning cars

Bob Brooks wheels Ed Carter's Proud American Chevy Corvette at the beach in front of the packed stands. Ed hailed from Newark, California, where he ran his Color Kart 65 Chevy II, which began life under the Blairs Speed Shop banner.

Jake Johnston pounds the asphalt while heating up the Goodyears in Gene Snow's Rambunctious II Dodge Charger at Irwindale Raceway. B&R Racecars (John Buttera and Dennis Rollain) constructed the chassis with a late-model Hemi by Keith Black for motivation.

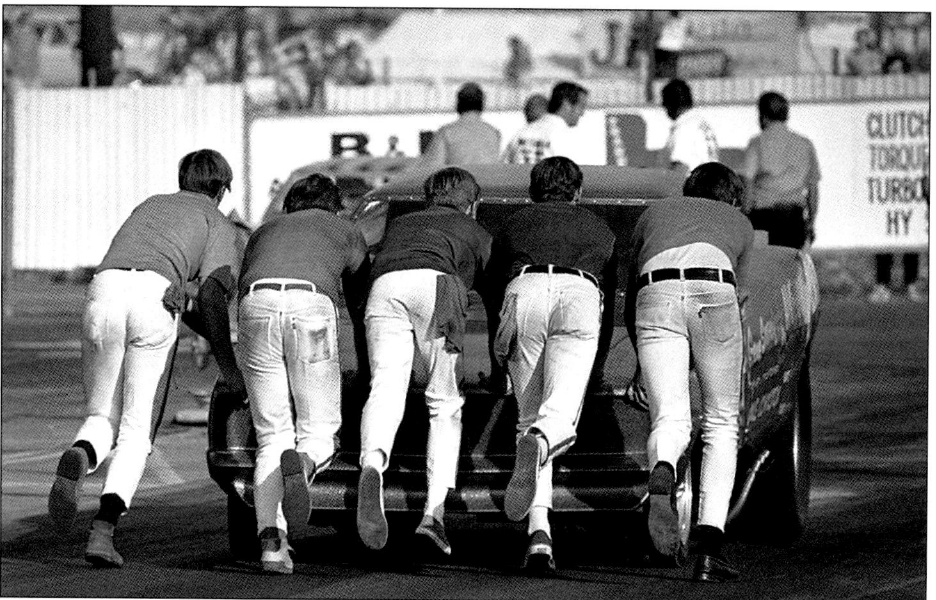

Without a reverse gear for the direct-drive transmission, crewmembers push Jake Johnston back to the starting line after completing his burnout. Paula Murphy was in the other lane, and both cars launched together at the green. As Johnston approached the lights, the engine erupted into a fireball when the crankshaft split in half, which allowed the complete clutch assembly to exit the car. The car went sideways through the lights and nearly rolled over, but when the chute deployed, Johnston corrected the car and kept it from rolling.

The Funny Honey Dodge Charger belonged to the brother-and-sister team of Bernie and Della Woods. Bernie handled the mechanics end with engine and chassis maintenance, while Della drove the Charger. Wolverine Diesel built the 128-1/2-inch wheelbase frame, which was completed with two one-piece looped roll cages designed to a large extent for driver protection. The car weighed approximately 2,400 pounds, which was extremely heavy for a Funny Car. A late-model 426 Dodge Hemi sat between the rails that Della drove to ETs of 8.90 at 167 mph.

were on the fairgrounds vying for one of the 16 spots to race on Sunday.

Several top-echelon owners and drivers of the AA/FD legion now brought their new Funny Cars to the class. Roland Leong, Tom McEwen, and Ron Rinauro now joined the earlier stars who made the jump on the bandwagon with the likes of "Big" John Mazmanian and Dave Beebe.

Early problems that plagued the Funny Cars were the driveline failures. Rear-end and automatic transmission brakeage was the weak link between a winner's circle appearance or going home early. Many went the route of a three-disc, slipper clutch setup that rapidly improved the performances with lower ETs and substantially higher speeds. The AA/FD stars noticed the Funny Car's surge in popularity and money and then offered "fire sales" on their rail cars and switched to Funny Cars.

New Blood

Danny Ongais, Connie Kalitta, and Gary Gabelich were now legitimate competitors with some of the best equipment that money could buy. The new-model-year vehicles for 1969 were real eye-catchers. Based on size and appeal, mid-7-second ETs and 200-mph-plus runs were knocking on the door. Ford stalwart Connie Kalitta brought out his combination of a new Logghe-built Mach I Mustang with the new Ford Boss 429 Shotgun engine, which was the same apparatus that powered his Top Fuel dragster.

Tom "the Mongoose" McEwen revamped the former record holder Barracuda of Leonard Woods and Paul Candies to enter the Funny Car brotherhood. McEwen repainted the body, made changes to the chassis, updated safety equipment, and discarded the TorqueFlite in favor of a direct-drive unit with a slipper clutch.

Dodge and Plymouth Aero Disadvantage

New problems arose for a few Mopar Funny Cars in 1969. They needed to find a way to win among the blown fuel Funny Cars and remain NHRA legal in competition. Many top runners had low wind-resistant Mustangs or Camaro/Firebird-sized bodies; however, the bulkier Dodge Charger–bodied floppers (Roger Lindamood, Nelson Carter, and Gene Snow) couldn't match the aerodynamics of the smaller models, so they were at a disadvantage.

One such case was Roland Leong, who won every major title in NHRA National competition as an owner of a Top Fuel dragster with different drivers. Leong built one of the most impressive Funny Cars for his newest rac-

ing venture. Larry Reyes, driver for Leong's new $15,000 *Hawaiian* flopper, was on his fourth pass down the quarter mile when the rear of the car caught air and lifted at 180 mph, went airborne, and flew more than 200 feet, which was longer than the Wright Brothers' inaugural flight at Kitty Hawk. The car crashed down hard on the strip. The mangled body separated from the destroyed chassis, resulting in a pile of tangled metal and plastic remnants. As fate had it, Reyes won the round against Mike Hamby in Larry Christopherson's Chevy II but couldn't return. Reyes suffered only shock and walked away without serious injury.

Coca-Cola

Drag racing and Funny Cars received a huge boost of revenue when the Coca-Cola and Sprite bottlers signed one of the largest non-racing contracts. The contract promoted the popular soft drink to the younger crowd and ran a series of eight All-Star Funny Cars touring across the county promoting safety, competition, and the refreshing soda products.

Toying Around

In the summer of 1969, another milestone for drag racing was taking shape behind closed doors when Don Prudhomme and Tom McEwen formed Wildlife Racing Enterprises. The duo was also in negotiations with the

Arizona Funny Car standout Larry Christopherson was one of the unsung drivers whose hard work and dedication reaped rewards in quality numbers. Mike Hamby wrenched on the 427 Chevy-powered Nova and climbed into the seat from time to time. One of Mike's memorable rides occurred at the 1969 Winternationals in Pomona against the Hawaiian *when Larry Reyes flew 200 feet in the lights, defeating Hamby.*

The tower-side grandstands at Orange County International Raceway quickly fill up with fans choosing their seats and quality spots along the fences, waiting for the action to begin. The fence was a great place to get up close and personal with the parade of cars, including the Beach City Chevrolet *Corvette,* Gas Ronda's Mach I *Mustang, and Pete Everett's* New Breed *Firebird.*

Memories: Steve Montrelli

Crew Chief on Jim Shue's **Hell Fire** *Corvette*

"I was working for Mickey Thompson at the time when Jim Shue and Johnny Wright got together and asked me to get involved with their car. The three of us formed a reputable team. I built the motors and maintained them.

"During the first few months, we had trouble just trying to get the car down the track. It wasn't due to the lack of power, but something was off with the car. I asked Mickey if I could borrow his scales from the shop. I put them under the race car and figured out what the problem was and fixed it.

"We went to Lions that weekend, and when we got the car to the line, Johnny did the burnout, backed up, and launched. The car rolled the rear end out and snapped the driveshaft. Wright got banged up on the butt by the driveshaft and went to the hospital to get checked out, but other than a few bruises, he was fine.

"Mike Case, who built the chassis for both the *Hell Fire* and *Invader* Corvettes, was at the track and noticed what happened. He helped us load up the car on the trailer and took it to his shop, which was right around the corner. The damage wasn't too serious. Case made all of the necessary repairs, and within three hours, were back at the track in time for qualifying at 6 o'clock. I hopped that baby up, and Johnny went out and put his foot into it and ran 203.61 mph!"

Johnny Wright watches the Christmas tree while staging at Irwindale Raceway in Jim Shue's Hell Fire *Corvette. Tuner Steve Montrelli and Wright were strong runners, and both complimented each other's talents. The conservative Wright and the fanatical passion of Montrelli combined to make the* Hell Fire *one of the strongest forces out on the West Coast.*

Mike Miller, an NHRA Division 6 Funny Car standout, ran a highly competitive 1969 Dodge Dart throughout the western states. Miller sought out Thayne Portier to build his Hemi-powered Dart. Miller raced the car for a few years before selling it to supercharger manufacturer Mert Littlefield.

Mike Brown took possession of a Dart from well-known Funny Car owner/driver Gene Snow. The car was likely a rolling chassis with the body and interior tin work in place. Refurbishing an old workhorse included adding a new engine and driveline components, fresh paint with bright colors and lettering, but in this case, the old paint and lettering survived. Brown could not wait to get racing with the Dart. He raced it with the original paint scheme, only renaming the Dart Mixed Emotions. Brown kept the existing striping and lettering, including the full line of sponsors and mechanic Jake Johnston's name, who no longer had any affiliation with the car. (Photo Courtesy Jake Johnston)

Mickey Thompson's confidence in drag racing returned when Semon "Bunkie" Knudsen (an old pal from Thompson's Pontiac days) became president of the Ford Motor Company. Knudsen brought back research and development with a high budget for racing, and that brought Thompson back to the Blue Oval. Thompson had been building Indy cars, boats, LSR-Bonneville cars, and dune buggies using Ford power, but his return to drag racing was now with a pair of Mach I *Mustang Funny Cars. Veteran chassis fabricators Pat Foster and John Buttera were brought on board to build the pair of digger-style chassis rather than the square frames, while engine builder Don Ratican induced power into the blown 427-ci SOHC Cammers. Shown at Irwindale, Foster puts the Mustang through its paces during a qualifying session.*

Mickey Thompson hired Danny Ongais to drive the 116-inch blue Mach I. "Famous" Amos Satterlee handled the tuning chores while Pat Foster handled the 120-inch red Mustang with John Kranenburg turning the wrenches. Ongais dominated. He captured Funny Car Eliminator titles in both AHRA and NHRA National events, taking home the big money in 1969.

world's largest toy company, Mattel. The goal was to bring the toy magnate into drag racing for 1970–1972.

The parties signed a lucrative two-year contract that provided a pair of Plymouth-branded fuel Funny Cars to match race cross country. While they had to wait until 1970 to the take to the strip in their Snake and Mongoose Hot Wheels cars, sales of their Hot Wheels toys and race sets instantly sold out to collectors and enthusiasts worldwide. With two of the greatest ambassadors representing drag racing, Prudhomme and McEwen became overnight rock stars, selling out every drag strip they attended.

More than Just Tires

Innovator and trendsetter Mickey Thompson developed a more modern chassis with safety in mind to run much quicker and faster than before. Thompson employed chassis builders Pat Foster and John Buttera to build two identical team Mustangs, both with the first dragster-style roll cage for a Funny Car.

Mickey hired Danny Ongais to drive his blue car while Pat Foster drove the red Mustang. This was the greatest one-two punch in the early history of Funny Cars, and it changed the face of Funny Car history. Ongais dominated practically every strip on which he competed, setting numerous ET and speed records on his way to the winner's circle.

Ongais's first major win with the Mustang was at the Stardust Open in Las Vegas, where he defeated teammate Pat Foster. Ongais went on to take wins at Bakersfield, the OCIR Nitro Championships, and Sears Point. He also dominated both the AHRA and NHRA Springnationals at Bristol and Dallas respectively. The Mangler went on to take the AHRA Grand American in Detroit and NHRA Indy Nationals. Ongais was the last non-Hemi winner in an NHRA Nationals event in the Funny Car nitro class.

September was an unbelievable month for Danny Ongais. The torrid Ongais drove Mickey Thompson's *Blue* Mach I to victory over rival Rich Siroonian in "Big" John Mazmanian's Plymouth Barracuda at the NHRA US Nationals at Indy, running an incredible ET of 7.25 at 203 mph, which astonished the crowd.

Two weeks later, on September 14, Danny drove through the magical 7-second barrier with a 6.96 ET at Kansas City International Raceway. Danny "the Mangler" also ripped three additional runs of 7.21 and two consecutive 7.11s before dropping into the 6s. No other driver up to this point in the history of Funny Car could boast a 90-percent winning record in a years' time.

The New *Hawaiian* Drops Pineapples on the Competition

Roland Leong was born in 1945 in Honolulu, Hawaii, has been involved in drag racing since the 1960s, and came to the mainland in his late teens. He landed a job welding tubing for dragsters with Jim Nelson at Dragmaster Chassis in Carlsbad, California. After spending time at Dragmaster, he moved on, building race engines for Keith Black.

Leong wanted to drive, so he put together his own dragster built by Kent Fuller. For Leong's first pass in the car at Lions, he ran a respectable ET of 8.01 at 191 mph, but he could not find the chute release to slow down. He went through a fence and wound up on the railroad tracks far off the end of the strip. The excruciating encounter was enough to give Leong a second thought on his driving career. At Black's recommendation, he stayed strictly as a team owner and tuner.

Leong went on to be one of the most successful owners in the business. His *Hawaiian* Top Fuel dragsters won both the NHRA Winternationals and the US Nationals Eliminator titles back to back in 1965 and 1966 with drivers Don Prudhomme and Mike Snivley.

A new dragster was in the works at Don Long's shop for the 1969 season, but Funny Cars were not going away. So, Leong changed his mind about the dragster and sold it to Don Prudhomme. He contacted Gene and Ron Logghe to build a Funny Car chassis for the Winternationals at Pomona.

Leong had an extensive history with Chrysler and Keith Black, so he went with a new Dodge Charger body and a Keith Black Hemi resting between the rails in the Logghe. With the car near completion, Leong needed a driver, and word traveled fast. Larry Reyes fit the bill and was hired.

The car made its debut appearance for the press with half pass and tune-up runs at OCIR. Gene Logghe and Keith Black were both present.

The forecast was bright with sunny times ahead for the new Charger 500. A few days later at Pomona, things quickly turned bad when Larry Reyes entered the lights with a first-round win over Mike Hamby driving for Larry Christopherson. When air entered under the body, the car became airborne in an instant. It first rolled nose to nose then barrel-rolled to a stop. Reyes was shaken but unhurt. The car was mangled beyond repair, but the roll cage did what it was intended to do: keep the driver out of harm's way. Within days, Logghe began construction on a new car that was ready by Memorial Day. The car was rushed from Logghe unfinished.

When it arrived at Black's shop, both the body and chassis were left unpainted. More refinements were wanted by both Leong and Reyes to the fiberglass body, underbody tin, and chassis to make everything fit prop-

With five years of experience in a Funny Car, Larry Reyes signed with Roland Leong to drive the new **Hawaiian II** *full-size Dodge Charger 500 Funny Car. The car only made four passes down the quarter mile before it was completely wiped out at Pomona. With more than 60 dates already booked to fill, Logghe took only three months to construct a brand-new car that was rushed back out to California. Reyes returned to the driver's seat in Leong's new* **Hawaiian** *in late May at Lions for testing. The chassis wasn't painted and the tin work needed modifications. The car now sported a new scaled-down Dodge Mini-Charger body complete with a new Keith Black Hemi nestled between the rails.*

Roland Leong and Larry Reyes's unfinished Hawaiian II *debuted in a three-day whirlwind tour around Southern California during Memorial Day weekend. Without aid of a transporter or pit crew, the* Armenian Army *of "Big" John Mazmanian jumped in and offered Leong a hand with the new car. Right out of the gate on Friday, May 30, at Irwindale, Reyes eased the Charger into the program but lost in round one. He returned for round two via the break rule, and that was all he needed. He ripped through the rest of the competition, including clobbering Ron Leslie in the* High Country *Cougar II in the final round to earn the $1,000. Reyes also claimed an extra $250 winner-takes-all bonus with a special match race against Bob Muravez driving the* Freight Train *twin-engine gas dragster. Reyes had no trouble, and he easily derailed the train.*

Larry Reyes continued his hot hand in front of the 10,000-plus onlookers on Saturday, May 31, at Orange County International Raceway's Hang Ten Funny Car Championships. Reyes not only set low ET (7.38) and top speed (200.06 mph) right out of the transporter but also prevailed over the opposition. The Keith Black–powered Pineapple/Armenian Army *Dodge was more than a match for Randy Walls's Chevy-powered Nova in the final round. Fans held their ears when Reyes blasted past Walls, who suffered from transmission woes.*

erly. Instead of returning the car to Michigan, it was sent to Ronnie Scrima's Exhibition Engineering in Van Nuys for competition.

The long-awaited return of the *Hawaiian II* happened at Lions on May 24. Leong and Reyes rolled up to the starting line with none other with "Big" John Mazmanian, Doug Cook, Stan Shiroma, and the *Armenian Army*. Reyes eased the Charger on its maiden runs with several soft passes, clocking an ET of 7.92 at 160.05 mph.

The following Friday night at Irwindale on Memorial Day weekend, Leong, Mazmanian, Black, Holly Hendrick, Cook, Shiroma, and the *Armenian Army* returned to iron out the kinks of the new Charger. Now sporting white shoe polish lettering on the blue gel coat body, Leong instructed Reyes to take it easy. Reyes lost in the first round but returned in the second round via the "break rule." It was the opportunity they needed. The car hooked up and ran like a rocket all night long.

Going into the final round, Reyes took out Ron Leslie in the Kenz and Leslie *High Country* Cougar to take home the $1,000 prize. The night was not over yet. John Peters, owner of the twin-engine *Freight Train* Top Gas dragster, and his driver Bob Muravez issued a $250 winner-take-all challenge. Both cars left on the green, but Reyes never looked back and collected the additional cash.

Saturday at OCIR's Hang Ten Funny Car 500 Championships, Reyes unloaded an ET of 7.40 at 200.00 mph right off the trailer. It put him in the number-one spot

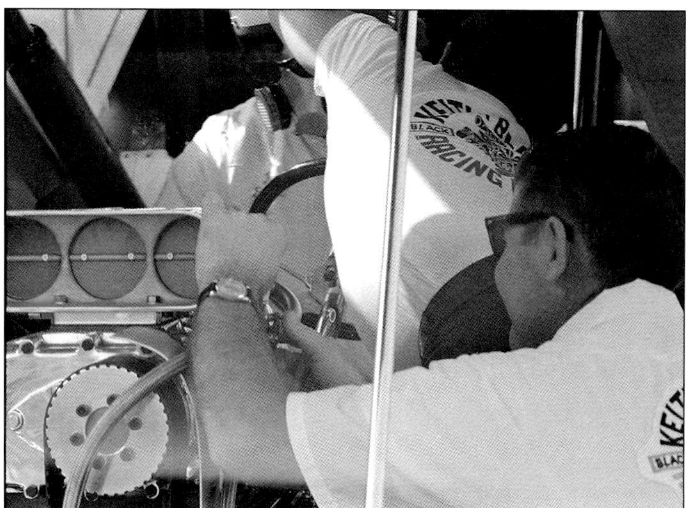

Keith Black adjusts the barrel valve, and Holly Hendrick straps Larry Reyes into Roland Leong's new Hawaiian II *Charger 500 flopper over the Memorial Day weekend in 1969. Reyes bankrolled nearly $5,000 for his amazing three days of racing.*

in qualifying, pocketing $1,000 for his efforts. Hang Ten offered an additional $500 for anyone setting low ET in the first round. Reyes once again ran low ET, turning in a super quick 7.38. The final round had the same results when Reyes beat Randy Walls in the final round and collected the $2,500 purse.

The conclusion for the weekend was Sunday's Commotion by the Ocean event at Carlsbad. The Super Team went for the trifecta and once again defeated everyone. Reyes, fresh off OCIR, clocked a 7.37 for low ET of the

meet on his way to taking home all honors, including the extra cash. In all, Leong bankrolled more than $5,300. Not bad for the three days' work. According to Leong, it was better than Vegas any time.

Detroit Dragway Produces Legends

Racing in the Midwest attracted the biggest names in Funny Car racing. Some of the best racing took place at the historical Detroit Dragway. Owner Gil Kohn opened the track in 1959, and the NHRA hosted the first and second annual Nationals events there in both 1959 and 1960 before moving the prestigious event permanently to Indiana.

In the late 1960s, Kohn and promoter Ben Christ collaborated and penned a famous phrase for a radio commercial, "Sunday! Sunday! Sunday!"

The Detroit strip hosted events for several sanctioning bodies during its history, including the American Hot Rod Association, the National Hot Rod Association, and the Midwest United Drag Racing Association. Overall, Detroit's top event was the AHRA's Grand American.

After a few years under AHRA sanction, Kohn and former field director of the NHRA Edward Eaton founded the UDRA in 1971. The UDRA had four national events at Detroit, including the URDA Nationals, which drew hometown favorite Connie Kalitta and the superstars Arnie Beswick, Roger Lindamood, Larry Arnold's *Super*

Clare Sanders drops the hammer, driving "Jungle" Jim's number-two Nova at Detroit Dragway. Chief mechanic Larry Petrich kept the blown Chevrolet Rat engine up to pace against the blown Hemis and SOHC products.

Arnie Beswick's 1968 Pontiac GTO competes against the Bounty Hunter *Mustang of Connie Kalitta at Detroit Dragway. Romeo Palamedes built the tube-type frame that incorporated the one-piece body built by Ron Pellegrini. The body was hinged to the front of the frame with two body latches mounted in the rear of the chassis to keep the top down at speed. The rear-lifted Poncho body allowed crewmen Fred Cooperman and Joe Palsgrove easier access to the blown 428 Pontiac engine.*

The Pontiac faithful cheered loudly for their superhero, Arnie Beswick, as his loyalty to run pure Pontiacs carried over to his latest flopper: the Super Judge. *Running a blown 428-ci Super Poncho for power, the Logghe Stamping Company built the 1969 GTO for Arnie, who was still one of the top draws on the match racing circuit. He averaged 80 match races throughout the year.*

The Super Cuda was one of the strongest runners out of Tennessee. It was campaigned by the team of Larry Coleman, Bill Taylor, and Pat Collins. The driver's seat was shared by several top-tiered drivers, highlighted by Larry Reyes, Larry Arnold, and Sidney Foster. Reyes recorded the better times and major wins with the Barracuda, including the "King of Kings" Championships at Capital, the AHRA World Finals, and here at the Super Stock Invitational at Detroit Dragway.

Tony and Russell Wahlay of Lakewood, Ohio, ran one of the strongest AA/Gas cars out of Cuyahoga County before switching to fuel Funny Cars with their Warlord Plymouth Barracuda. Tony, who was a self-employed cement worker, drove the wildly painted, dragon-themed flopper, which had a Logghe chassis.

Connie Kalitta's entry into the Funny Car wars was this 1969 Ford Mustang built by the Logghe Stamping Company. The Bounty Hunter *was one of the few cars to run the Hemi-head 429-ci Shotgun engine and the only one to compete in the Boss 429 and both Funny Car and Top Fuel classes. The Ypsilanti, Michigan, legend remains active in drag racing today, owning and competing several championship-quality Funny Car and Top Fuel dragsters.*

From his roots in Super Stock, A/FX, and the early days of Funny Car, pioneer Roger Lindamood had been representing Chrysler throughout most of his career as a test pilot and consultant. The Color Me Gone *icon ran this full-bodied fiberglass flip-top fueler with a Logghe Stamping chassis with a late-model 426-ci Dodge Hemi.*

Bill Lawton had been around since the early days, driving everything from Stockers, Thunderbolts, and A/FX machines to the early flip-tops when they arrived on the scene. The Rhode Island native's Mystery 7-, 8-, 9-*numbered Mustangs were running under the Tasca Ford banner owed by Bob Tasca Sr. Lawton's* Super Boss Mach I *relied on the 427 SOHC engine with ace mechanic John Healey tuning for power.*

Two of the winningest Funny Cars from 1969 were Don Schumacher in his Stardust Plymouth Barracuda and Danny "the Mangler" Ongais in Mickey Thompson's blue Mach I Mustang. Both cars were at the top of their game, as they both qualified in the number-1 position of their respected teams at the third annual Funny Car Manufacturer's Championships.

Corvette-bodied Funny Cars were known for being damned, jinxed, or cursed, but if any car fell under that label, it was the Beach City Chevrolet Corvette roadster of Bud and Don Kirby. The original Beach City entry, with motorsports driver Gary "El Scoundrel" Gabelich at the controls, ran incredibly well with constant 7.50 ETs and speeds above the 200-mph barrier. A change in luck took down the Corvette one night at Irwindale. Gabelich was approaching the finish line when the engine blew in the lights, resulting in a massive fire. Gabelich slowed the car to just under 40 mph and jumped out of the rolling inferno that eventually melted the body and burnt the remains to the ground. Gabelich was an accomplished multi-skilled driver from drag racing cars to off-road buggies and motorcycles. He set the quarter-mile drag boat record of 200.44 mph in 1969 and the land speed record of 622.407 mph driving the Blue Flame rocket car at the Bonneville Salt Flats on October 23, 1970. When Gary was not racing, he was also a volunteer skydiver for NASA's Apollo space program.

The Genuine Suspension AMX-1 of Bob Walker accelerates to an ET of 8.35 at 177.16 mph down the fabled strip at Lions. With the measured length of 100-1/2 inches, the AMX was one of the shortest-wheelbase Funny Cars that ran in the fuel ranks. The Kenosha Cadillac ran an early 354 Chrysler Hemi for muscle with the likes of Kenny "Smokey" DuBose and Tom Ferrero spending time behind the wheel.

"Stormin' Norman" Weekly stepped up for an ailing Ron Rivero in the K&G Mustang at Irwindale's East versus West Funny Car Championships. Rivero suffered a case of the dreaded kissing disease, mononucleosis, which knocked him out of the driver's seat. Rumor had it that former K&G AA/FD pilot Mike Danylo was seen on the premises ready to step in.

Memories: Jim Shue *Owner of the* **Hell Fire** *Corvette Funny Car*

"In the early days, I was making a decent living, making about $3,000 a month. I wanted to go racing and build a Funny Car, so I dedicated a certain amount of money into building the *Hell Fire* Corvette. We scrimped and saved every penny, even with my wife and small daughter. We were cashing in pop bottles just to eat on!

"I met Johnny Wright at the Stardust Raceway in Henderson, Nevada. Johnny was campaigning another car when I approached and talked to him. I took his phone number, as we really hit it off. I told him I was building the *Hell Fire* Corvette and that I would like to get him involved.

"Johnny was committed to running the other car at that time, but on a full-throttle pass, the car's engine expired and blew up, which led to the car burning to the ground. With no commitments, Johnny came aboard to help finish the car. Steve Montrelli soon came into the deal, so we now had the combination of a good driver and tuner. I supplied the money and creativity; they did the rest. Wright wanted to be conservative, and Montrelli wanted to go crazy, so we met somewhere in the middle and were able to be successful without damaging many parts."

Jim Shue's Hell Fire Corvette was not only one of the most beautiful cars in drag racing but also was a top hauler. Steve Montrelli power and Johnny Wright pedaling made the flamed pearl purple and white car a record setter. (Photo Courtesy Tim Pearl Collection)

Ron Rivero has all the comforts of safety when racing behind the wheel of the K&G Speed Associates' Frantic Ford *Mach I Mustang*. It had the combination of the Logghe Stamping Company chassis and the power of the early Chrysler 392-ci blown Hemi.

Gene Conway sold his battle-worn *Destroyer Jeep* but continued campaigning roadsters with his Sticks Unlimited–backed *Corvette Stingray*. The Corvette curse was alive, but the so-called superstition did not faze Conway. His roadsters won more races than any other Corvettes of the day, defeating some of the biggest names on the West Coast.

"Big" Mike Burkhart kept his allegiance, running Chevrolet-powered Funny Cars throughout his drag racing career, including his 1969 Camaro with a blown fuel 427-ci Rat. Burkhart, who was from the Dallas area, was a larger-than-life legend of the 1320 but also was a giant of a man, topping the scales at more than 300 pounds. His car featured a driver's door that opened, allowing Mike easier access entering and exiting the car. His size never overshadowed his driving abilities.

Journeyman fuel driver Gary Read spent many times behind the wheel of several big-name fuel cars. He drove for the AA/FDs, Groundshakers, Over the Hill Gang, and several AA/FAs (Groundshakers Jr., Mother-in-Law, and the Nutcracker Javelin Funny Car shown here at Lions). The American Motors entry ran a 392 Chrysler Hemi for power, and Read ran ETs in the upper 7.70s with a top speed of 180 mph.

Independent "Rapid" Ray Doyon from San Antonio, Texas, started his Funny Car career when he purchased the ex-Fritz Callier–J.E. Kristek Chevy II fastback and match raced the car throughout the Southwest. Doyon eventually retired the tired and outdated Chevy II and replaced it with an updated Don Hardy–built Mustang, Old Glory.

Jim Maybeck's Screaming Eagle Corvair makes a pass at Irwindale without the familiar Hilborn scoop fixed into the interior tin. Maybeck ran an L88 Chevrolet motor punched out to 488 ci. It was mounted to the rails of the Rollie Lindblad chassis. The Fiberglass Trends Corvair body was sprayed with patriotic red, white, and blue colors by Ron Gina. The modifications still had Maybeck looking around the tin work to get an unrestricted view of the track, and it was uncertain if performance improved.

Barry Kelly was one of the strongest independents running from Southern California who stayed with Chevrolet power. He ran a blown 427-ci Rat engine in his Machine Gun Kelly Corvair. Kelly drove the car throughout the end of 1970 before parking the non-competitive Corvair. Later, he built a series of hemi-powered Vega-bodied products before an exploding engine at the Professional Racing Organization Nationals in Long Island turned him into a high-speeding fireball that crashed into another car on the track. (Photo Courtesy Tim Pearl Collection)

Charlie Allen and "Big" John Mazmanian were gladiators, drawing each other many times in the money rounds out on the West Coast. Allen and Mazmanian were the top-running Mopars from Southern California who both ran Keith Black Racing Engines and chassis built by Ronnie Scrima's Exhibition Engineering.

"Big" Ed Lenarth ran one of the successful Kaiser products in the quarter mile with his **Holy Toledo Jeepster**. Brian Chucha's Four Wheel Drive Center in Fullerton, California, sponsored the Jeep Commando, which was a far cry from Kaiser's version with four-wheel-drive and a 160-hp 225-ci engine. Dick Fletcher Racecars built the constructed tube chassis with a Lenarth-inspired 392-ci Hemi that produced 1,400 hp hidden under the tonneau cover. The Hayes-clutched Donovan direct-drive unit transferred power to the Oldsmobile rear end.

Frankie Pisano plants his foot down on the Moon pedal in the Pisano Brothers Chevy Corvair at Lions Drag Strip. Joe Pisano tuned the 427-ci Rat to ETs of 7.40 at 195 mph. The Corvair was one of the strongest-running Chevy-powered Funny Cars from the West Coast.

The ex-Destroyer Jeep of Gene Conway was now in the capable hands of new owner and driver Ken Coleman. Since Jeeps were outlawed in the fuel Funny Car class, Coleman soon abandoned the fuel ranks in favor of bracket racing, where he enjoyed moderate success.

Dick "Poll Cat" Poll was a Southern Californian who began his professional Funny Car career with the ex-Gas Ronda fuel-injected Mustang. Poll added a blower to the Cammer engine, but it lagged behind, as it was too heavy to keep up with the lighter tube-type cars.

Supercharger wizard Mert Littlefield ran one of strongest Hemi-powered Dodge Darts on the West Coast. The ex-Dodge Dart of Mike Miller became the first of Mert's Funny floppers: the Rapid Transit Dart. The car ran with moderate success, but Littlefield raced to have fun instead of making it his career.

Cuda, the Wahley Brothers *Warlord* Barracuda, and a cast of others.

Southern California held spectacular displays of horsepower when it came to Funny Cars. Whether at Lions, Carlsbad, Fontana, OCIR, or Irwindale, the action was always fast and furious. Every strip had a personality. Lions was a stone's throw from the port of Long Beach, Carlsbad had the hillsides, OCIR had modern amenities, and Irwindale had the reverberation sounds of power bouncing off the San Gabriel mountains.

Drag racing now had several sanctioning bodies throughout the country: the NHRA, the AHRA, the UDRA, and the IHRA. Each held their own governing rules and laws.

Danny Miller was a top standout and contender from the Midwest who made the trek out west to Orange County International Raceway with his MCS Dodge Dart. Miller spent his time racing mainly in the UDRA, where he finished second in UDRA points for 1968 with the former Ramchargers Dodge.

With time well spent behind the wheel in the Hemi-Cuda, *drag racing's first rear-engine Funny Car, Tom McEwen returned to the "fiberglass furors" with a more conventional flopper: the ex-Candies and Hughes Barracuda. McEwen debuted the Barracuda at the 1969 NHRA Winternationals at Pomona, where he promptly recorded low ET at the meet (7.79 at 193.96 mph), which set a buzz around the pits. McEwen also performed double duty when he alternated time between his record-holding 6.64-second AA/Fuel dragster and his new fiberglass Mopar, which had a 392 Hemi and produced mid-7-second runs.*

Nelson Carter's revamped Dodge Charger for 1969 featured a wilder, more vibrant color scheme than his original candy green machine. With driver Dave Beebe leaving the seat, Carter moved behind the wheel. The crew of Nelson; his wife, Pam; and old-time friend Chuck Ridgeley kept the Super Chief *on the rails with runs above 200 mph.*

Dave Beebe lights 'em up in the staging lanes at Irwindale in the Dodge Fever Charger of Dean Hofheins and Dallas Furgeson. The Charger featured some of the best products available for a Funny Car: a Logghe Stage II chassis and a Keith Black 426 Chrysler Hemi.

Dick Loehr's Stampede Mustang was another product from the Windy City (Chicago) that was built and run out of Chapman Performance Products. Loehr had been running Ford-powered products for several years, and his newest Midwest steed was no different with a stout 427-ci SOHC powerplant. At one stretch in time, Loehr ran 12 consecutive runs at 4 different tracks, collecting 8 wins in a row with ETs in the 7.30s and top speeds of 202-plus mph.

The wives of Jim Shue, Johnny Wright, and Steve Montrelli kept the Hell Fire Corvette polished and cleaned prior to each run down the strip. Wives and girlfriends were an integral part in drag racing but went relatively unnoticed for all their hard work and dedication.

Mel Perry began his racing career in a low-class stocker and worked his way up the ladder to unblown (gasoline and fuel) Funny Cars and this blown 1968 Camaro. The Norwood-backed Chevrolet reigned terror on the East Coast under ace mechanic Ken Zaborski with an ET of 7.90 at 185 mph at Cecil County Drag-O-Way, which was dubbed as the "Traction Capital of the World."

Chris Karamesines campaigned dragsters for what seemed like an eternity. So, when the "Captain of the Greek Fleet" needed a flagship, he hired Kent Fuller to build him a new Barracuda and placed Ron "Snag" O'Donnell at the helm. A new 1969 Chrysler Hemi was built by both Karamesines and top mechanic John Nykaza. The versatile O'Donnell drove many floppers out of the Midwest for Don Schumacher, Chapman Automotive, Mr. Norm, Ron Pellegrini, and several more. O'Donnell set sail with the "Greek Fleet" 'Cuda that earned him the eighth slot for Team Plymouth at Orange County International Raceway Manufacturer's Funny Car Championships.

Miss STP Paula Murphy stepped up her Funny Car program when she replaced her outdated Mustang with this Barracuda that she purchased from Larry Reyes. Reyes had only raced the car a few times before accepting a driving job with Roland Leong. Murphy sold her Mustang to the owner of Suffolk Dragway, who later sold it to Butch Kernodle. The new Barracuda was built by Don Hardy in late 1968 and was powered by one of Fat Jack Bynum's 392 Chrysler Hemis. Murphy was the first woman in Funny Car history to qualify for a spot on the Chrysler team at the 1969 Orange County International Raceway Manufacturer's Funny Car Championships. She turned an ET of 7.62 for the fourth spot, which placed her well ahead of Chrysler's heavy hitters, such as Richard Siroonian, Leonard Hughes, Pat Minick, and Ron O'Donnell.

Glenn Solano was a 27-year-old sheet metal worker when he entered the Funny Car world around the same time the popular ABC television series The Invaders took to the airwaves. Solano and associate, Walt Williams, shared the namesake The Invader, which was built with a 122-inch Mike Kase tubular chassis and a 1969 Corvette Fiberglass Trends body resting onto the rails. Carrying the load was the power of a blown late-model 427-ci Chevy that unleashed 1,100 hp running on a 50-percent load of nitro. The alluring 'Vette was first under the tutelage of Bill Nash and later replaced by the talented "Mighty" Mike Van Sant, who smashed several low ETs and speed records at several tracks. (Photo Courtesy Tim Pearl Collection)

Larry Fullerton briefly spent time in the seat of Mickey Thompson's Mach I, mostly testing the combinations of the bodied Mustang with the new Ford 429 Shotgun engine that Mickey redesigned and modified himself. The Mustang was the original red Mustang driven by Pat Foster that crashed at Dallas. (Photo Courtesy Tim Pearl Collection)

"Mighty" Mike Van Sant deployed the laundry in The Invader Corvette after another 200-mph pass at Lions Drag Strip. The Corvette was one of the most recognized in a series of Funny Cars co-owned by Glenn Solano and Walt Williams. "Mighty" Mike's driving qualities made The Invader one of the most-feared Funny Cars from the West Coast. (Photo Courtesy Tim Pearl Collection)

Ron Leslie puts 5 feet of daylight between him and the ground, demonstrating the super bite of Irwindale's track conditions. Bill Kenz and Ron Leslie were one of Mercury's early pioneer teams that received one of early Logghe tubular chassis that rewrote the history in Funny Car safety and performance.

Tom Strum stepped forward from his A/FX Chevelle with his first flip-top flopper, the Just 4 Chevy Lovers Corvair. Driver Bob Smith debuted the new Strum and Fischer wild Chevrolet on June 28, 1969, at Lions in grand fashion. Smith qualified off the trailer in the fourth slot with a stout 7.94 ET. He went on to collect $1,000 when he flashed past Gary Gabelich as the Beach City Chevrolet Corvette detonated the Rat engine at the eighth mile.

Lee Jones from Los Angeles, California, powers through the water box in Malcolm Durham's Strip Blazer VI Camaro at Orange County International Raceway. Jones ran as an independent owner and driver from his earlier years with a blown nitro Firebird with Chevrolet power. Later, Jones and Durham formed a partnership to have identical themed Camaros for Jones to race out west while Durham concentrated mainly to race on the eastern seaboard.

"Flash" Gordon Mineo outdistanced Johnny Wright in Jim Shue's Hell Fire Corvette in the final elimination round of the first field of eight Funny Cars at the Drag News Nationals at Lions Drag Strip. During the closest match of the night, Mineo tripped the win lights, turning an ET of 7.61 at 192.11 mph to Wright's 7.74 196.50 mph. Mineo earned $1,000 for his efforts.

The jubilant crew of Flash Gordon receives roaring approval from the fans as the car drives down the strip to meet Mineo after he defeated the Hell Fire *Corvette* in the money round.

"Doc" Leroy Hales rides the Firestones at Irwindale in the Wild Breed *Mercury Cougar. Chevron station owner Pete Everett purchased the ex-Keaton's Cougar and campaigned the car for several years. He added major upgrades that kept the Cougar competitive. Everett used an early 392 Chrysler Hemi.*

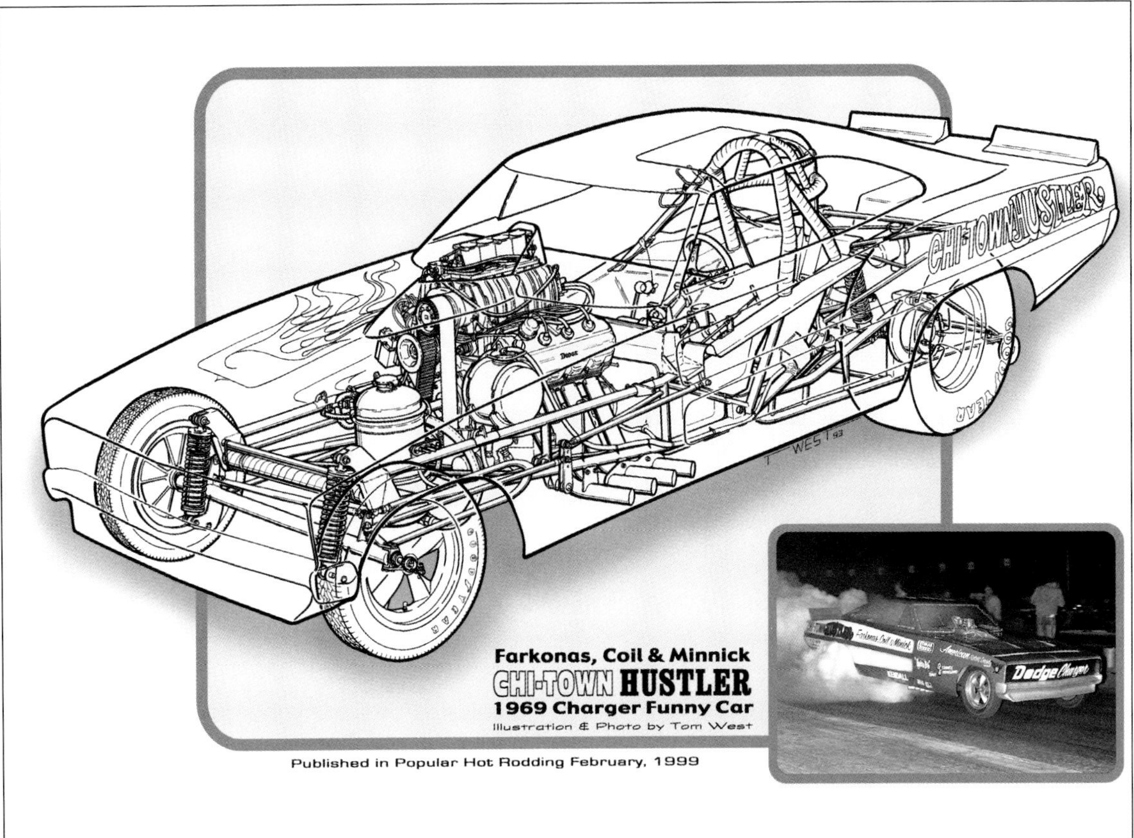

The name Chi-Town Hustler *brings back memories of Pat Minnick obliterating the slicks during the Charger's patented quarter-mile burnouts! Illustrator Tom West's X-ray drawing shows the detail under the body of one of the most famous Funny Cars in drag racing lore.*

Dale Armstrong flat-bladed the butterflies to an ET of 7.72 at 182.39 mph in Gary Crane's Travelin Javelin at Irwindale. "Wild" Bill Carter painted the AMC product with an array of bright colors of purples, yellows, pearl white, and multi-levels of pearl tangerines. A unique feature with the Javelin was how both the front running lights and rear taillights were operational. The car stood out during night races when the Javelin disappeared down the track in the dark.

Bob Bedell's Wild Thing Camaro was one of the most brightly colored Funny Cars from the West Coast. Bedell ran an early 392 Chrysler Hemi to ETs in the mid-7.60s at top speeds in the 180s. Bedell was one of the low-budgeted racers who raced without much flair but ran hard against the top runners.

Gas Ronda put his Mach I Mustang through time trials at Irwindale's East versus West Funny Car Championships. Ronda, racing on his home track, scored a win for the West Coast in front of 12,681 delighted fans in the number-two Eliminator bracket. His Ed Pink Ford-powered Mach I cracked into the 200-mph bracket, turning an ET of 7.44 at 202.49 mph on a holeshot that put Ronda into the winner's circle. There, he defeated Gene Snow's quicker-but-losing 7.38 ET.

Rusty Dellings gets the bite on Irwindale's sticky surface driving Marv Eldridge's Fiberglass Trends AMC Javelin. A seasoned veteran of the flopper wars, Dellings's rides included the Fiberglass Trends Corvair, Little Jon Corvette, and the Mister T Corvette. The Mister T Corvette met its demise by crashing at Lions and causing serious, career-ending injuries to Dellings.

The infamous Chi-Town Hustler of John Farkonas, Austin Coil, and Pat Minick made its debut at Irwindale at the 1969 East versus West Funny Car Championships in front of a record crowd of 12,681. Minick became the instant crowd favorite after he laid down a smokey burnout. I remember that when the Hustler rocketed past me after snapping this photo, I stretched out both my arms and couldn't see my fingertips in the clouds of smoke.

Feudin' Floppers

Drag racing feuds in the 1960s were a common sight. Rivals mixed it up either physically or psychologically (or both), getting into each other's heads.

One of the most publicized feuds in 1969 was between Danny Ongais, Mickey Thompson, and tuner "Famous" Amos Satterlee against "Big" John Mazmanian's *Armenian Army*. No matter how well Mazmanian performed, the blue Mach I was one step ahead of the Candy Red Barracuda. At nearly every event the pair were entered, they wound up facing each other, including at the famed March Meet.

Ongais beat Rich Siroonian in Mazmanian's 'Cuda in the final round, setting low ET at 7.56. Throughout the summer, the results ended up the same with Siroonian always the bridesmaid against the blue Mach I. Frustration peaked for Mazmanian when both met up once again in the final round at the NHRA Nationals. The strong-running Siroonian laid down an unreal 7.24 in the final, but it was all for nothing when he red-lighted, giving the automatic win to Ongais.

Finally, the streak broke at the United States Professional Dragster Association Championships at OCIR when Dave Beebe in the Barracuda put away the Mustang in a come-from-behind win in front of the standing-room-only crowd. A week later in *Drag News*, Thompson, Ongais, and Satterlee graciously posted a half-page letter congratulating "Big" John and the *Armenian Army* for a well-deserved win.

"Big" John Mazmanian, Dave Beebe, and Doug Cook (behind Beebe's left shoulder) smile as they receive the $1,200 check from lovely race queen Bonnie McDonald for winning the PDA Nitro Championships. Hysteria broke out as the crowd gave the Armenian Army a standing ovation that lasted nearly five minutes after Beebe defeated heated archrivals Mickey Thompson and Danny Ongais. Beebe was also a gifted baseball player and was drafted by the Pittsburg Pirates as a catcher but declined pursuing his baseball career to continue racing.

The intense rivalry between Mickey Thompson and "Big" John Mazmanian reached new levels at the United States Professional Dragster Association Championships, which were at Orange County International Raceway. Danny Ongais (in Thompson's Mach 1) and Dave Beebe (in the candy red Barracuda) easily defeated the competition and met in the final round. Both drivers fired up the cars simultaneously and brought the record crowd of 19,447 to their feet with the anticipation of what had been building for months. At the green light, Ongais got the jump out of the gate, but Beebe thundered pass Ongais to win. Beebe's final top speed of 205.01 mph was the quickest time ever for the Barracuda.

The largest gathering of Funny Cars ever assembled at one place for the richest all–Funny Car purse in drag racing history, the 1969 Manufacturers Funny Car Team Championships, was November 6 and 7 at Orange County International Raceway. The independent race was expanded to a two-day event. Qualifying was on Friday night for the quickest 32 cars earning team spots and all racing three rounds on Saturday evening to decide the Manufacturer's Championship.

The 1969 OCIR Manufacturer's Meet

The success of past Manufacturer's Meets at OCIR now expanded to a colossal two-day event, which was the largest gathering of Funny Cars at one location. Qualifying took place on Friday night, and team competition runoffs concluded on Saturday night. Pre-race activities included marching bands and driver and team introductions of the qualified cars that were lined up on the track with their bodies raised.

Sixty-one Funny Cars entered and were wanting part of the record $30,000 cash purse. The finals were nearly a

Norm Cowdry's Blue Fox *Corvette roadster fell into the category of the Corvette curse. Cowdry lost control of his roadster midtrack at Irwindale, plowed into the guardrail, and rolled over. The body separated from the chassis. There wasn't much damage to the body, but the chassis was severely damaged. Cowdry received several abrasions and walked away without serious injury.*

Bad Bascomb's Ghost *was a Western movie that was filmed in the 1940s about a tough outlaw with a soft heart for a little girl. Wallace Beery and Margaret O'Brien starred in the Hollywood production. When the team of Engle, Bagnard, and Bradford went racing with its new Chevy II flopper, it borrowed the name* Bad Bascomb's Ghost, *which became one of the coolest names for a Funny Car. The* Ghost *was a product of chassis fabricator Dick Fletcher and Bill Thomas. The* Ghost's *biggest win was on August 2 at Irwindale's Gold Cup Championships when Pete Bagnard met Dave Beebe driving "Big" John Mazmanian's heavily favored Plymouth in the final round. Beebe experienced unexpected staging problems and rolled through the staging beams, setting off the unwelcomed red light.*

repeat from the previous year that resulted with another major upset.

From the beginning on Friday night, only one team car for Ford made it into the race. Gas Ronda experienced engine woes from a new SOHC engine. After switching out the engine and replacing the well-used Cammer, Gas outdueled some of biggest names to reach the final round. There, he faced the heavily favored and feared *Chi-Town Hustler*. What seemed a sure win for the Windy City Charger was a back-and-forth battle that swung toward the West Coast underdog. Ronda tripped the win light when he knocked off the powerhouse from the Midwest!

Steve Bovan arrived on the exhibition scene in late 1964 with his blown fuel-burning 1965 Chevy II running out of the Blair's Speed Shop. When the Nova became too heavy and outdated to keep up with the competition, Bovan built and campaigned several Camaro-bodied Funny Cars, including his 1969 Mister T Chevy Camaro, which was billed as the world's longest Z28. Bovan continued to run blown Chevrolet engines, but toward the twilight of his profession, he pulled the plug on the GM powerplants and switched to run a Keith Black Hemi. Financial, personal, and legal problems forced him to quit racing altogether in 1971.

Gene Snow qualified his Rambunctious Mini-Charger in the second spot on a slippery, damp track with a 7.58 ET at Orange County International Raceway's Manufacturer's Funny Car Championships. The largest independent Funny Car race in the country was now a two-day event with qualifying rounds held on Friday evening and team racing on Saturday night.

One of the "good ole boys" from New Orleans, Louisiana, Sid Foster began his professional drag racer career in 1964 with Super Stocks and quickly moved up to driving Funny Cars. Foster posted multiple runs in the low 7s at 210 mph in Larry Coleman's Super Ford Torino, which was impressive considering that the Torino weighed nearly 2,300 pounds. Foster was a stout believer of a non-cross bred car. Sidney once said, "If you run a Chrysler engine, you should run a Chrysler body. [It's the] same for running a Chevrolet body—it should have Chevrolet power, [and its the] same with Fords and other makes."

Junior Brogdon's Phony Pony 1969 Mustang was a more conventual Funny Car than his previous radical Funny Car, which was more of a match racer than a legal competitor. Brogdon's newest mount ran a 392 Chrysler powerplant but still fell short of being a serious threat.

Terry Hendrick astounded everyone by running a 7.30 ET to be the overall low qualifier at the 1969 Orange County International Raceway Manufacturer's Funny Car Championships. Under damp conditions and overcast skies, it took more than six hours of constant qualifying, as more than 60 Funny Cars in attendance that were attempting to make one of the 32 spots on one of the four teams.

Mart Higginbotham was one of the greatest drivers and fuel floppers that came out of the state of Texas. Higginbotham is shown driving the number-2 team car, a Chevrolet-powered Chevy II, for "Big" Mike Burkhart, the "Gentle Giant," at the third annual Funny Car Manufacturer's Championships at Orange County International Raceway.

Lew Arrington drove his *Brutus Firebird* with a 7.55 ET, which was good enough for the second slot on the Wacky Racers team at Orange County International Raceway's third annual Funny Car Manufacturer's Championships. The Wacky Racers were defined as cars of dissimilar body and engine combinations. The highly competitive team included "Mighty" Mike Van Sant (Invader Corvette), "Big" Eddie Lenarth (Holy Toledo Jeep), Dick Bourgeois (Javelin 2), Rusty Dellings (Fiberglass Trends AMC), Norm Weekly (K&G Frantic Ford *Mach I Mustang*), Gene Conway (Corvette roadster), and Clyde Morgan (AMC Javelin).

Gas Ronda enjoyed the biggest win of his Funny Car career as an underdog. Ronda shocked the crowd of more than 14,000 at the third annual Funny Car Manufacturer's Championships when he trailered the odds-on favorite, the Chi-Town Hustler *driven by Pat Minick. Ronda jumped out with a slight advantage over Minick, but the big Charger caught the Mustang at midtrack and grabbed the lead. The Mustang's well-raced Cammer and regained the lead from Minick and never looked back in the win. They were the two quickest runners of the night. Some of those celebrating with Ronda in the winner's circle include Billy Pink, Gwen Ronda, Skip Burroughs, race queen and model Sue Bridges, Ken Cassidy, Ed Pink, and Gas Jr. (Photo Courtesy Tim Peral Collection)*

Countless workers across the country dreaded returning to work on Monday mornings, especially knowing there were five more days till the weekend. However, for Gas Ronda, one Monday morning at the office was the icing on the cake. A few days earlier, he shocked the drag racing community and won the largest two-day Funny Car Championships in the United States at Orange County International Raceway. Sitting at his office desk at Russ Davis Ford in Covina, the high-performance sales manager finalized another great deal for a satisfied customer on a brand-new Boss 302 Mustang. Ronda's successful racing career put the city of Covina on the map and into folklore history.

The Top Eight AHRA Funny Car drivers for 1971 included (from left to right): Mart Higginbotham (Drag-On Vega), Larry Reyes (Super Cuda), Dick Harrell, Leroy Goldstein (Ramchargers), Dick Bourgeois (Mickey Thompson's Mustang), Gene Snow (Rambunctious), Dale Pulde (Mickey Thompson's Pinto), and Tom Hoover's (White Bear Dodge) Charger.

Chapter Four

1970–1974

Performance, Growth, and Surprises

The 1970s brought on a new outlook that ran more toward professionalism with a decreasing emphasis on the plain Joe or little guy. Struggles for power were waged between the Fuelers and Funny Cars with the rails trying newer technologies in an attempt to win back the crowd appeal.

Even within the Funny Car ranks, there were many of the plastic cars, and they had to be more innovative and creative to keep the public from getting surfeited with the increasing numbers of cars and diluting of the class. With more variations of direct-drive units available, 6-second ETs were more than inevitable with speeds hitting the 220-mph mark.

"Terrible" Tommy Grove heats the M&H Dragmasters when he drew the "bad" lane during first-round eliminations against Bob Pickett. Paula Murphy exploded the transmission in her Barracuda during her last attempt to qualify for the Irwindale's New Year's Day Meet. Grove displayed his expert handling abilities on the slick track when he cut a great light on the tree and pulled off the run of his life with a smokey, out of shape, sideways pass with an ET of 8.45 at 192.76 mph to defeat the Javelin's quicker 7.40 at 202.49 mph run.

Jim Kirby displays smoke and noise while exiting the water box in Nathan Valdez's Mustang at Irwindale Raceway. The local Southern California match racer featured a Jim Kirby chassis powered by an early 392-ci Hemi. For being a low-budget team, the Mustang rans mid-7-second times with speeds in the 190-mph range.

Marc "the Kid" Susman competes against Larry Reyes in the Hawaiian Charger during the first round at Irwindale. Both cars left together at the green, but Susman went up in a cloud of smoke and lost with an ET of 8.34 at 190 mph.

When the NHRA added a separate eliminator bracket for the Funny Cars for 1969, rules were for standard body sizes, more sophisticated machinery, and updated safety requirements and equipment. The new chassis being built were simplified compared to ones built just a few years earlier. An additional safety factor was tighter driver confinements. Even with all the updated safety advancements, the number-one concern was the ever-present problem of fire that was on the mind of every Funny Car driver from leaving off the starting line through the top end.

To improve safety, the Specialty Equipment Market Association (SEMA) along with Simpson and Deist Safety Equipment manufacturers developed pressurized on-board Dupont FE-1301 freon fire extinguisher systems. The systems put out flash fires immediately after activation. Roof escape hatches were also added to the fiberglass bodies.

Gone were the old-style of fire suits. They were replaced with Simpson's new 30-second, four-layer fire suit. The outer layer of fabric was 100 percent polished Nomex, which looked better and had fire-stopping layers. The layers were aluminized beta cloth, Teflon-coated asbestos and rayon foam, a polyvinylchloride Kynol insulator, and Nomex inner layers that protected the driver from oil and fuel absorbing into the material. The suits kept out temperatures of 2,000 degrees for half a minute.

Mickey's the Boss

Always the innovator, Mickey Thompson was never one to rest on his laurels after his *Blue* car, without a

Bob Pickett qualified deep into the field of 16 at Irwindale Raceway's New Year's Day show, where he competed against Tommy Grove in the first round. Pickett had the makings to put Grove's Going Thing *Mustang* on the trailer, as Grove was in the oiled lane from the previous runners. However, Grove's slick driving denied Pickett and the overpowered *Javelin* the win.

Ex-Top Fuel driver Hank Clark made his West Coast appearance at the March Meet. It became a successful one, as Clark drove the Chapman Automotive Camaro past the Snively & Annin Dodge Challenger in the final round to take the Eliminator title. The Chicago-based Clark weeded through the tough field before meeting up with the low qualifier Snively for the trophy and coins.

Lil' John Lombardo always displayed colorful graphics and wildly painted colors on his Gassers and Funny Cars. His Dodge Challenger certainly fit the bill.

Funny Cars were more of an art. Designs were more sophisticated, using strengthened and improved metals without sacrificing safety. Mickey Thompson's monocoque Mustang Funny Car weighed 500 pounds less than his typical fleet of 2,300-pound Mustangs from the previous year. Mickey's white Mach 1 served as a model for Nye with nearly the same engine and driver location but with the key addition of a "tub." The wheelbase measured 115 inches with separate fiberglass body pieces. Thompson chose the Boss 429-ci engine to power the Mustang and tabbed Mighty Mike Van Sant for driving duties. The car was never built to be competitive. It was part of an agreement with Ford to get a certain amount of magazine covers and press coverage. It was not the easiest to work on, and the performance and handling were terrible.

The West Coast's counterpart to the Chi-Town Hustler was the L.A. Hooker Dodge Charger that was campaigned by Gene and Richard Beaver and with cousins Steve, Dave, and Billy Condit. The big Dodge was once owned by Nelson Carter as the Super Chief. Former Top Fuel driver Dave Condit occupies the seat shown here at Irwindale blasting the Goodyears with the approval of Uncle Gene Beaver, Paul Bagger, and Terry Harrison.

doubt, was the most successful car in the country for 1969. In keeping steps ahead of the competition, Mickey prepped no less than three cars: a Boss 429 Maverick, a Boss 429 Mustang, and the most interesting one of the lot, which brought the marriage of Grand Prix, Funny Car, and Can-Am technology together. This monocoque Mustang had an untested 429-ci Shotgun engine. The idea was right on track, but the car's poor performance and overall handling was doomed from the start.

The success of fabricator Pat Foster, who was then working over at Woody Gilmore's Race Car Engineering, gave the Logghe Brothers a real run for their money with quality if not quantity.

Into the 6s

Elapsed times were averaging around the 7.20s in the beginning of 1970. By June, times were knocking on

"Smokey" Joe Lee was an ex-Top Fuel pilot who earned his nickname with some of the wildest burnouts performed in both dragsters and Funny Cars. The San Diego standout took top Funny car honors at Irwindale's second rendition of the "Potpourri of Drag Racing" show when he defeated Jack Chrisman in the last round. The potpourri event brought together five of the most popular classes in the sport of drag racing (Top Fuel, Funny Car, AA/Fuel Altered, AA/Gas Supercharged, and the upcoming Pro Stocks).

Warren Gunter's Durachrome Bug *was a Funny Car with characteristics of a Fuel Altered. It was a rush of pure adrenaline every time it made a run down the quarter mile! It was always an adventure for the world's fastest and quickest Volkswagen, not knowing what direction it would take to the finish line. Crowds held their breath in anticipation to see if the Bug ran straight, avoided the centerline and guardrails, or just stayed in its own lane.*

Tom Strum and driver Dale Armstrong picked up their first Funny Car Eliminator title with the new Swapper *Dodge Challenger at the Tom Ferraro Benefit Invitational at Irwindale Raceway. A crowd of 5,600 fans saw Armstrong dump Donnie Hampton's twin-motored Corvette in the final round, setting the low ET of the race (7.73 at 187.50 mph).*

the door of that magical 6-second barrier. At the NHRA Springnationals in Dallas, Texas, three cars pushed the envelope, as all three came within three-hundreds of a second. The Springnationals winner, Leroy "the Israeli Rocket" Goldstein, came the closest, turning a run of 7.03 in the final round against Gene Snow.

One week later, on June 21, at the US Funny Car Championships at York US 30 Dragway, it finally happened, not once, not twice, but in three back-to-back winning runs. The Israeli Rocket officially became the first into the 6s, driving the candy red stripe and white *Ramchargers* Dodge Challenger.

Black Solves Oil Starvation

Many tried to run quicker, and the wear took its toll on engines. They suffered from lack of oil at speed. Many used a larger-cubic-inch stroker motor with aid of a new trick oil pump system developed by Keith Black. The oil pump system solved the oil starvation problem that normally took out numerous bearings and/or complete engines. The system added 6 to 8 additional quarts of oil, and the pump cost a hefty $1,000, but it was well worth the investment.

In past years, fuel systems lacked the volume and starved the motor of the oil required for high-end RPM, so Enderle brought out the cure with an overdrive fuel

Kenny Safford races in the Grand Spaulding Dodge–backed Mr. Norm's Super Charger. *The Windy City Mini-Charger was built by the Logghe Brothers with a 426 Hemi powerplant that was maintained by Gary Dyer. The Dyer and Safford combination won its first time out at Irwindale, defeating Charlie Allen in the eliminator round with an ET of 7.48 at 191.56 mph.*

pump that directed fuel back into the fuel tank. The major engine builders (Ed Pink, the Ramchargers, Sid Waterman, and Keith Black) all made major improvements to the late-model stroker Hemi engines. Many top Funny Cars settled on running one of the three top builders' bullets, and records were set nearly every weekend.

The Ramchargers were represented by their flagship *Ramchargers* Dodge Challenger driven by Leroy Goldstein, Hot Wheels star Tom McEwen, and Harry Schmidt had *Blue Max*. The Black Elephants included Roland Leong's *Hawaiian*, "Big" John Mazmanian, and Don Prudhomme's *Hot Wheels 'Cuda*. Don Schumacher, Gas Ronda, and Barry Setzer flew under the Ed Pink Banner. The engine suppliers and builders war was just as intense as two Funny Cars facing off in the final round.

Larry Fullerton's Ring Free/Galpin Ford Maverick exits the water box at Bakersfield during the 12th annual March Meet. The Maverick suffered from traction bite throughout the weekend and failed to make the show.

Here Comes the Money

By the early 1970s, the number of licensed drivers and new cars nearly tripled, as professionals were making a good living and still having fun doing it. The

Charlie Allen was one of the first Mopar stars to get a new Dodge Challenger body for a Funny Car with backing from Saddleback Dodge. Jeff Crowther tuned and maintained the Challenger 1 shown here at Irwindale with an ET of 7.65 at 170.15 mph.

Vic Gibson's new Quick *Dodge Challenger was driven by Elgin Freeman with Bill Lowery handling the maintenance and tune-ups on the early 392-ci Chrysler Hemi, which was bolted to a Crowerglide unit. The Challenger posted its best performance with an ET of 6.98 at 225 mph.*

Dave and Tim Beebe's Dodge Fever II *competed against Ray Alley, Clyde Morgan, and Marc "the Kid" Susman for the title of the "King of Garden Grove" at Lions Drag Strip's Garden Grove Challenge night. Dave Beebe piloted the new Challenger that was built by the Logghe Brothers with a Sid Waterman Hemi mounted between the frame rails. Unfortunately, the victor of the "Special" was the weatherman when the predicted rain washed out the festivities.*

fuel cars were now at the top, playing major roles in drag racing with increased television coverage, expanded printed media exposure, and now with the movie makers and motion picture studios exploring the sport with film pilots.

Major races, such as the US Indy Nationals, were seen as paid television shown in movie theaters. Fans were identifying with the personalities as well as their favorite brand of cars. Spectators came out in droves to see the top names and cheer for their favorites, who were compared to rock stars and professional sports personalities.

Don Schumacher carries the front wheels in his new Logghe-built 'Cuda at Irwindale. The "Shoe" ran a two-car operation with Arnie Behling driving his blue Stardust Barracuda.

The unpredictable excitement generated by "Jungle" Jim Liberman is shown at the fourth annual Winternationals warmups at Irwindale. Jim arrived at the track with his freshly painted Chevy II. Tacky to the touch, the red color was sprayed the night before and had overspray on the grille, lights, headers, and front and rear bumpers. With the crowd on its feet, Liberman went up in a massive ball of smoke all the way down the track against Dick Bourgeois. (Photo Courtesy Tim Pearl Collection)

Memories: Kenny Youngblood

Sign Painter, Artist, and Illustrator

"I've had several titles starting with 'sign painter.' I love lettering, and amazingly, I went to Pasadena City College, which had a fabulous sign arts course, but I didn't take it because I wanted to draw cars. But back then, the place you could draw cars was in Detroit. I wasn't really into new iron. I just loved hot rods, so I ended up being a sign painter and learned the hard way.

"I learned mainly from watching the other guys at the time, such as Steve Feinberg, who lettered the original *Hell Fire* Corvette; Dennis Jones; Tom Kelly; and a few others. I was at the right place and time there in Bellflower, California, where I had painted and lettered a slingshot dragster for my friend Gary Messenger.

"Painter Dick Olsen saw what I had done, called me up, and asked me to go to work for him. He was tired of waiting in line at Kelly's. I credit Tom Kelly for being that good that I got into this business. Everything took off from there.

"I worked with Don Kirby and Olsen. Man, they were both hard workers, and we made sure we'd get the cars out there on time and looking good. We were an overnight hit, and guys knew they could bring their cars to us.

"Back then, the Funny Cars would go on tour match racing, and in the winter, they came out here to build new cars. We'd get the bodies done up for them, and of course, you don't appreciate what you got when you got it. It was amazing times back then with all these famous race cars, and I certainly cherish those days!"

Kenny Youngblood is one of the most talented artists and illustrators in the history of drag racing. Known for his detailed painting, lettering, and drawings of race cars for more than 50 years, Youngblood remains passionate with his brushes and spray guns. Along with keeping busy with his self-taught trades, Youngblood is also a practicing ordained minister.

Jim Nicholl and Chris Karamesines (back left) check out the performance of Don and Roy Gay's Infinity IV GTO, as Roy uncorked an unreal 7.23 ET. That run was the low ET of the meet and set a new track record at the 1970 AHRA Winternationals in Beeline. Unfortunately for Roy, the Keith Black Hemi-powered Pontiac was defeated by Gene Snow in the first round of eliminations.

With Funny Cars making astonishing performances, the demand for them was higher than ever. Ron and Gene Logghe, Jay Howell, and Tom Prock built their own experimental research and development 200-mph rolling test lab with the Warhorse Mustang. Prock was given the seat assignment with Howell wrenching on the stock Hemi that was built by Diamond Racing Engines. At the second-annual AHRA Grand American and Lions Drag Strip, the one-race-only driver and tuner combination of Larry Reyes and Roland Leong succeeded putting the car deep into the 16-car field. Larry defeated Marv Eldridge in the first round of eliminations with a respectable ET of 7.35 at 196.59 mph.

Fellow Texans "Big" Mike Burkhart and Harry Schmitt each ran a successful operation with a fuel-burning Chevy-powered Camaro, so when Schmitt ventured out on his own, he commissioned Don Hardy to build a new Mustang flopper and hired veteran tuner Jake Johnston to drive. With Johnston committed to another temporary ride, interim drivers Paul Gordon and Mart Higginbotham took turns behind the wheel. Gordon is shown at Orange County International Raceway, blistering the hides on Harry Schmitt's new Mustang. Unfortunately for Schmitt, the Mustang was soon destroyed on a highway accident in New Mexico when an oncoming driver crossed the median in front of Schmitt, who veered off the highway and hit an overpass embankment. The Mustang dislodged from the transporter, and all was destroyed except the engine.

Many fans came out to the drag strip to spend the day or evening being entertained. The Funny Car drivers wanted to give the fans something to remember with intense performances and displays of showmanship, which gave the onlookers something to talk about on Monday morning at the office around the coffeemaker or water cooler.

Fame and Funny

There was always a flair of Hollywood around the strip when actors, actresses, and TV celebrities made appearances, arriving by helicopters, biplanes landing on the strip, or with police escorts that featured wailing sirens and rotating lights. At the All-Pro Championships Series Finale, the Southern California Dodge Dealers filmed one their highly favored commercials using the actual action on the strip. The clip featured Sheriff Joe Higgins, a salty, gruffly voiced actor posing with a trio of well-known masked Dodge Funny Car drivers with assistance of race queen Vicki Holloway.

The All-Pro Series for both Funny Cars and Top Fuel Dragsters was a four-race series kicking off at the end of the previous year, and it completed in early April, which was prior to the start of the spring and summer match racing tour schedule. Each driver accumulated points to become series champion. The All-Pro races were attended with high turnouts of fans and racers.

One of the top-running Chevrolet-powered Funny Cars in the All-Pro events was Randy Walls. Walls, along with wife Cherri, were possibly the first Funny Car husband-and-wife team owners. She primed the injectors, backed up the car, packed the parachute, and handled public relations.

Memories: Randy Walls *Owner, Tuner, and Driver of the* Super Nova II

"I've always considered AA/Dale Armstrong one of the best there was driving and tuning a Funny Car. I had not seen Dale in nearly 25 years, so when he was named grand marshal at the 14th annual California Hot Rod Reunion, I wanted to go up and say hello and see him.

"He was sitting in the hospitality tent with the other honorees, signing autographs for a long line of fans. I was about 50 feet down in front of him, waiting for the line to thin out. I did not want to go up and bother him. Suddenly, I heard this loud, 'Walls, get your dumb ass over here.'

"I was looking all over the place to see who said that and where it came from.

"Then, I hear it again, 'It's me—Dale. Get over here, Walls. I want to talk to you.'

"I sat down next to Dale and the next thing I knew we were bringing up our old battles, laughing about all the crazy times we had. By now, he had me signing autographs with him as we carried on. When the line thinned out, Dale leaned over to me, looked me in the eyes, and said, "I always wanted to tell you how much respect I had for you. Also, several drivers told me the same sentiments about you. One guy even told me that he would be about 300 feet away with binoculars watching you, trying to figure out how you got your car to run that well."

This trio of masquerading Dodge Funny Car drivers assist race queen Vicki Holloway and masquerade TV personality Sheriff Joe "You're in a heap of trouble" Higgins with the Southern California Dodge dealers' commercials during prerace ceremonies at Orange County International Raceway's All-Pro Finale. The American character actor played recurring roles on the popular Rifleman and Arrest and Trial television series. Orange County was home to several TV and movie productions.

Dave Beebe, "Mighty" Mike Van Sant, and Tom "the Mongoose" McEwen shed their masks and reveal their identities. Beebe drove the Beebe Brothers' Dodge Fever II Dodge Challenger and went on to win the All-Pro Championships Series Finale easily against McEwen when the Mongoose lost the transmission converter on the starting line. Beebe began his driving career at the age of 16, when his grandfather, who owned a sprint car, was at the track and his driver was a no-show. Without much experience, Beebe jumped right into the car and won the main event!

Danny Ongais was the Drag News *Funny Car Driver of the Year for 1969, and he was the one to beat at Orange County International Raceway's All-Pro opening race. Ongais advanced to the second round against a red-lighting Dr. LeRoy Hales, but the engine went silent on his first burnout against the Durachrome Bug of Warren Gunter.*

Keith Black prepares to take off to congratulate the Beebe Brothers for winning the All-Pro Championships Series Finale at Orange County International Raceway. Black was one of the top iconic engine builders in drag racing. He was well-known for his Black Magic Elephant Chrysler Hemis that powered the top legions of dragsters and Funny Cars into the winner's circle. Black made his first impressions building boat engines. By the late 1950s, the success of his engines allowed Black to open his own engine shop. KB Racing Engines found its way into the top-running Funny Cars, including Roland Leong, Nelson Carter, Gene Snow, "Big" John Mazmanian, Candies and Hughes, Don Prudhomme, and many others.

Independent Randy Walls was the quickest and fastest pure Chevrolet-powered Funny Car qualified in at Orange County International Raceway's All-Pro Finale on the West Coast. The El Cajon, California, resident was an early runner in the infancy days of the match bashers. Walls was one of the few who knew how to tune and maintain a blown Chevy without damaging parts and kept the heat on the Ford- and Chrysler-branded cars. He retired from drag racing in early 1971 to take on other ventures. Today, Walls lives in Kentucky, actively driving his yellow and green 1969 Super Nova II Funny Car.

Arizona State Funny Car Champ Bob McFarland drove his Chevy-powered Chevy II to top honors at Orange County International Raceway's Big 4 Funny Car Championships. Race favorite Rich Siroonian in "Big" John Mazmanian's new 'Cuda lost the clutch and broke the differential at mid-track.

The Corvette Curse

All athletes have superstitions. Some have their daily routines. For example, some never change out their lucky socks and shoes or undershirts, some never stepping on chalk lines, and others only eat certain foods. Drag racing also has superstitions, especially when it involves a certain breed and brand of Funny Car: the famous Corvette curse!

From 1967 through 1970, the early day of Corvettes had unceremonious finishes, non-parachute deployments, uncharacteristic handling and traction problems, engine explosions and fires, unexplainable failures within the electrical systems, transmission blowups, crashes, rollovers, and numerous unexplainable incidents. It was like having a full moon or Friday the 13th hovering around the Corvettes. No one could ever figure out why these cars were so marked with doom.

The unluckiest Corvette was Don Kirby's infamous *Beach City* Corvette. It crashed and burned three times, all with different drivers. The popular Corvette was a fan favorite. They cheered if the car made it down the strip without incident or if it went up like a Roman candle. Either way, it was a sight to watch.

The third annual Corvette Funny Car Nationals event has hit by "whammies" when it was postponed twice, both by wind and rain—who says it never rains in Southern California? On race night, several of the advertised Funny Corvettes were no-shows or arrived at the track too late to compete. Without the "no-shows," time trials were permitted because there was no qualifying.

When it came time for the Kirby's red roadster to put tracks down on the surface, new driver Ron Goodsell lined up in the lane that had rosin on it. Goodsell waved

Vic Morse peppers the Bakersfield fans with rubber from the Goodyears in the Mister T Corvette during Saturday's qualifying rounds at the 1970 March Meet. Minutes later, the curse made an appearance when the beautiful Corvette lost control at the three-quarter mark and rolled over on its top, causing a total loss to the body. Both Morse and the chassis were okay. (Photo Courtesy Tim Pearl Collection)

Corvettes are status symbols that cruise down the highways, countryside, drive-ins, and burger hangouts. They dominated road courses, rallies, and Trans-Am races, but in the Funny Car class, they were branded for being the unluckiest bodied floppers to run down the 1320! An example of infamous Corvette curse was at the third annual Corvette Funny Car Nationals at Orange County International Raceway, and it affected seven out of the eight invited floppers on and away from the track. After two consecutive rain outs, the All-Corvette Nationals finally were underway minus several top-name Corvette Funny Cars that were booked at other commitments. One to suffer from the jinx was Gary Densham. During his licensing pass in the new Densham, Plugger, and Zeller Corvette, the jet-black coupe attempted only one pass before the curse sidelined Densham with unrepairable brake failure.

The Corvette Curse CONTINUED

for more of the powered dust, rolled into the added gold, and nailed the pedal. After all the tire smoke, clutch dust, and rosin cleared, the damaged 'Vette was found upended on the guardrail, facing back toward the starting line, and knocked out of competition.

The next weekend, Goodsell returned with the repaired Corvette to compete at the All-Pro Championships finale. He qualified well into the show, where he ran an unreal 208 mph for the Chevy-powered roadster. During the elimination rounds, facing the *Too Bad* Corvette of Donnie Hampton, Goodsell was on one of his best runs ever, motoring through the lights when the engine coughed and blew up like a bomb.

It drove off the track, knocked down several chain-link fences, dodged two road signs, and climbed up the shoulder of northbound lanes of Interstate 5. It came to a stop and burnt down to the ground once again. Traffic backed up on the I-5 for miles with people stopping to get out of their cars to see what all the commotion was about. Goodsell was transferred to a local hospital, treated for burns, and later released. It was rumored the CHP issued several citations to all in involved.

The list of no-shows included Ed Carter's Proud American with driver Kip Brundage. Vic Morse's Mister T arrived minutes before the first round but did not race. Dick Bourgeois, driving for Don Cook, experienced traction woes right off the trailer in both lanes, suffering quality bite that failed to get him down the track during eliminations.

Marv Eldredge experienced the hex when he was crossed up in the right lane that had been laced with a heavy dose of rosin by one of his crewmembers during time trials. Eldredge repeatedly hit against the guardrail, as evidenced by the scuff marks on the right front tire. During eliminations, the undamaged Corvette switched lanes against Gene Conway and promptly red-lighted, which ruined his chance of advancing to the finals.

Fresh from a successful Hawaiian tour, Donnie Hampton's Too Bad *dual-engine Corvette delighted the crowd on this single pass with an ET of 7.91 at 191.89 mph, which was the top speed of the night. Hampton was all in on the final round with Conway but blew a head gasket after his burnout and had to shut off, which ended his day.*

Ron Goodsell, subbing for Pat Foster in the Beach City Chevrolet Corvette, was one of the six cars participating in the third annual Corvette Funny Car Nationals. Qualifying runs were not necessary with the under-count field, so drivers were allowed time trials to get acquainted to the track surface. This was suitable for Goodsell because this was his first time at the wheel of the topless Corvette. The previous run in the right lane by Eldridge left a small dusting of rosin, and Goodsell decided he wanted more (approximately 30 feet more) of the magic powder. He lined up into the runway of the crush and let it all out during his burnout with owner Don Kirby keeping tabs. When the smoke and dust cleared, Goodsell was found to have completely spun around, and he was on top of the guardrail facing back toward the starting line. Unfortunately, the Corvette was too far damaged and was knocked out of contention for the night.

Billy Holt ran his successful Gasser program before he decided to build his first Funny Car, the Alabamian I 1970 Corvette, which featured a Logghe chassis with a 392 Chrysler for power. Gary Fowler, shown here at Indy, handled most of the driving duties and at times shared the seat with Clayton Harris. The Corvette met its demise at Gainesville, Florida, during the track's annual Turkey Trot Nationals when the engine exploded into a fireball in the lights, which destroyed the car.

Arnie Behling turned in a stellar performance on the Fourth of July Nitro Championships at Orange County International Raceway when he took down all comers for the Mazmanian mob. Behling's ET of 7.25 at 202 mph defeated the red-lighting Ray Alley in the final round. (Photo Courtesy Tim Pearl Collection)

The dynamic team of "Diamond" Jim Annin and Mike Snively dominated the action on the West Coast Funny Car scene at every track in which they competed. From Sears Point in March, WCS at Bonneville Raceway Park, and Irwindale in October, the team made regular visits to the winner's circle.

Mattel Hot Wheels Supernationals Introduced

NHRA founder and president Wally Parks proudly hosted the national and international press corps with an open house for the inaugural NHRA Mattel Hot Wheels Supernationals at Ontario Motor Speedway, the state-of-the-art $25 million superspeedway. The press was offered hands-on and upfront conversations with Funny Car stars Gene Snow and Steve Bovan. Concluding the tour of the facility, the press was treated with a fuel Funny Car fire up and burnout.

A Month of Records: Schumacher's 6.93 ET at 211 mph

After experiencing unsatisfactory results with his latest Logghe-built 'Cuda, Don Schumacher and "Colonel" John Hogan made the rare road trip to Southern California during the busy match race season. There, they took delivery of Schumacher's first Buttera-built 'Cuda at Ed Pinks.

Before heading back to Chicago, Schumacher made an unannounced weekday stop at OCIR for bracket night to log on a few passes on the new car. Straight off the trailer, the 'Cuda dropped an ET of 7.18 at 206 mph. On the second pass, Schumacher equaled the track speed record of 210 mph with a 7.12 ET.

The delighted Schumacher stuck around until Saturday night's Funny Car feature. If any car broke into the 6-second zone, resetting the track record, the driver would be awarded a $1,000 bonus plus the posted $1,100

NHRA founder and president Wally Parks welcomed pho-tojournalists, local and foreign television news crews, and newspaper reporters for the introduction of the new $25.7 million multi-racing facility called Ontario Motor Speedway. The media day festivities highlighted the upcoming NHRA Mattel Supernationals with tours of the strip, the state-of-the-art timing tower, and the permanent garage facilities.

The mid-summer appearance by Don Schumacher not only surprised the crowd at Orange County International Raceway's Top Fuel/Funny Car doubleheader but also put the him as the favorite for the $1,000 bounty offered by the strip for any Funny Car that could set the first 6-second record at the strip. Coming straight off the trailer, Schumacher nailed down an ET of 7.02 at 211.76 mph for low qualifier. He backed it up in spectacular fashion when he unleashed an ET of 6.93 at 210.28 mph in the first round over Johnny Wright at the wheel of the Fiberglass Trends Javelin. With the loot under his belt, Schumacher was now in OCIR's record books for holding both the first 6-second record and top speed record.

Don Schumacher, the "Windy City Kid," recorded one of the most successful months in Funny Car racing. Schumacher and ace mechanic "Colonel" John Hogan made the trek across the country in late August to take delivery of Don's new revolutionary 'Cuda Funny Car built by "Lil" John Buttera. It was complete with a new Ed Pink Elephant Hemi. With encouraging results during midweek testing at Orange County International Raceway, Schumacher stuck around until the weekend to collect a $1,000 bounty offered by the county for the first Funny Car to break into the 6s. The "Shoe" proved that sticking around was worthwhile by setting the new ET record with a stout 6.93. The following weekend landed Schumacher in the winner's circle, capping top honors at the 16th annual NHRA Nationals in Indy. A month later, the Stardust gang celebrated once again with Schumacher, Ed Pink, and the crew taking the Eastern Funny Car Championship Title.

Larry Reyes unleashed the thunder and the clouds of burnt rubber in the Taylor, Collins, and Wolfe Super Duster at Irwindale. Lightning literally struck near the strip after this photo was taken, as the inclement weather moved in and postponed the race.

The toolboxes of Funny Car teams included many expensive specialty tools, but two of the most important tools cost less than $10: a roll of 200-mph duct tape and a bottle of liquid shoe polish. Danny Miller brought his new Ford Maverick to the West Coast for the 1970 Manufacturer's Championships at Orange County International Raceway. The Maverick received a coat of paint without lettering on the body. Miller improvised the misspelled lettering on the Plastic Fantisic with fresh shoe polish.

Big races have their hard luck victims, and the Manufacturer's Meet was no exception. Ray Alley lost control of his Engine Masters Plymouth Duster during Friday night's qualifying round and ran into the opposite guardrail, which caused considerable damage to the body and front end that knocked Alley out of the show.

INSET: The Long Beach Junior Marching Band performs the National Anthem at the Manufacturer's Championships at Orange County International Raceway. Driver, car, and crew introductions and fireworks were all part of the pomp and circumstance festivities that made the team championships a special race for all.

Chevrolet hopefuls kept tabs on the Texas team of "Big" Mike Burkhart, Mart Higginbotham, and driver Charlie Therwhanger at the 1970 Manufacturer's Funny Car Team Championships at Orange County International Raceway. Therwhanger earned the third slot on the GM team with a 7.36 time running a blown Chevrolet engine.

The scoreboard says it all! Fans react to what they just witnessed on the quickest run ever between Jake Johnston in the Blue Max and Richard Siroonian in "Big" John Mazmanian's Plymouth 'Cuda during the final round of the history of the Manufacturer's Funny Car Championships at Orange County International Raceway.

The closest race in the history of the Manufacturer's Funny Car Championship series took place in November 1970 during the final round for top individual honors. That's when 21-year-old Jake Johnston powered the Blue Max Mustang of Harry Schmidt past Richard Siroonian in "Big" John Mazmanian's Plymouth 'Cuda in front of more than 25,000 spectators, which was the largest crowd ever in the facility. Johnston laid down a slight holeshot against Siroonian that did the trick, running an ET of 6.89 at 217.91 mph to the quicker but slower 6.88 at 212.26 mph. Earlier in elimination rounds, Johnston became the world's quickest Funny Car, running a 6.72 blast backed up by a 6.84 time.

Memories: Jake Johnston

Driver and Tuner of Harry Schmitt's **Blue Max** *Mustang*

"Harry contacted me and knew I was the mechanic working for Snow. I knew how to work and tune on blown late-model Hemis. Harry and Mike Burkhart were racing Chevys then, but Harry wanted to build his own car. Harry received an inheritance and called me to come over to his house and talk about me working and driving for him. Don Hardy was commissioned to build Harry's new car, so I was able to get my license in Mike Burkhart's Camaro.

"In the meantime, I became Burkhart's mechanic. With Harry's car taking a lot longer to build, Snow gave me an offer that I could not refuse. I was to drive his second car, the Gelcoat Mini-Charger, which ended up blowing up at Irwindale with me in it. Harry's car was finished and both Mart Higginbotham and Paul Gordon took turns in the car.

"Mart left when he was offered to drive Burkhart's new Nova, and Harry kept with Gordon, with whom I went to high school. After Snow rebuilt the Charger, we did not really want to take it out on tour. I called Harry, and we got back together. We packed and loaded up every spare part and car onto the ramp truck, and we were ready to race.

This sequence of photos took place in the first round of eliminations at the inaugural NHRA Mattel Supernationals at Ontario. Sush Matsubara drove the Pisano and Matsubara Camaro against Leonard Hughes in the Candies and Hughes 'Cuda when the rear end broke. Matsubara careened into the concrete barrier, which destroyed the new Camaro. Matsubara hung on for the ride of his life but was able to exit the remains of the car practically unscathed with the aid of the OMS safety team. The only other injury was to NHRA photographer Leslie Lovett, who was in the wrong place at the wrong time. He was shooting photos past the finish line when a sheared-off shock absorber from the car bounced and struck his foot, resulting in a fracture.

"We were in Tennessee traveling on the interstate with Harry driving. I was asleep in the camper when a car from the other side of the freeway came across the wide, grassy median. To avoid colliding with the car, Harry had to abruptly swerve, which woke me up. I heard a loud noise when he hit the embankment under a bridge. The truck went sideways, and the car was dislodged when the hold-down straps broke away. The car rolled off the truck and was destroyed in the process. The only salvageable part was the engine.

"The good thing was that nobody was seriously hurt, but the bad news was that we had all these bookings on tour and no race car. Harry called Don Hardy, and imme-diately we headed to Hardy's shop in Floydada, Texas, which is a amall town located in the panhandle. We all worked on the car 16 to 18 hours a day and stayed at the hotel across the street just to sleep.

"Don never made a digger-type chassis like this one before, building it from scratch for the next two straight weeks just by looking at pictures of Mickey Thompson's Mach 1s. When the new body arrived at the shop, we cut it down, removed the biggest section of the body, and narrowed it. When the car was finished, it looked identical to both Thompson's Mustangs. We were able to get back on tour after those two weeks, and we did fairly well."

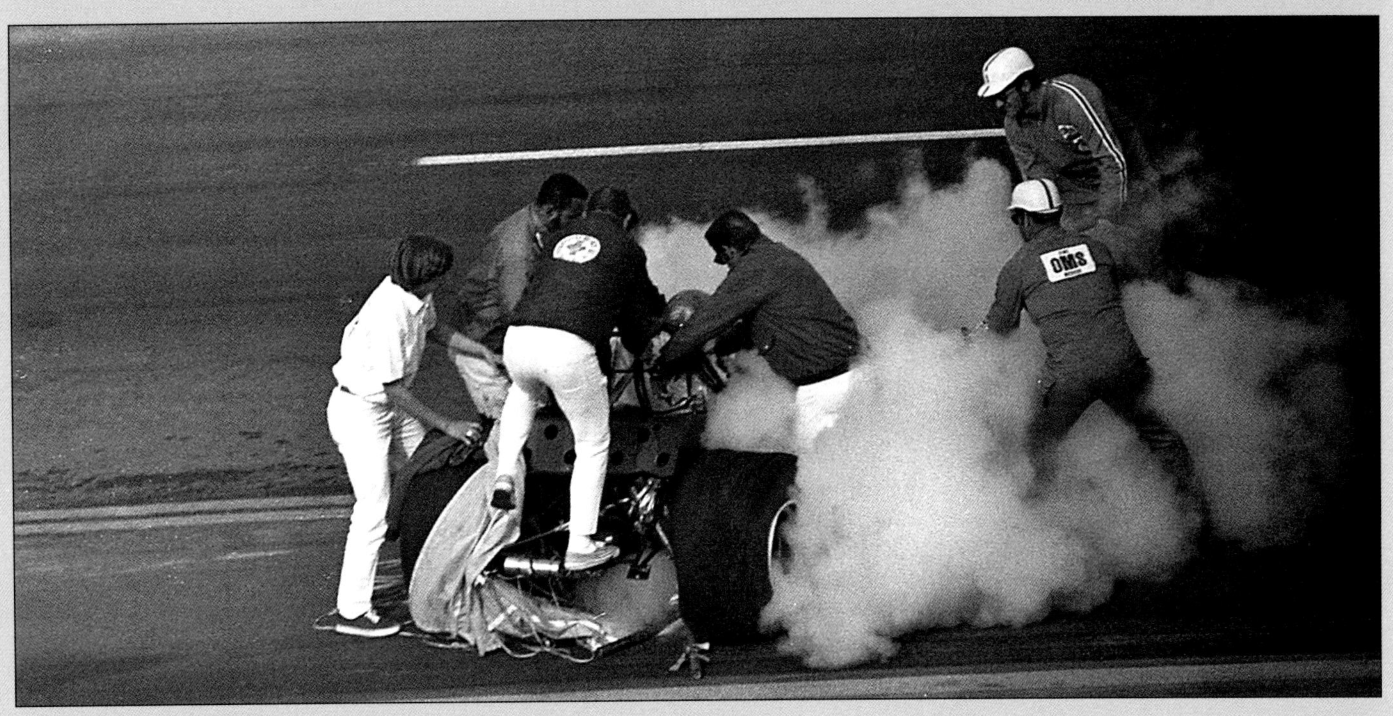

for taking the Top Eliminator title. Schumacher not only outperformed the local competition but also burned his name into the OCIR record books, blasting to an ET of 6.93 at 211 mph.

Funny Cars Reign in 1971

The year 1971, in several opinions, could be viewed as the pinnacle year of Funny Cars. Funny Car numbers were hitting top strides in the first days of the year with ETs of 6.60 at 215 mph right out of the gate.

On January 10, the AHRA Grand American kicked off 1971 in fine fashion at Lions. First, Funny Car driver Gary Gabelich was selected to the 1970 All-America Auto Racing Team for his contributions to drag racing. Gabelich received his award in front of the sellout crowd and garnered a standing ovation.

The 16-car field was led by the top 8 seeded Funny Cars for the first AHRA Grand American Series, including Tom Hoover, Dale Pulde, Gene Snow, Leroy

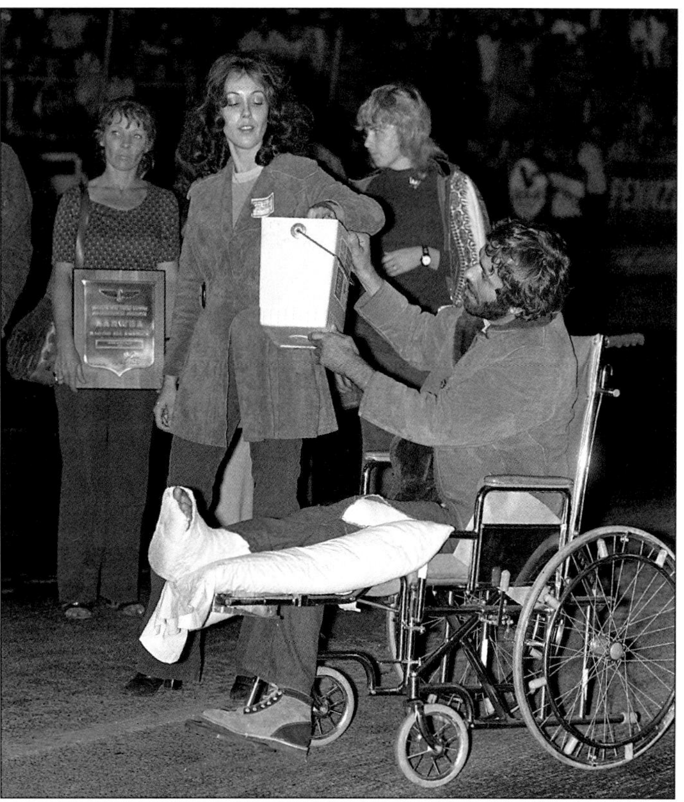

Gary Gabelich was selected in 1970 to the All-America Auto Racing Team for his accomplishments in drag racing. Gabelich was born August 29, 1940, in San Pedro, California, and grew up in south Los Angeles. At age 16, he hot rodded his dad's 1957 Pontiac down the strip and won his first trophy, which did not sit very well with his dad. The trophy wound up into the trash. Gabelich has done it all: skydiving, scuba diving, motorcycle racing, various stints behind the wheel of Top Fuel rails and jet cars, and spending time in the infamous Beach City Chevrolet Corvette Funny Car. Not only was Gabelich a noted driver but he also assisted with pulling the winning raffle ticket after accepting his American Auto Racing Writers and Broadcasters Association award at his home track, Lions Drag Strip, in front of a packed house despite having a broken left leg from a motorcycle accident.

Late afternoon activities around the bridge are buzzing with activity as drivers, crews, and cars prepare to run during the 1971 AHRA Grand American at Lions Drag Strip. Among the first to check out the well-prepped surface was Dave Boncosky's Boss Bird and the Corvettes of Plugger and Griffis and Don Cook. (Photo Courtesy Stormy Byrd Photography)

Al Bergler, Tom Prock, and Pete Seaton made the trek from frigid Michigan to Southern California to shake down their new Logghe-built Super Shaker Vega with Prock at the wheel at Lions Grand Premiere.

Goldstein, Larry Reyes, Mart Higginbotham, Dick Harrell, and Dick Bourgeois. Tom McEwen led the eight unseeded cars when he dropped an unofficial 6.55 ET during qualifying, but he failed to back it up it for the record. Six of the eight unseeded floppers netted times in the 6s.

Funny Cars Close Gap with Top Fuelers

Interesting comparisons took place in February 1971 at OCIR's third All Pro Series race when Don Prudhomme set track records for both ET and top speed (6.62 at 226.13 mph). Only 0.16 of a second separated each division (Top Fuel and Funny Car), but Top Fuel winner Gary Cochran

John Collins suffered a broken back when he crashed "Big" John Bateman's rebodied Atlas Oil Tool Special *during qualifying at AHRA Grand Premiere at Lions. Bateman replaced the Maverick body with a newer, lighter Challenger body, but it immediately failed when the bracing broke apart at speed and disintegrated into fragments. Pieces from the collapsed body lodged against the throttle linkage, keeping the injector at wide-open throttle. The car impacted the guardrail, ripping out approximately 12 feet of railing and taking out two poles that launched the motor completely out of the car. It bounced down the return road, nearly knocking out dragster great Don Garlits.*

Dave Boncosky flat blades the injectors during the Grand Premier at Lions Drag Strip. Boncosky purchased Phil Bonner's Daddy Warbucks *Ford Talladega Torino and retired the car from the show car circuit. Wasting little time, Boncosky sent the car back to Logghe to receive modifications. The 427 SOHC was removed and sold to Ford standout Connie Kalitta. Logghe swapped out the engine plates and mounted the 426 Chrysler Hemi plate and engine. Needing a lighter and more attractive body, the Torino was replaced with a 1970 Pontiac Firebird Trans Am body painted Polar White with blue stripes. Boncosky, with longtime friend Arnie Beswick, struck a deal to lease both Arnie's and the* Boss Bird *name to go match racing under the Beswick banner. Beswick set up most of the racing dates, including spots on the Coca-Cola Cavalcade of Stars Tour team.*

Memories: Al Bergler
Race Car Body Fabricator, Owner/Driver of the **More Aggravation II** *AA/C and* **Motown Shaker** *Vega Nitro Funny Car*

"When Jay Howell and Tom Prock split from campaigning the Logghe Brother's *Warhorse* Mustang Funny Car, Tom and I went in as partners. We bought all the stuff from Logghe, which included the first narrow digger-style chassis built by Logghe.

"Pete Seaton, who I rented out part of my shop to, wanted to be in on this deal. So, we put this together and bought the first Vega body from Ron Pellegrini in Chicago. We hauled the *Seaton Shaker* out to California in 1971 for at Lions. It was cold that night, and Pete had a blanket across his knees while sitting in the truck. He got out of the truck and said he'd had enough of this. Tom and I took the car the Kirby's to repaint it and debuted the Bergler & Prock Vega at the NHRA Winternationals."

Dodge and Plymouth standouts Gene Snow, Richard Siroonian, and Leroy Goldstein share good times, laughs, and stories in the staging lanes before getting to the serious side of racing at the 1971 NHRA Winternationals.

and Prudhomme's Funny Car averaged only 0.03 of a second apart in their three runs in competition (6.68 to 6.71). Another side note is that the Prudhomme's three runs were all above the top speeds by any dragster at the recent NHRA Winternationals and 0.01 slower than the lowest ET

Throughout 1971–1974, performances with the Funny Cars were skyrocketing. Nearly every weekend, the record books were being rewritten at nearly every track coast to coast. Digger-style chassis of light alloy tubing were being built at a record pace.

Long before GoPro cameras were used as an important tool on a race car, the crew of Roland Leong's new Hawaiian Charger mounted a Super 8 movie camera to the left rear of the car that chronicled the data. Butch Mass, the latest driver for Leong, put the new car back into to the winner's circle for the second consecutive year in the Funny Car Eliminator. Mass defeated the Leroy Goldstein, who drove the Ramchargers Challenger at Pomona. Mass set low ET and top speed (6.93 at 212.76 mph).

Young fans line up to collect an autograph from one of the all-time drag racing greats, Don Prudhomme, during the 1971 NHRA Winternationals at Pomona.

Larry Arnold erupts from the bleach box at Irwindale in the King Fish *Barracuda of T.B. Smallwood. The Memphis-based 'Cuda went on to the runner-up position at the inaugural 1970 NHRA Supernationals, losing to Gene Snow in the final round.*

Aluminum cast engines, heads, and internal parts were the ticket to low ETs and outrageous speeds. To remain competitive, big-name sponsors were needed to keep the flow of money going along with payouts at the track. Proprietors increased admission prices, which topped an all-time high. It was getting crazy, but the spectators loved the racing! Drivers had their followers, obliging to take a photo with or giving an autograph to a happy fan.

Unsettled Waters

Darks clouds loomed on the horizon, signaling the downslide for drag racing. For one, the federal government placed into law the Clean Air Act of 1970, which resulted in major changes of air pollution control. Controlled emissions devices had been around since the mid-1960s starting in California, but every year, more stringent requirements lead up to the Clean Air Act.

The 1971 model year vehicles from Detroit were now manufactured with lower-compression engines and with additional smog devices. The high-compression and high-horsepower engines were on their way out. The death of the muscle car was now as real as ever and eventually phased out with a shell of their prestigious past.

With heat from the federal government, Detroit now focused on building subcompact, gas-efficient vehicles for the years to come. GM and Ford suffered the embarrassment with the Chevy Vega and Ford's Pinto. The Vega experienced defective rear axle shafts that literally separated, wheels that sheared off, and carb throttle linkages that jammed the throttle to stay open.

Even through the Ford Pinto got an estimated 20 mpg, it was considered the worst car ever manufactured for the consumer. Cost cuts and flaws in the fuel tank location caused major grief for Ford. But to the drag racer and fiberglass manufacturers, the downsized Vega and Pintos made outstanding lightweight and aerodynamic Funny Car bodies.

Cragar Industries also launched an experimental program testing a completely different induction system using high compressed air in the tanks mounted on both sides of the chassis. Bob Bowen, Andy Crum, Bob Keane, and Jake Johnston tested the air-powered Funny Car at Irwindale.

When Johnston hit the pedal for the first time, the car backfired through the air delivery system. It blew both the plenum from the manifold and the body completely off the chassis. The team continued to test the car without the body. It ran on alcohol and sounded more like an injected alcohol engine. It was relatively quiet compared to the blown fuelers.

The brand-new Corvette AA/FC out of Hyder's Garage was driven by "Nitro" Nick Harmon, who was another victim of the dreaded Corvette curse. The first full pass on the new car (shown at Orange County International Raceway) was likely its last. After Harmon left off the line, the clutch exploded, and the car made an abrupt right into the guardrail that chucked off the body. The bodiless car continued bouncing along the guardrail, tearing it up even more before coming to a complete stop. Harmon was not hurt, but the car was a total loss. Notice the damaged mounting studs of the bellhousing and clutch can.

Orange County International Raceway track personnel remove the remnants of Nick Harmon's Hyder's Garage Corvette. A violent clutch explosion ripped the clutch can and bellhousing completely out of the race car. Nick Harmon was shaken up but not seriously hurt. (Photo Courtesy Steve Reyes Photography)

Omar "the Tentmaker" Carrothers of Joplin, Missouri, made his first trip out to the West Coast an unforgettable one at the 32-car Big 4 Funny Championships at Orange County International Raceway. Facing Ron O'Donnell in the Super Chief during the second round of eliminations, the week-old 'Cuda broke the pinion shaft, which slammed the car into the guardrail, careening Carrothers back onto the track, minus the car body. Both the chassis and body were demolished.

Orange County International Raceway's superb track crew quickly cleans up the twisted wreckage after Omar Carrothers' encounter with the guardrail that demolished both the chassis and body. Omar walked away without serious injuries with aid from Nelson Carter and Ed Pink. The remains of the car were loaded onto the hauler and sent back to Missouri.

Power and Safety Research

Driver Jake Johnston experienced one of the worst fires at the 1973 NHRA World Finals in Tulsa, Oklahoma. He was driving Gene Snow's number-two *Revell Snowman* Charger when the engine burnt a piston that resulted in a blazing inferno.

"The fire was so intense [that] it burned all the stitching out of my gloves," Johnston said. "When I finally got out of the car and stopped, I took off my gloves and found out the Nomex and the layered retardant materials in the suit did their job. I looked down at my gloves and realized both gloves weren't held together, they just flopped open."

Johnston was one of the lucky drivers; others weren't so fortunate.

The high costs of nitromethane, engines, parts, and replacement bodies skyrocketed; finding alternatives to increase safety and avoiding the engine bombs and fires caused a few to turn to experimenting with other means to power Funny Cars and dragsters.

Turbochargers had already been used in Indy car racing for several years. Gene Adams, the head foreman at Hilborn, developed and perfected a turbo system used on his Adams & Enrique's AA/Gas dragster. However, it was a hit and miss, and several times the car was either underpowered or overpowered. Adams installed a dual turbo system for testing purposes to one of Gene Snow's earlier chassis using a Charger body.

Adams, Johnston, other crewmembers took the car to OCIR for testing only. The car never ran in competition, but it ran fairly decently, running in the high 6s. For an alcohol turbo car, it wasn't bad at that time. The major complaint was that it was too quiet for the fans; it didn't make any noise or vibrations normally felt from a fuel car. Also, the car didn't give the driver that addition nitro headache.

Memories: Jake Johnston
Veteran Tuner and Funny Car Driver

"Gene Adams, the head supervisor at Hilborn, developed turbochargers for Indy Cars. For some time, Gene had already been running a turbo system on the Adams-Rasmussen and Enrique's Top Gas dragster. Adams focused to develop a turbo system for a Funny Car with one of Snow's old Logghe cars for Snow to run. Adams and two other team members from Hilborn aided with tuning and had me driving it, testing at OCIR.

"Right out of the gate it ran strong—I believe runs in the high 6 seconds. The only problem with the car was that it was way too quiet for the spectators. [It was] far from the noise, vibration, and power from a traditional fuel car."

Jake Johnston tests Gene Snow's experimental Dodge Charger Funny Car without the aid of a nitro fuel supercharger but with a twin turbocharger setup that was developed by Gene Adams with Hilborn and Cragar. Adams ran a similar turbo system on the Adams-Rasmussen and Enrique's Top Gas dragster.

Cragar Industries' Cold Air Research was its latest project. It involved a conventional Funny Car that utilized a series of in-line stainless-steel bottles that were filled with compressed air that forced air into a specially designed intake manifold in the place of a blower. The first time testing at Irwindale, at the initial launch, the car backfired through the air delivery system, which exploded like a bomb that blew off the body. (Photo Courtesy Jake Johnston)

Leroy Chadderton navigates Roland Leong's Hawaiian *through the bleach box at the 1972 Super Stock Nationals at York US 30 Dragway. Chadderton was the first driver of a blown Fuel Altered who cracked into the 7s when he drove the* Magnificent 7 *in 1966. Leroy achieved another first for a Fuel Altered by cracking the 6-second bracket in 1969.*

Dale Pulde drives Mickey Thompson's Revellaser *Ford Pinto at Orange County International Raceway. The Revell model company built a series of models saluting drag racing "Superstars" both for Funny Car and Top Fuel dragsters. While the* Revellaser *appeared one time only with this paint scheme, the Pinto sold 10s of thousands of its kits.*

Aerodynamics Reach the Next Level

Funny Cars were now far away from their original stock appearances. They were now built with added aerodynamic modifications: shorter and narrowed bodies, raised rear-wing spoilers to put power to the ground, canard wings, hood and nose extensions, and wheel bubbles that dropped the nose of the body to a couple of inches off the ground.

Modifying a body at the track was commonplace, and many went the creative route. This may have included unfolding an empty box that previously contained quarts of oil and using a roll of trusty "200-mph" duct tape to attach the cardboard extension to the existing rear spoiler to add down force. It was crude, but it achieved results. Creativity had no boundaries.

Women in Drag Racing

Women played a large part in drag racing back to the early days. Barb Hamilton, Shirley Shahan, and Judy Lily were tough combatants in the Gasser and Super Stocker wars, respectfully.

This elite group of the Funny Car fraternity take in the between-round action at the 1972 Northern Nationals at Fremont. This gathering of greats includes (left to right) Don Prudhomme, Jim Wolfe, Kelly Brown, Steve "Okie" Bernd, Tom McEwen, "Jungle" Jim Liberman, "Jungle" Pam Hardy, Gene Snow, and Jake Johnston. (Photo Courtesy Steve Reyes)

Barry Setzer owned one of the most successful textile operations in North Carolina and had a passion for drag racing. He watched his hero Don Garlits as a teenager and raced a 1955 Chevy in the process. Setzer, who was one for detail and superb quality, built and funded one of the baddest Funny Cars on the strip. Barry hired "Lil" John Buttera and Ed Pink to collaborate with each other on the Vega. Veteran fuel pilot Kelly Brown was hired to drive the car and quickly drove to the runner-up spot at the 1971 NHRA Springnationals in Dallas. Test sessions at the county included legendary Don Schumacher with seat time for Ed Pink.

Pat Foster sits at the helm of Don Cook's Damn Yankee Plymouth 'Cuda. He was one of the top performers from California using Ed Pink power. Woody Gilmore built the chassis; lettering and paint was by Don Kirby. Foster was one of the top qualifiers in Funny Car at Indy for 1971.

The "Israeli Rocket" Leroy Goldstein concentrates on the countdown on the tree in the Candies and Hughes 'Cuda during the 1971 Orange County International Raceway's Funny Car Manufacturer's Meet. The audience of photographers and racers, including "Jungle" Jim, anxiously wait for the hit of the Houma, Louisiana, 'Cuda during round-robin competition. Goldstein made the jump to the Candies and Hughes team from the Ramchargers and quickly became one of strongest teams from the South.

Clarence Bailey charges off the line at Orange County International Raceway behind the wheel of his King Boogaloo *AA/FC Mercury Cougar. Bailey was mostly a local match racer, and he competed in events around the Southern California area. Bailey was one of the few African American drag racers who campaigned a nitro fuel Funny Car without major funding.*

Memories: Dave Boncosky

Driver and Owner of the Mr. B's Hemi-Tractor Boss Bird *Pontiac Funny Car*

"Being in California during the fall months, we had a good time there. I remember running the car quite a bit, but I really needed to return home to Illinois. Around the time of the Manufacturer's Meet at OCIR, you had to run the race for the big money, and I said no to race.

"Lots of us stayed at the Marco Polo Hotel in Anaheim, which was a wild place. I shared a room with Tommy Smallwood with Austin Coil next door. Coil said, 'I'm not going either.'

"It was all about the money for us to stay, and OCIR kept calling us, and our answer was the same: 'No.'

"Finally, they agreed to pay us more to race, and to be honest, it was quite a bit more.

"Coil and I ran the first race that night and the car ran fast. Another thing, Arnie had a deal with Crane Cams and always ran them, so right after the race at OCIR, Joe Lunati approached me and asked me to try one of his cams. I told him about the Crane deal, and Joe told me to leave the Crane decal on, so I did. He sent me five cams for about $20. The car's speed at that time averaged 195, but it jumped up to 200 to 215 mph using the Lunati camshaft in early 1971. Arnie still built my motors, never knowing the Lunati cam was in the engine. It was something that only Joe and I knew."

The Castronovo brothers, Phil and Fred of Utica, New York, ran one of the most-feared Funny Cars in drag racing. Phil garnered the 1970 NHRA Division One Funny Car title and set track records at nearly every track on which the team competed. Phil and expert mechanic Phil Roberts (shown Orange County International Raceway) gave the Dodge faithful something to cheer about with the brothers' new 1971 Dodge Custom Body Mini Charger, which was 300 pounds lighter compared to their Division 1 Championship car.

Memories: Steve Reyes *Photographer*

"After photographer Alan Earman shot Tom McEwen's Top Fueler in 1972 with a herd of cheetahs at Lion Country Safari for the publication *Drag Racing USA*, I wanted to do something there with the *Rat Trap* Funny Car, so after a couple of calls to Lion Country's public relations department, our request was set up.

"Fowler was notified, and we all met out at the Lion Country offices. They explained the rules to us and let us know that the park was to be open and the traffic would not be stopped for us to shoot. It was a weekday, so there would not be a lot of traffic anyway.

"We decided on elephants because of the name of the *Rat Trap* Funny Car. You know, the old story of elephants being afraid of rats and mice. Anyway, the car was unloaded and put in place now, so all we needed were the elephants.

"Within minutes, the elephant handler showed up—a small man who probably weighed 100 pounds—and asked us where we wanted the elephants? We picked the spot and then had his guys put down the elephant chow or something like that around the car. As soon as the elephants saw the food, they came. The herd had been called for lunch!

"The car disappeared behind the herd, and now there are elephants everywhere along with the smell that is not very pleasant, but we were there to make Fowler famous, so we started shooting around these huge, smelly animals.

"Well, now there was one huge bull elephant that was clearly was not a Funny Car fan, so he wandered over to the front of the car and raised up his massive right front leg. The handler saw what was about to happen and started yelling at the bull, running up with a bamboo stick raised up, threating to hit the elephant. I figured now this guy was going to be toast, as this huge animal was going to stomp him into little pieces. However, the bull turned and ran away with his tail between his legs. So, there were no death photos after all; it was a good day to be an elephant."

When the Fuel Altered class died out in the early 1970s, Dennis Fowler and Don Green continued the **Rat Trap** tradition. This time, they used a Plymouth Satellite flopper and hired former Fuel Altered pilot Tom Ferraro to drive. (Photo Courtesy Steve Reyes Photography)

On Tour with Drag Racing Photographer Steve Reyes

"I believe it was 1972 when fellow photographers Bob McClurg, Jeff Tinsley, and myself were always out 'attacking' Funny Car owners for shoots and features. So, while on tour at Rockingham, North Carolina, in 1972, we approached Malcolm Durham about shooting a feature on his new Camaro Funny Car. Malcolm was all for it, so we all had to hook up in Washington, D.C., where Malcolm lived on Tuesday after the race at Rockingham.

"On Malcolm's last pass on Saturday night, his chute failed and spun the car out near the end of the track. All we could see was a huge number of sparks, as it was so far down the strip, and it was dark. We figured that old Malcolm screwed up his new car, and we were out of a feature. However, only the wheelie bars were bent. Malcolm was a bit excited that he had not crashed his car. The only thing now was that we needed a place to shoot the car in D.C. on Tuesday. So, me being rather forceful, I told Maryland resident Tinsley, 'Hey we should use the US Capitol building as a background.' Well, Jeff thought about it and said, 'Why not?'

"On Monday after the race, Tinsley got on the phone and started making calls to find out what we had to do to use the Capitol building as a background. Well, it took him most of the day, and 13 permits later from different government offices, it was a go the next day.

"Malcolm was called to let him know our plan, so we all met Tuesday morning with the Capitol police department. We found out quickly that they were extremely easy to work with, plus they really liked Malcolm's car. The Camaro was put in position, and we started our shoot. The Capitol police assigned a few officers to keep people away from our photo area so we would not be disturbed. Mal-

Malcolm Durham, along with fellow teammate Lee Jones, pose in front of the US Capitol in Washington, DC, with Durham's latest **Strip Blazer VIII** *Camaro. Durham spent his time mostly match racing on the East Coast while Jones was a stellar performer on the West Coast, running more eliminator events. (Photo Courtesy Steve Reyes Photography)*

colm was going to bring both of his cars to the Capital shoot, one being Lee Jones's team car, but that one was not finished, so Jones was there with his fire suit and was photographed with Malcolm."

Jimmy Boyd's Turkey Plymouth 'Cuda Funny Car was another momentary car that only made a few passes down the track. The home-built creation had a shortened wheelbase and ran an early Hemi for power. The Turkey debuts at Orange County International Raceway, making shakedown passes. On its next outing at Lions Drag Strip, the 'Cuda met its doom when Jimmy pitched the blower at halftrack, lost control, and crashed into the track railing. It folded into a pile of wreckage.

The remains of Jimmy Boyd's Turkey sit on the trailer in the pit parking lot at Lions Drag Strip. Although Boyd was shaken up, he stepped away from floppers and retired from drag racing. Later, Boyd returned to pilot a nostalgia front-engine Top Fueler. (Photo Courtesy Steve Reyes)

Memories: Ross Howard

Owner of the Custom Body 1972 Challenger Funny Car **Fulfilling a Wish**

"I purchased the 1973 Castronovo Brothers Custom Body Enterprise AA/FC in 2014. I had been on the lookout for a race car of notoriety for several years. I wanted a car of prominence in drag racing, and it had to be a Chrysler product.

"The car had been sitting idle for years at the NHRA Museum located in Pomona, California. The owner at the time decided it was time to sell the car, and I acquired it. I knew the car was incapable of running as it was and enlisted the aid of longtime racer friend Larry 'the Okie Smoker' Brown. Larry was a former Top Fuel and Funny Car shoe in the Golden Era. He proceeded to put his expertise into the Keith Black Hemi and prepare it for its next life as a cackle car.

"Soon after, Okie's pal and 1974 NHRA US Nationals Top Fuel winner Marvin 'WHO' Graham joined us in forming the trio of 'Okie's on Nitro.'

"In 2016, the car was invited to the NHRA US Nationals for the 50th Anniversary of the Funny Car class. The last time the car was at the US Nationals was 43 years earlier. Crew chief extraordinaire Jimmy Prock (Tom's son) started the car, while grandson Austin Prock was in the driver's seat.

"In the summer of 2017, the Challenger returned to its birthplace of Utica, New York, where it was reunited with the Castronovo family. Former owner Fred Castronovo saw his race car one last time. We even fired the car up in downtown Utica, just as the Castronovo did

In the early Funny Car years, Shirley Muldowney was the top female driver in the class and frequently schooled her male counterparts. Muldowney teamed with one of the best that ever sat behind the wheel of a race car: Connie Kalitta. Dubbed the *Bounty Hunter* and *Bounty Huntress*, both were main draws at the strip. Not all were racers, but many served as goodwill ambassadors, trophy gals, media writers, and crewmembers who supported husbands and boyfriends. Also seeing the ladies at the strip brought fans to the stands.

It wasn't all glamor with the hot-pants, go-go boots, and halter tops. The girls thrashed on the race cars, not afraid of getting dirty or breaking nails. They were a credit to the sport; they were remarkable times.

No Gas

Panic from the oil embargo in 1973–1974 by the Organization of the Petroleum Exporting Countries (OPEC) affected every driver when the price of a barrel of crude increased

Women in motorsports were as important to a racer as the parts and pit crew. The fans loved them too! These gorgeous ladies promoted racing as goodwill ambassadors that acknowledged crowds, waving and handing out the hardware and cash to the victors in the winner's circle. Miss Hurst Golden Shifter, the lovely Linda Vaughn, highlights "Lil" John Buttera's craftmanship and the Chevy Vega of Barry Setzer during a Drag Racing USA photo session by photographer Steve Reyes. Reyes snapped some of the greatest action and explosive shots seen in major publications, but he gave many drivers that "uneasy" feeling when they spotted him standing at the finish line. (Photo Courtesy Steve Reyes)

in the good old days. Neither of the family reunion moments had a dry eye in the house. We have been from coast to coast, from the paddocks of Laguna Seca to the Greens of Legends on Amelia Island Concours d'Elegance . . . it's still making history."

The current owner of the Custom Body Challenger, Ross Howard, reunited the last of the original brothers, Fred and Vic Castronovo, with the 1973 Custom Body Challenger during the return to its birthplace in Utica, New York. The Castronovo family was legendary in the East Coast world of drag racing. According to Howard, Fred stared at the car without an expression until the car fired and came to life. Then, Fred gave the largest smile. As the fuel ran out and the car shut off, Fred yelled "Let's do a burnout!" A little over a year and half later, Fred passed away. (Photo Courtesy Franca LaBarbera)

Women played a major role in helping husbands and boy-friends around a Funny Car. Photographer Tom West took this candid shot that shows the reaction of Joe Winter's wife to his good luck pat while tightening his lap and harness belts.

Shirley "Cha-Cha" Muldowney had a long journey working her way up the ladder as a professional drag racer. Despite fires, crashes, and setbacks, her determination and perseverance propelled her to be the quickest and fastest female Funny Car driver of her time. In 1971, she became the quickest woman in Funny Car history with an ET of 6.82 at 219.50 mph and the only woman to capture a major Funny Car Eliminator title. When Muldowney experienced an engine fire that destroyed her 1972 Mustang, the Bounty Huntress returned to the scene with her new John Buttera–built, candy gold/red 1973 Plymouth Satellite that was built with the best of everything, ranging from safety equipment to all-out performance. (Photo Courtesy Steve Reyes)

National Dragster and Drag News columnist "Friendly" Fran Rooks flashes one of her trademark smiles while hanging out with the Texas-based Brand X Mustang Funny Car of David Sein and Cecil Langford. Rooks was the "Rona Barrett" of the happenings in drag racing. (Photo Courtesy Steve Reyes)

NBC's Rowan & Martin's Laugh-In comedy television show aired from 1968 to 1973. It featured silly humor, pranks, and behavior. Along with the comedy skits, body painting was used every week on the show, so the idea carried over to this Drag Racing USA magazine photo with bikini-clad Stefanie Rose covered with the green and yellow paint to match the Super Chief of Nelson Carter.

Members of the Beebe clan celebrate Dave Beebe's win in the Whipple and Mr. Ed *Plymouth Satellite entry at PDA OCIR. Partaking in the celebration is PDA promoter Doug Kruse, Keith Black, Barbara Roufs (OCIR's trophy queen), Dave and Judy Beebe, Art Whipple, Tim Beebe, friends, family, and crew members. (Photo Couresy Kathy Beebe-Harris)*

Funny Cars were at peak of popularity in 1973. Several non-racing major corporations took notice of the age levels of crowds that were attracted to the fiberglass fliers. Having a sponsor's name plastered to the side of a 225-mph missile increased sales. Don Rackemann and Glenn Way promoted the idea to International Telephone and Telegraph (ITT), the world's largest corporation during the time, and its parent company for Wonder Bread. A major deal was struck with ITT, and a pair of Chevy Vega Funny Car panel trucks were painted to resemble Wonder Bread delivery trucks. Chassis builder "Lil" John Buttera built both **Wonderwagon** *trucks on a $28,000 budget, and each was equipped with a 494-ci Ed Pink Chrysler Hemi. Kenny Youngblood designed the paint scheme and Don Kirby applied the paint. Kelly Brown and teammate Glenn Way drove the panel wagons. Out of gate, both cars were plagued with handling issues during test sessions. The aerodynamics led to handling woes. The trucks were compared to a shoebox, as the back end wanted to come around. Adding spoilers to the roof had no effect on performance, so the idea was scrapped.*

The **Chi-Town Hustler** *and its mind-boggling, tule fog–styled burnouts that engulfed the starting line all the way past the 600-foot mark will always be embedded in the minds of Funny Car fans. The* **Hustler** *was an elite Funny Car not only with the billowing smoke clouds of burnt rubber but also because of some overly impressing numbers. For the 1972 season, the Chicago trio built a new assault missile, a low and slippery Dodge Challenger that replaced the familiar Dodge Charger. John Farkonas, Austin Coil, and Pat Minick now had a new driver: the 1970 NHRA Winternationals Funny Car Eliminator champ Clare Sanders.*

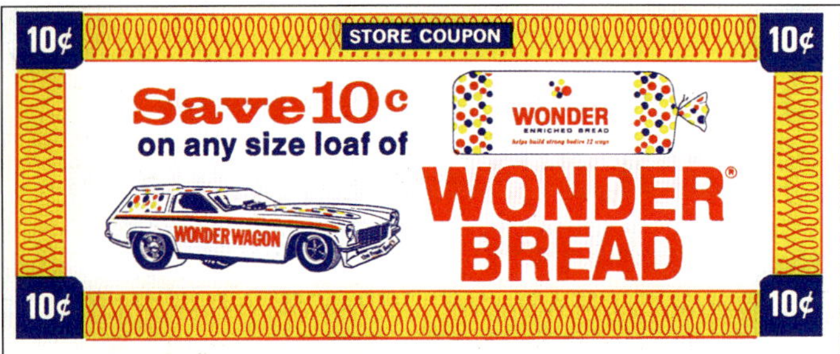

Wonder Bread's promotional coupon was a drag racing first. "The Fresh Guys" Wonderwagon Vega Panel Funny Car illustration was found in each loaf. It offered the customer 10 cents off future purchases of a loaf of Wonder Bread that "helps build strong bodies 12 ways." (Coupon Courtesy the Dale Kunesh Collection)

In the semifinal round at the 12th annual NHRA Winternationals, Jake Johnston strikes the tires off the line and clicks it off against Ed "the Ace" McCulloch. During Johnston's burnout out of the bleach box, the parachute pack came off the car and opened. With the car backing up to the starting line, the entangled straps wrapped around the differential. Johnston was unaware on what was happening because Richard Tharp and Don Schumacher grabbed the chute and released the cords just as Johnston was prestaging. Starter Buster Couch (in the background on the left) knew the rule in Funny Car that states no one could a run without a chute. However, during the chaos, he was not aware that Johnston did not have a second chute pack to slow the Charger down. Back on the starting line, both Tharp and Schumacher received the wrath of Couch for the incident. Notice the chute cords dragging under the rear of the car and Johnston's NHRA AA/FC Competition license approved by Division IV Director Dale Ham.

Denver Schutz concentrates on the tree in Charlie Proite's Telstar Dodge Challenger in the first round of action against Connie Kalitta at the 1971 Orange County International Raceway Manufacturer's Meet. Schutz turned in an ET of 7.40 at 205.74 mph to his opponent's 7.52 at 193.15 mph, earning a point for Team Dodge.

Don Prudhomme hits the asphalt for one of the last times in his black Snake III at Lions Last Drag Race on December 1–2, 1972. Twenty-four hours later, the curtain closed for good on the stellar venue with 17 years of history at 223rd and Alameda in Wilmington, California.

Teamwork comes in all forms, especially in drag racing. Assisting Twig Zeigler in the pits was the talented Art Whipple and Ed "the Ace" McCulloch. This lovely backup girl carefully lines up Zeigler back to the starting line. (Photo Courtesy Steve Reyes Photo)

The Twig Zeigler topped Dave Beebe in Ray Alley's Charger in the third round of team racing, recording the third-quickest ET of the meet (6.72 seconds) at 215 mph at the 1971 Orange County International Raceway Manufacturer's Meet.

Chula Vista's Bill Leavitt recorded the quickest time in Funny Car history when he blasted an amazing 6.48 at 213 mph win against Henry Harrison at Lions Grand Finale Funny Car Meet. Leavitt's Quickie Too Mustang pumped new life into the 392 users when he first ran an ET of 6.53 on his way to setting the record.

Dale Pulde exits the water box blazing the Goodyears while prepping for his quarterfinal encounter against Don Prudhomme at the Supernationals at Ontario Motor Speedway. Prudhomme and Shirl Greer were nearly locked together in the points championship, but Pulde pulled past the Snake with an ET of 6.16 at 233.76 mph, which set the national ET record. The win also secured the banged-up Greer the NHRA Funny Car World Championship. Pulde qualified number six but lost in the semifinals against Dave Condit.

Tom Prock obliterates the tires through the bleach box in Phil Castronovo's latest version of the Custom Body *Dodge Challenger in front of the standing-room-only crowd at Orange County International Raceway. Castronovo retired from driving a few months earlier when his 1972 Challenger that won the highly touted Best Appearing Car Award and was the number-1 qualifier at the Indy US Nationals blew up in the finish lights and crashed into the guardrail. With the increased dangers of engine explosions and fires, it was a family decision to remove Castronovo from the car and put Tom Prock into the seat.*

nearly 300 percent (from $3 to nearly $13 in the United States). The economy was squeezed, and many felt that drag racing could go into extinction.

Attendance at the strips dropped across the nation. The prices of parts and cars reached all-time high levels. The "Boomer" generation was older and now raising families, paying mortgages, and having responsibilities with little time or extra cash to spend to go racing. Several top-named Funny Car players were forced to cut back their participation, trying to build major funding. Many became hired guns or dropped out of racing completely.

In 1975, the country was hit with a severe recession that took a toll in all motor sports. There were now decreasing attendance numbers, higher gate costs, and noise and pollution complaints. Property values skyrocketed, leading landowners to close local racetracks and drag strips and sell them off.

R. J. Reynolds/Winston Jumps Aboard

Times were gloomy. Then, the biggest news to come out of the offices of the NHRA was that R. J. Reynolds/Winston Drag Racing inked a lucrative deal as the new series sponsor. This gave new life and money to the stag-

nant series with extended television and advertising coverage.

End of the Greatest Era of Funny Cars

It is anyone's calculation what the future of the Funny Car holds. It has been nearly six decades since Jack Chrisman strapped himself into the Sachs & Son's *Super Charged* Cyclone and made that inaugural run in a true Funny Car. Chrisman averaged high-10-second runs in the quarter mile while today's editions cover the refigured distance (1,000 feet) for a fuel flopper at an average run of 3.90 at 325 mph. It was exciting back then, and it is a pure adrenaline rush today.

No matter if you are an advocate of days past or a fan of the present day, Funny Cars were and still are exciting to watch. Drastic changes have taken place in the last 50-plus years, but they share many of the same characteristics.

The early Funny Car body configurations were right on for a stock model with bright colors sprayed with actual paint with hand detailed lights and grilles. Today's renditions are futuristic molded cookie-cutter designs nowhere close to a production model and wrapped with vinyl lettering, colorful paint schemes, and graphics.

"Animal" Al Marshall pushes the pedal wide open at halftrack at Tulsa in Dale Creasey's Tyrant *Mustang. The professional group of Coca-Cola stars used an intensified points system. Points were awarded to the overall event winner who totaled toward bonus money that was awarded to the series champion at the end of the year.*

The Coca-Cola Cavalcade of Stars

The Gold Agency in Evanston, Illinois, was one of the largest and oldest agencies that served nearly every drag strip in the country. It promoted talent and races, did publicity (radio commercials and printed publications), and gave trophies.

In the summer of 1967, Ben Christ, the head of the agency, brought his idea to drag racing's super-agent Ira Lichey. Christ wanted to seek out major sponsorships that would benefit both the sponsor and the drag racing industry. With their sights on the youth market, which was hitting its all-time high, Christ and Lichey sought out what was popular with younger movement. They discovered that Coca-Cola was their choice of soft drinks.

When the executives from the Gold Agency and Coca-Cola met, the major concerns of the soda giant dealt with

Norm Kraus's 1968 Dodge **Super Charger** *unleashed a new trend of the ultra-modern Funny Car that was built by Race Car Specialties. The 128-inch tubular chassis with a digger-style roll cage was built by Frank Huszer. Fiberglass LTD in Illinois provided the Charger body that was narrowed 10 inches. The red and silver colors that covered the Windy City Charger were sprayed by acclaimed painter "Molly." Both Kraus and Ron Rinauro spent a short time driving the Charger until Gary Dyer returned to the Coca-Cola tour in the driver's seat on June 7 at Thompson, Ohio. Dyer defeated Kelly Chadwick, Fred Goeske, and the Stone, Woods, and Cooke Mustang in the final round. Both Dyer and Sid Waterman performed their magic on the 426 Dodge Hemi that ran on an 80-percent blend of nitro. Dyer went on to win the Inaugural Coke Championship, capturing a total of 11 wins out of the 32 scheduled event series. (Photo Courtesy Steve Reyes Photography)*

Kelly "the Professor" Chadwick of Floydada, Texas, was employed during the week as a high school teacher and coach, but on the weekends, he was an avid drag racer "schooling" the opposition. As his passion grew for speed racing down the quarter mile, he retired from the classroom and became a professional driver of nitro Funny Cars (both injected and blown versions). Chadwick's latest model was built with a 124-inch-wheelbase chassis by fellow Texan Don Hardy. The candy apple red lacquer paint was sprayed over the Fiberglass LTD stretched body that hid the 427-inch Rat motor. Chadwick was the Coca-Cola series runner-up, posting nine event wins.

Jess Tyree of Fullerton, California, owned his own exhaust header business. He also built his own race cars, including his 1969 Pontiac Firebird AA/FC. The soft-spoken Tyree was the perfect fit on the Coca-Cola tour because of his professionalism with the fans and his racing on the track. Tyree fit mostly into the underdog role, but he always raced hard while giving the fans a memorable show.

Dick Bourgeois has driven an array of high-quality race cars in his career for several predominant owners, including "Big" John Mazmanian's Willys A/GS and Doug Thorley. Bourgeois, with top wrench Earl Wade, produced some serious power numbers that made the Corvair one of the strongest Chevys in Funny Cars. When Ira Lichey selected Bourgeois and Wade to represent the Coca-Cola USA traveling show, the Corvair was replaced with a new red, white, and blue–themed American Motors Javelin body.

Jack Chrisman's presence on the Coca-Cola Cavalcade brought quality and leadership to the traveling troupe of all-stars. Chrisman's 1969 Mach I was one of the top-performing Funny Cars under the Coke and Sprite banner. As a 15-year drag racing pioneer, Chrisman was elected to lead the program at a gala black-tie dinner and press party for team owners and drivers hosted by the Coca-Cola USA and Sprite bottlers in Atlanta, Georgia.

accidents and liabilities under the Coca-Cola name. The agency provided an insuring agreement to the Atlanta-based company, stating that the project would make a large amount of money to protect the company.

Don Wilson, the general manager of the Sprite division of Coca-Cola, was a huge racing fan. He was the force behind the project who took the proposal to the president and vice president of Coca-Cola. Not long after, the dream became a reality with a major deal.

Within the year, the Coca-Cola Cavalcade of Stars was formed. Bottlers from Coke and Sprite sponsored the selected group of eight touring all-star Funny Cars and two alternates. The teams match raced three rounds for points and guaranteed prize money. Appearance money for each team was $1,000 per race, and if the driver went on to win the three round-robin events, he took home an additional $1,400.

Lichey set up, organized, and handpicked the eight teams and the drivers. He also handled the promotional side for Coca-Cola. The weekly schedule of the tour ran at least two races but could sometimes be up to five races, depending on travel miles and time between locations.

Several ground rules were put in place. All team members were required to wear uniforms and act as professionals because Coca-Cola and Sprite had representatives watching at each race to see if the company wanted to

put their investments back into the sport. With the tours arranged in advance, the drivers and crews were able to plan their free time away from the grueling schedule to relax, spend time with family and friends, and race as an independent at NHRA, AHRA, IHRA, and UDRA meets.

Owning and operating a fiberglass manufacturing business that produces lightweight body products that ranged from doors, fenders, and bumpers to complete one-piece bodies meant that Marv Eldredge, the owner of Fiberglass Tends, supplied them all. Eldredge also built, drove, and owned some of the most beautiful Candy Red Corvettes and AMC products that were available right off the warehouse shelves.

Fred Goeske's Plymouth Dealers Association *Plymouth Road Runner toured extensively on the exclusive Coca-Cola Funny Car circuit in 1969. Ronnie Scrima's Exhibition Engineering built the 120-inch chassis. The unique Plymouth Road Runner body was built by Contemporary Fiberglass, which also fabricated the interior tin. The body was sprayed Omaha Orange, which was a regional Los Angeles Sales District color, before being rolled out for Plymouth production models.*

Fred Stone, Tim Woods, and Doug "Cookie" Cook's New Dark Horse *hemi Ford Mustang won its share of Coca-Cola gold in the inaugural year of the Coca-Cola All Stars with Kenny Safford at the wheel. Safford went on to drive Norm Kraus's* Mr. Norm's Super-Charger *with tuner Gary Dyer. (Photo Courtesy Steve Reyes Photography)*

The Coca-Cola Cavalcade of Stars card from the October 18, 1969, issue of Drag News *promoted the only West Coast appearance and the series season finale for Cola Cavalcade at Lions Drag Strip. Series champion Gary Dyer was replaced by Bob Smith driving the* Uncola Invader *Corvette, and Steve Bovan's* Mister T *Camaro was in as an alternate when Jack Chrisman coughed up the supercharger in the lights and blew the roof off his Mustang. Kelly Chadwick closed out year by taking the check for the win at the beach.*

The inaugural season lineup representing the "Elite Eight" in no particular order was Norm Kraus-Norm Weekly-Gary Dyer (Mr. Norm's Dodge Charger), Kelly Chadwick (Chevy-powered Camaro), Dick Bourgeois and Earl Wade (Chevy-powered AMC Javelin), Jack Chrisman (Ford-powered Mach I Mustang), Jess Tyree (Pontiac-powered Firebird), Fred Goeske (Plymouth Roadrunner), Marv Eldridge (Hemi-powered Corvette Roadster), and Kenny Safford (Stone, Woods, and Cooke Mach I Mustang).

The popular touring group match raced approximately 25-plus dates a year around the country. They toured from May through September at the nation's top drag strips.

Jon Lunberg, the "Voice of Drag Racing," was hired as the official announcer for all race dates. The tour kicked off on April 27, 1969, at Amarillo Dragway in Texas. Texan native Kelly Chadwick defeated the Plymouth Road Runner of "Fearless" Fred Goeske in the final round.

By the end of May, the racing was far more successful than Coca-Cola ever imagined. When the tour stopped in Atlanta, Georgia, Bob Brandon of Coca-Cola and Don Wilson of Sprite hosted a black-tie press party and dinner for all the team drivers and owners. At the conclusion of the dinner, 15-year veteran drag racer Jack Chrisman was elected by a majority vote by the drivers to head up the program.

Lions Launches Coca-Cola to the Heavens

The last stop for the Cavalcade of Stars in its inaugural year was at Lions Drag Strip on October 18. The management team of Lions had ingenious ideas about how to draw the spectators to the strip, so it got creative advertising the upcoming Coca-Cola Cavalcade race. The team hired a helicopter and attached a bright neon billboard sign to the bottom. The helicopter flew on Friday night before the next day's finale. The helicopter was spotted flying above several highly populated locations around the southland, including Hollywood, Los Angeles, Pasadena, and Long Beach.

The helicopter flew south into the Orange County area above the city of Anaheim, which included flying over a crowded Disneyland. After a few passes around the "happiest place on earth," the pilot noticed bright lights coming from Angel Stadium. Since it was well past baseball season, the curious pilot and sign operators flew the copter directly over the stadium and hovered above to find Billy Graham's three-day Crusade well under way in front of the standing room–only crowd.

Right around that time, the evangelist Graham was on the stage leading tens of thousands in prayer with all eyes closed. Suddenly, Graham shouted to "open your eyes and lift your arms toward the high heavens!"

When all eyes opened, low and behold, there was the helicopter hovering perfectly still with the brightly displayed message for Saturday's Coca-Cola Cavalcade of Stars. "Come see and hear the refreshing sounds of real "soul music" . . . the real loud eight-cylinder music!"

At Saturday night's finale, all eight cars participated with three complete rounds of racing. The lineup of the top eight cars from the first to eighth position was Kelly Chadwick–substitute Bob Smith (driving the "Uncola" *Invader* Corvette), Marv Eldridge, Dick Bourgeois, Ken Safford, Fred Goeske, Jess Tyree, and Jack Chrisman.

Alternate Steve Bovan in the *Mister T* Camaro replaced Chrisman in the second round when the roof blew off Chrisman's Mustang after the blower backfired in the lights. When the racing concluded, Gary Dyer won the overall Coca-Cola/Sprite Series Championship.

Enjoy Coca-Cola Drag Racing Again

The Coca-Cola Company and Gold Agency felt the tour greatly helped both companies in 1969 with increased sales and higher interests of the Coke All-Stars. So, the series was brought back to the strip for the next year. For the 1970 Coca-Cola Cavalcade, the scheduled lineup of participants was penciled in with three new members: Johnny Wright, driving Mickey Thompson's white Mustang; Bobby Wood's *GT-1 Rebel* Chevy II; and Dale Pulde at the wheel of Stone, Woods, Cook Mustang with Dee Keaton.

The returnees were now sporting new looks and cars. Jess Tyree's 1970 Firebird was still under Pontiac power. Fred Goeske was now in a Plymouth Duster. Jack Chrisman had his 1970 Mach I. Marv Eldridge was now with a Dodge Challenger. Dick Bourgeois had a newly painted red AMC. Kelly Chadwick filled out the rest of the field without major changes to his 1969 Camaro.

The Coke tour once again opened in Amarillo, Texas, with several new rules in effect. One major change was that the four lowest ETs from the opening secession automatically advanced to the second round, regardless of whether the cars won or lost. Another first for the tour was recognition by the three major magazines of the Peterson Publishing Company: *Hot Rod*, *MotorTrend*, and *Car Craft*. Each carried full-page color advertisements that featured Kelly Chadwick's Camaro. When the smoke cleared from

Mickey Thompson and Johnny Wright were invited to fill one of the eight spots on the Coca-Cola Cavalcade tour for 1970. Wright had already won several outings in the Mickey Thompson white Mach I Mustang, including the January 1 Funny Car Festivities at Irwindale Raceway. The revamped Mustang of Wright, Thompson, and Steve Montrelli made the trio strong contenders on the touring All-Stars.

Captain of the second Coca-Cola Cavalcade season for 1970 was "Fearless" Fred Goeske. He was now sporting a slippery, lightweight Fiberglass Trends Duster body after ditching the heavy Road Runner body. Goeske's $25,000 Duster met its demise at Capital Raceway in Maryland when a violent engine explosion set the car on fire in the lights and burnt down. Goeske escaped without injury, but the car was a total loss.

The newest member to the Coca-Cola Cavalcade of Stars in 1970 was personable Bobby Wood from Birmingham, Alabama. When the tour kicked off the series at Amarillo, the confident Wood predicted he would clean house at the troupe's motel, wowing the crowd with a couple of burnouts in the parking lot. Good to his word, Wood put his Kendall GT-1 Rebel Chevy II into the winner's circle when Dale Pulde red lit in the Stone, Woods, and Cook Mustang. Wood sailed to the finish line, posting the low ET of the meet with a 7.81 for a new Amarillo Dragway record despite a slick track and battling 35-mph crosswinds.

Marv Eldridge switched from his familiar Corvette roadster to a new Dodge Challenger that sported pearl white paint instead of the candy red of his Funny Cars from the earlier days. Eldridge's L.A. Challenger *featured a late-model 426 Hemi with B&M 2-speed TorqueFlite transmission. Embracing the Hemi was a new Exhibition Engineering chassis with a measured 122 wheelbase. The* Challenger *averaged 7.20 ETs with speeds above 200 mph. (Photo Courtesy Tim Pearl Collection)*

New on the tour was veteran driver Dale Pulde at the controls of the Stone, Woods, and Cook with Dee Keaton *Mach I Mustang. The* Tinkerbell *was one of a select few Coca-Cola Cavalcade Funny Cars that was featured in full-page advertisements representing the cast of traveling stars that targeted the younger generation.*

"Mr. Pontiac" Jess Tyree, returned for his second tour of the traveling all-stars with a new 1970-1/2 Firebird body painted with outlandish, bright colors. Tyree remained loyal, running Pontiacs from his earlier days of S/S and A/FX trials and now campaigning a blown 428-ci "Big" Chief engine.

the evening's racing, Chadwick brought home the win and Gary Dyer was crowned the 1969 Coca-Cola/Sprite Series champion.

For most of the cars and the stars of the tour, racing went on as normal without any hitches. However, one tour member took a punch to the gut twice within a week's schedule. Fred Goeske, one of the original players of the Cavalcade, was booked at Capital Raceway in Maryland when his $25,000 Plymouth Duster experienced a massive engine explosion, caught fire, and burnt down due to the flaming magnesium parts and fiberglass body. The on-board fire system prevented injury to Goeske, but the track fire crews emptied 25 extinguishers trying to save what was left of the car.

Goeske continued to fulfill his obligations when he was able to buy back his old ride (*Hemi Cuda II*) from Joe Bush, the proprietor of Speed Sport of Chicago. The following week, Goeske was right back at it at Detroit Dragway in Michigan on Saturday night for a high-stakes Funny Car meet. Several delays on the track prolonged the race that concluded after midnight.

Goeske needed to be in Suffolk, Virginia, the next afternoon for a scheduled Coca-Cola race, but it was after 1 a.m. when he was loaded up and pulled out of Detroit Dragway. Knowing he had an 11-hour, 700-mile trek in front of him, Goeske pushed the pedal to the floor, trying to make up lost time. When he entered Sussex County, New Jersey, a pair of rotating red "gumballs" lit up behind him, and he was pulled over for speeding, doing 72 mph in a 55-mph zone.

When Dale Pulde was released from the **Stone, Woods, and Cook** *ride, it didn't take long to fill in for the injured Dick Bourgeois and make a statement to the troupe. Driving Bourgeois's 1970 AMC Javelin on one of the stops of the Coca-Cola tour in the Midwest, Pulde promptly went out and ran an ET of 7.29 at 201.78 mph, which was the quickest the car ever ran. He took home the cash, winning the event.*

Fred Goeske suffered a violent engine explosion and fire that destroyed his $25,000 Duster Funny Car at Capital Raceway. He was pressed to find a replacement Funny Car to fulfill his racing commitments. He reached out to Joe Bush, the owner of Speed Sport, on the south side of Chicago, who was also the owner of Goeske's old **Hemi-Cuda II**. *Goeske was able to strike a deal with Bush and picked up where he left off, keeping his next Saturday night of racing at US 131 in Martin, Michigan.*

Goeske immediately paid the fine (of a sum of $37.50) and quickly continued on his way. Rolling into Suffolk Raceway shortly after noon without much sleep, his mind was on how he was going to get around his transmission problems.

Goeske's first-round opponent was Jess Tyree, but Tyree left early, turning on the red light. Goeske thought he could bluff his way through round two against Cliff Zink, driving the Stone, Woods, and Cook Mustang. The antsy Zink also suffered the jitters and jumped too soon, red-lighting his chances away for the win. Without high gear, Goeske chuckled to himself, knowing that he lucked his way into the final round and coasted through the win lights with an enormous 17.02 ET!

The only chance Goeske had in the money round against Kelly Chadwick was to try to outfox the "Professor" like his previous opponents in the previous rounds. Both cars fired, performed their burnouts, and lined up together. When the last amber light went to green, the Plymouth jumped out of the hole but instantly fell flat, as Chadwick shot past unchallenged for the win.

Pulde Falls but Jumps Back into the Race

Dale Pulde was released from the of Stone, Woods, and Cook Mustang in Chicago and was heading back home to California when he received a call from Dick Bourgeois. Bourgeois had burned his hands and arms in

David Ray became a regular on the tour after Marv Eldridge succumbed to injuries in the fall of 1970 while testing an Anglia Gasser that crashed at Hawaii's Raceway Park. Ray, the driver of Bobby Steakley's Camaro out of Texas, replaced the late Eldridge's Fiberglass Trends Challenger.

Kelly Chadwick was still one of the top cars to beat on the Coke circuit. He now was driving a brand-new Don Hardy flopper with a second-generation Camaro Z28 body and a fresh 427-ci Rat engine. The former high school teacher was now a performance consultant for Steakley Chevrolet in Fort Worth, Texas. (Photo Courtesy Steve Reyes Photography)

a fire while cleaning parts using gasoline at Joe Bush's Speed Sport Shop in Chicago, which sidelined him from driving duties. Bourgeois brought in a few drivers, including Ron O'Donnell and Marc Susman, but neither could get the car to perform well due to mechanical issues.

At the next Coke event, Keaton came over to watch Pulde's run. Keaton saw how it wanted to turn hard when it got out down the track, hanging on to keep it straight. The problem was that the rear shocks were not set correctly. When Pulde pulled back to the pits, Keaton came over and said, "The left rear shock is the problem. You need to screw the spring up about six turns and see what that does."

Pulde raced Kenny Safford driving now for Keaton the very next round. Pulde and the Javelin ran as quick as ever, easily disposing the Stone, Woods, and Cook Mustang with a 7.29 ET!

That is one example showing that the Coke guys were all business, serious racers on the track, but they were always sharing information in solving problems with the other team cars to provide the best racing for the fans in attendance.

For the Fans

The Coke racers had many adversities of their own but still gave it their all to make sure the fans and sponsors got to see the best in racing. This group of racers committed to race the night before at various venues before Sunday's giant Coke show at Aquasco Speedway, Maryland.

Tommy Grove was in South Carolina during the witching hour, cashing in the coins and gold; the Hill Brothers raced late into the night in Hartford, Connecticut; and Tom Sneden, Dave Reitz, and their crew built a complete engine past midnight in the Bob Banning Dodge Challenger. All of the teams drove overnight, arriving early the next morning at the track, taking interviews, smiling, and talking with everyone without letting anyone how weary they were!

On the promotional side, the Coca-Cola bottlers were overzealous for the sport of drag racing. The company printed nearly 50 million soda cans and bottle cartons that featured a discount coupon for a diecast Funny Car. If the coupon was sent in along with 70 cents, customers would receive either a Mattel Hot Wheels Don Prudhomme or Tom McEwen diecast Funny Car.

The Final Tally

Throughout the years of the Coca-Cola circuit, many drivers raced, including Roger Lindamood, Raymond Beadle, Bobby Rowe, and Don Schumacher (with all *Stardust* 'Cudas); Dave Condit's *L.A. Hooker* Mustang; Tommy Grove; Leroy Goldstein's *Ramchargers* Challenger; Bobby Steakley; Al Bergler's *Motown Shaker* with drivers Tom Prock and Butch Mass; Ron O'Donnell; Al Hanna's *Eastern Raider*; David Ray driving for "Big" Mike Burkhart; Al Marshall in Dale Creasy's Mustang; "Flash" Gordon Mineo; and dozens more.

Memories: Dale Pulde

In my early teen years, I'd help my lifetime neighbor Skip Watson, who built a nitro Junior Fuel dragster, which was a real popular class out here on the West Coast. Skip worked on trucks at International Harvester and in his spare time. He was and still is a great mechanic. Along with all of his buddies, he pitched in by working nights on the car and went racing on the weekends.

I was able to sit in the car many times doing push-starts, warming it up, and helping where I was needed. Not long after that, Skip got drafted and went into the army. He decided that since everyone helped with the car, everyone would get the chance to drive the car. I didn't think anything of it, as I was the smallest guy there and weighed roughly 115 to 117 pounds, while the other guys weighed 170 pounds or more. Skip was a tall guy (about 6 feet, 6 inches) and weighed more than 200 pounds, so with a Jr. Fuel dragster, anything to save weight was a good deal. I made a few passes, and I ran well in the car—in fact, it ran really well!

Skip finally went into the service and had taken on a partner, Glenn Dobbs, where he and his family owned General Engine Power in Long Beach. They were the local Detroit Diesel dealer to service the Long Beach Harbor rigs in the harbor and anything else. Glenn was also a pretty darn good mechanic, and he maintained the dragster. I drove the car, went to San Fernando for a few races, and ran Lions a little bit. Overall, we did okay with the car, rather well for out of his pocket and for not knowing all that much.

I was able to meet various people, and at that time, Funny Cars were becoming popular. I started going to races with Bob Pickett when he had his 1960 Corvette. It had a tricked-out 327 Chevy with Rochester injection and was equipped with a good roller cam. I would help Bob show it at car shows.

Later, Bob put a blown 354 on nitro in the car to run the Funny Car class. At that time, I was approached by several people who noticed that I drove the Jr. Fuel dragster for Skip Watson, which led me to meet Charlie Wilson. Charlie invited me to go to the races with them at Orange County International Raceway (OCIR) to help on his car, the *Vicious Vette* Funny Car.

I was promised a shot at driving the car, which was stretched out for more than a year. I was told that I was going to drive the next weekend, and when that time came time, it became the following week, and so on. By then, I said, "To heck with it," and I quit going. Charlie asked me what the problem was. I told him, "I want to drive a race car. I can go work on anyone's race car."

Charlie was painting down at Clyde Morgan's shop, where I met Joe Pisano, who also became a close friend. I could go with them to help any time.

Clyde Morgan was driving for Charlie at that time, and he was not happy thinking I was out to steal his ride. I never looked at it that way! I was 17 years old and just wanted to drive eventually. Charlie said, "Okay, come on down here and help me with the car. I will help you get your license in the car."

At that time, Charlie kept the car at Von Fritch Automotive in Fountain Valley. The guys, including Ronnie Roseberry, got the car ready, and when I showed up at the shop, we loaded up to go to Orange County International Raceway.

I will never forget standing in the speed shop when photographer Bob McClurg walked in, as I did not know who he was.

"Where's Clyde?" Bob asked.

This kid is going to get his license in the Corvette," they replied.

"Oh, I have to go see this!" Bob responded.

After making the runs in the car, Bob admitted that I did very well. We went out and ran it at a few more races, and then I ended up being the permanent driver. Charlie ended up moving to the valley. He was a fantastic body man, and both he and my dad got a shop.

At that time, Charlie and Ron Roseberry were finishing building the new *Vicious Too* Camaro. I was getting ready to graduate from high school. Around the same time, the Vette was parked because we started to run the new Camaro in a few match races.

I graduated and was going to grad night at the high school. Right down the street from the high school was John Mitchell's dragster group (Red Mountain

Boys), so I went by his garage and stuck my head in the door. All the dragster guys were hanging out, and I ended spending my grad night drinking red mountain wine!

We went racing that weekend, and after a few weeks, we went on tour. While on tour, it was a whole different way of life. I met many good people, including Terry Hedrick, Dickie Harrell, Charlie Therwhanger, Dale Emery, and J. E. Kristek. Of all people, I also met my future wife, Valerie Harrell!

It is not like it is today. Back then, everyone liked to have a good time, and everyone liked to race. If you hurt or damaged something, everyone usually was there to help you in the best way they could.

Now, I worked with the Cooke Mustang on the Coca-Cola Cavalcade of Stars tour. I also drove for Dick Bourgeois in the Doug's Headers Javelin. Both were extremely hard to work for, but Dee Keaton was intolerable to work for even though I learned a lot from him.

Dee took over the Stone, Woods, and Cook car, and everyone said, "That's a big money car; they just throw money at it while you just drive the car."

I was a paid driver, but Dee was basically a partner, tuner, and crew chief. The way those deals worked was that he took the car with everything that came with it and carefully looked over everything. He knew what was there and knew what you were taking. When we were on the road, the owners split the bills with him 50-50, so if the car killed a transmission or blew a blower, which let's say a blower costs $800, it would be $400 out of his pocket.

Dee was an extremely great mechanic, deeply knowledgeable, and had the car running well when we were committed to run the Coca-Cola Cavalcade of Stars. We didn't run the major events, racing all of the big guys, but I got to race a lot of people, including "Jungle" Jim, Schumacher, Gene Snow, and more. When we went match racing, it was basically with the Coca-Cola Cavalcade guys. Out of all the guys who I worked with, Dee Keaton was a great mentor. The main thing that he taught me was how to race the car without beating up parts or tearing it up.

After all was said and done, Dee decided that I wasn't good enough for him. He fired me in either June or July of that year. It pretty well put me to my knees, but I was the young kid. I went home at the same time Dick Bourgeois got burned in a fire at Joe Bush's Speed Sport Shop in Chicago while cleaning parts with gasoline. A few people came in to drive for Dick, including Ron O'Donnell and Marc Susman, but both never could get the car to drive right, which wasn't their fault.

I got the call from Dee to come in, as apparently my relationship with him was still good. I just did not drive to his satisfaction. The car did the same thing to me. It would go out a ways and try to make a left turn. If you were lucky enough to get all the way down the track, you would have to really hang to keep it straight.

Like most of the cars in that time, the Javelin had a sprung suspension. As time went on, the shocks took a dive, so they rebuilt the shocks, but nobody knew how to set them up. At the next Coca-Cola tour event, the car still wanted to make a hard turn. When we came back to the pits, Dee came over after watching me make the one run and said, "Dale, take off the right rear shock and screw the spring up about six turns and see what that does."

Well, we raced Dee the very next round and smoked his butt off. The car ran as quick as it ever did, running a 7.29 ET, which for a Chevy car was good! That proved to me that Dee wasn't mad at me, it was just part of a business deal. Everyone else who drove for him ran into the same situation: no matter what you did, you couldn't make him happy.

If anyone deserves to be in the hall of fame, it's Dee Keaton! He was a real underrated man who would look at something and figure it out. He had only a ninth or tenth grade education, but he could figure out machinery and equipment. Jack Chrisman told me, "Dale, if you had to tell Dee something that couldn't be done, he'd be over at your shop tearing your stuff apart and showing you that it could be done. That was the way he was."

Dee worked for Chrisman for quite a while, and they were incredibly good friends. Dee was great man.

Memories: Dave Boncosky

Participant in the Coca-Cola Cavalcade of Stars

"I bought Phil Bonner's Ford Torino in 1970 that he never raced, and I replaced the Torino body with a Firebird body. I took the car to Logghe to have them switch out the Ford engine plate to one for a Hemi. Many people thought Arnie Beswick owned the car, but he did not. I leased the name *Boss Bird* from Arnie, which got me most of race dates for a year. Arnie's a great guy, and his cars were Pontiac GTO–bodied cars. In late 1970 or early 1971, he switched over to a Firebird body like the one I ran, but he still ran the Pontiac motors while I was running a Hemi, so there were two Birds.

"When I bought the Ford, it had a complete SOHC motor. I removed it and sold it, possibly to Kalitta, but I'm not sure. Heck, that was over 50 years ago. We toured out in Southern California in the fall of 1970, racing at Irwindale Halloween race, OCIR's Manufacturer's Meet, and finishing up the Coke series at Lions Drag Strip.

"Speaking of racing on the Coca-Cola tour during the summer, we raced several nights during the week, especially on every Wednesday night at different tracks. I raced with my good friend Dick Bourgeois on the Coca-Cola tour when he asked me to come out to California to race after the tour finished. At that time, I lived in Illinois just west of Chicago with my wife and our three little kids. I remember calling her to tell her I am going to California, and she told me you stay there!"

*Dave Boncosky bought Phil Bonner's **Daddy Warbucks** show circuit Torino to live his dream of match racing on the Funny Car circuit. Boncosky had Logghe remove the SOHC engine and install a late-model Chrysler Hemi. Dave sold both the 427-ci Cammer and the bulky Torino shell and installed a sleeker 1970 Pontiac Firebird body. Boncosky and Arnie Beswick were friends, so to book dates, Beswick leased his name to Boncosky, including races on the Coca-Cola Cavalcade tour.*

Tom McEwen and Don Prudhomme, who also had Coca-Cola as a major sponsor, made appearances from time to time on the tour from their busy Hot Wheels schedule. When the Coca-Cola Cavalcade made a stop in Gary, Indiana, at US 30, the *Goo$e* was an unannounced entry to the field of eight and proceeded to win all three rounds, taking home over $3,000! McEwen also set low ET with a 6.88 at 233.88 mph in round two and backed it up when the Ramchargers-powered Duster ran a 6.91 at 221 mph in the final round.

The series officially came to an end after seven years in late 1976. Tripp Schmake was the Cavalcade's final champion driving Dennis Fowler's *Sundance* Chevy Monza. More than 40 drivers, including alternates and standbys, participated in the popular series.

Butch Mass and Al Bergler rolled into Amarillo Dragway as an alternate, but they left holding the big bag of coins. Mass was inserted in the field during the first round when the Stone, Woods, and Cook Mustang suffered mechanical failure on the starting line and couldn't start. Butch promptly disposed Tim Beebe's Fighting Irish Camaro and defeated Dave Condit's L.A. Hooker Mustang in the semifinals. The final round had all the makings of a record run between Mass and Bobby Rowe, but Rowe's 6.99 ET went to waste when he fouled his chances away driving Don Schumacher's blue Stardust II 'Cuda. Mass blasted to a 6.97, which was low ET of the meet.

One of the heavy hitters on the Coca-Cola excursion was the Beaver Brothers' L.A. Hooker Mustang driven by Dave Condit. The Mustang was a strong representative from the West Coast for its two seasons running the Cavalcade tour. Shown in February 1972, Condit hooks up the Goodyears. Runs with ETs of 6.86 at 202 mph and 6.81 at 208 mph worked out the new-car bugs at Lions Drag Strip.

Captain of the 1975 Coca-Cola Stars Roger Lindamood blisters the big M&H Racemasters in his Color Me Gone Dodge Charger along with "Animal" Al Marshall in Dale Creasey's Tyrant Mustang. Side-by-side racing at dusk was the greatest time during summer months when the nitro ground pounders displayed 6-foot header flames at full throttle passes into the evening.

Tom McEwen (blue jacket, white pants) and Don Prudhomme (blue jacket, dark pants) view a document while standing in front of their matching haulers. The two 1970 Plymouth 'Cudas were marketing cars to be used by the Snake and the Mongoose.

Wildlife Racing Enterprises Brings Hot Wheels into Drag Racing

Since the early days of drag racing, Don "the Snake" Prudhomme and Tom "the Mongoose" McEwen were heated archrivals from the first time they lined up against each other. Their battle of words and actions led to the most intense rivalry in the AA/FD ranks. They formed a close friendship and respected each other, noting that neither could survive without the other. Prudhomme was the more serious racer, while the McEwen took more of a business approach to drag racing.

Formed in the summer of 1969, Wildlife Racing Enterprises merged a pair of archrivals into one of the greatest teams in drag racing history! Tom McEwen and Don Prudhomme approached toy magnate Mattel with the idea of bringing a pair of Hot Wheels–themed Funny Cars to the drag strip. After several months of intense meetings and negotiations, a two-year partnership was established, bringing one of the country's largest non-racing sponsors into drag racing. Both cars made their debut at the 1970 AHRA Winternationals at Beeline. A week later at the 10th annual NHRA Winternationals at Pomona, Prudhomme's bright yellow 'Cuda was an instant crowd pleaser.

Fast-forward from those early dragster days to the spring of 1968, when toy magnate Mattel brought out a new line of 16 miniature die cast Hot Wheels toy cars. Millions were sold throughout the world. The toy cars were quickly snatched up by the younger generations and even drew the interest of the older collectors too. All ages were trying to get their hands on these products.

Seeing the opportunity to merge the hottest toys on the planet with the two largest names in drag racing, McEwen, the marketing genius he was, approached the toy company. He presented the idea of sponsoring a pair of Hot Wheels–themed drag racing cars for the 1970 racing season.

The initial proposal to Mattel was for a pair of dragsters for McEwen and Prudhomme. But Mattel, seeing the popularity of Funny Cars, liked the visual appeal of a racing car with all the bright, colorful designs and graphics as opposed to the dragsters.

While McEwen had spent time in a Funny Car, Prudhomme balked at the idea, describing Funny Cars as "leakers." Prudhomme had never spent time in a Funny Car before, so both sides pondered the overall concept. They hashed out the logistics, going back and forth like two prize fighters exchanging punches. With all of the pieces laid out on the table, a deal was struck and both parties agreed to a lucrative two-year sponsorship.

Mattel became drag racing's largest non-automotive sponsor. With the deal, Wildlife Racing Enterprises was created by McEwen and Prudhomme. They then brought on board another giant non-automotive sponsor: Coca-Cola. From there, everything else steamrolled.

Tom McEwen qualified well into the field of 16 Funny Cars at the NHRA Winternationals at Pomona with his new Hot Wheels Plymouth Duster. However, he dropped the first round to the **Blue Max** *of Jake Johnston when Johnston's 7.57 ET smothered McEwen's 7.83. Both Hot Wheels Funny Cars suffered from handling problems due to the roof top spoilers, and they were removed not long after their debut. The* **Wynn's Duster II** *featured a Fiberglass Trends 1970 Plymouth Duster body that was graced by Cerny's Custom Paint along with the tin work by Tom Hanna. The Plymouth 426 Hemi was built by John Hogan of Ramchargers Racing Engines with a 118-inch Exhibition Engineering chassis by Ron Scrima.*

Don Prudhomme debuted his latest hot rod built by John Buttera at the 1970 Orange County International Raceway Manufacturer's Funny Car Championships. Making the big splash for the Plymouth Team, the Snake's second run off the trailer netted an unbelievable 6.93 ET. The new car was garnished with the familiar yellow paint job for the remaining year, including the inaugural NHRA Mattel Supernationals.

Ronnie Scrima's Exhibition Engineering shop in Van Nuys built two state-of-the-art cars. Both cars ran under the Plymouth brand: a 1970 Duster for the Mongoose and a 1970 'Cuda for the Snake.

Included in the Mattel/Wildlife venture was a transporter to get the cars to the track. When the Chrysler Corporation built six Dodge ramp-style transporters for both their factory NASCAR and drag racing teams, two used trucks became available. NASCAR champ Richard Petty's blue truck went to Prudhomme, and the Sox & Martin rig went to McEwen. The transporters were painted and lettered to match both cars, and the crews wore matching uniforms. When the Snake and the Mongoose hit the track, the duo became instant rock stars of drag racing.

The Toys

Toy Hot Wheels Funny Cars were available individually or in blister packs at most leading retail outlets. Snake and Mongoose Drag Racing sets were the hot ticket. They included 32 feet of orange track with loops and parachutes. Sales of the sets went through the ceiling, exceeding the corporate predictions.

Attendance at the strip was at an all-time high when parents brought their kids to see the real Hot Wheels Funny Cars up close and in action. Along with the brightly colored cars and the noise, youngsters got to see

the Hot Wheels Drag Racing sets come to life—only without the loopdy-loops.

Both cars ran well and made a lot of money driving thousands of miles touring to sold out bookings. Marketing hit an all-time high with the two cars.

Don Prudhomme sported a freshly painted white, blue, and red color scheme on his 1971 Plymouth, shown here at Irwindale. Mattel was simply blown away with the demand. There were record sales from individual toy Funny Cars to complete racing and stunts sets. Track owners raked in the bucks with sellout crowds wanting to see the touring stars.

Tom McEwen stepped up in 1971 with a chassis built by John Buttera. The car featured a straight front axle with a Hali-brand solid mount, quick-change rear end. The 1,600-pound rocket was painted blue with added red accents along with the familiar Hot Wheels graphics. Wynn's petroleum products was now a major sponsor, joining Mattel and Coca-Cola for both team cars. The Mongoose II debuted here at Irwindale.

If fans could not make it to the track, displays were set up at local shopping centers with both cars on display. Hot Wheels drag racing tracks were set up to give kids a chance to show off their skills and win trophies and Mattel prizes.

On the Track

The Mattel/Wildlife team launched it's colors for 1971 when Prudhomme kicked off the season February 7 at Lions Drag Strip. He put his Hot Wheels 'Cuda into the number-one qualifying spot with an ET of 7.23 at 206.04 mph. In the first round of eliminations, the Snake set a new track ET record of 7.18 at 208.81 mph against Richard Siroonian in "Big" John Mazmanian's Plymouth 'Cuda. Round two brought the team cars of McEwen and Prudhomme together, and Prudhomme earned the win with an ET of 7.20 at 207.36 mph against a shut off, out-of-shape McEwen.

The final round pitted the favored Snake against Pat Minnick's *Chi-Town Hustler,* but Prudhomme lost a motor mid-track. The excitement from the stands let drag racing know that the Mattel/Wildlife team was the most popular attraction at the strip.

The strength of Mattel's financial backing mixed with record performances of the Hot Wheels cars helped the Snake and the Mongoose become the hottest commodity

Don Prudhomme not only nabbed the coins at Orange County International Raceway's 3rd All-Pro Series race but also hit a milestone of becoming the all-time world's quickest and fastest Funny Car on the planet, running an unbelievable ET of 6.62 at 226.13 mph. Just weeks prior at Irwindale, the Snake's Hot Wheels Top Fueler tied a best ET of 6.62, which was identical to his flopper.

The crowd of more than 7,000 spectators not only witnessed Don Prudhomme winning the 1971 Third All-Pro Series Race but also watched him enter a new era of Funny Car when he established both world ET and speed records. Celebrating in the winner's circle were (from left to right): Holly Hendrick, Steve "Okie" Bernd, and the "Snake."

The Mongoose and the Snake paired up once again in this round-robin match up at Orange County International Raceway's Manufacturer's Funny Car Championships. Their longtime heated rivalry on the track was often filled with drama when the two legends squared off, but they were close friends away from the track.

Don Prudhomme drops the laundry in his black Snake III after completing shake down passes at Bakersfield. The Buttera-built 'Cuda sat mean and low from all angles—from being parked to doing smoky burnouts and halftrack bursts.

around. Strip owners were vying for the opportunity to book the excitement at their tracks. During a three-week span in the hottest months of the summer, the pair made appearances at several drag strips (Capital Raceway, Rockford, Union Grove, and Norwalk) that drew the largest crowds in the history of the facilities.

For 1971, both Prudhomme and McEwen were hotter than ever. Two brand-new Funny Cars were ordered from John Buttera, along with two new Top Fuel dragsters that complemented their Wildlife Racing Enterprises.

The Wildlife Racing Enterprises team landed another major sponsor. CEO and president John Troth of the Wynn's Oil Company signed the remunerative agree-

Legends, friends, and teammates Tom McEwen and Don Prudhomme greeted fans at the 2011 Wizard World Comic Con at the Anaheim Convention Center to promote the 2013 movie Snake & Mongoose. *The story portrayed the lives of the two Southern California drag racers during the golden years at the track, business ventures, and personal lives.*

ment along with the Mattel and Coca-Cola to fully fund both Hot Wheels Funny Cars and the new pair of Top Fuel dragsters at all drag racing events into which the team was booked.

When the word got out that Tom McEwen would make a rare appearance on the Coca-Cola Cavalcade tour on May 16 at Gary, Indiana, the track was packed. Legions of fans wanted to see the Hot Wheels legend. The *Goo$e* didn't disappoint anyone in attendance, as McEwen won all three rounds of his match action racing at US 30. He set low ET with a 6.88 at 233.88 mph in round two and backed it up when the Ramchargers-powered Duster ran an ET of 6.91 at 221 mph in the final round.

What a Run: Closing out an Epic Era

The Wildlife Racing partnership lasted only three years (from 1970 to 1972), but the sponsorship's lasting impression to the racing community and toy collectors is still as popular today as it was at its inception. Mattel remained an associate sponsor for both the Snake and the Mongoose for several more seasons. The end of 1972 brought closure to the Wildlife Racing Enterprises with a storybook ending that no one in Hollywood could write.

One of the premier drag strips in Southern California, Lions, held its Last Drag Race on December 2, 1972, after a stellar 17-year history. How fitting it was to close out the final round ever in Funny Car with both Prudhomme and McEwen going for the gold. It was well past midnight, into early Sunday morning, when starter Larry Sutton barked out the command to fire up the last pair of Funny Cars. Both the Snake and the Mongoose completed their burnouts, and the stage was set.

Everyone was on their feet when the lights counted down the tree. At the green, both cars launched into the night. At the top end, the win light illuminated for McEwen, who ran his best ET of 6.35 at 225 mph, turning away Prudhomme's off-pace 6.97 ET.

Although the deal with Mattel as their major sponsor had run its course, the toy magnate continued as associate sponsors along with Coca-Cola. The Wildlife Racing partnership continued when the Hershey Company, makers of Carefree Sugarless Gum, signed a one-year deal for 1973. When the season concluded at the end of the year, McEwen and Prudhomme dissolved their partnership and went their own ways. They have remained friends and rivals on and away from the track.

In 2013, both received recognition of their years in drag racing when Hollywood released the full-length motion picture drama *Snake & Mongoose*. Actors Jesse Williams and Richard Blake portrayed the famed drivers at their peak years of racing and personal life experiences, including the successful Wildlife partnership.

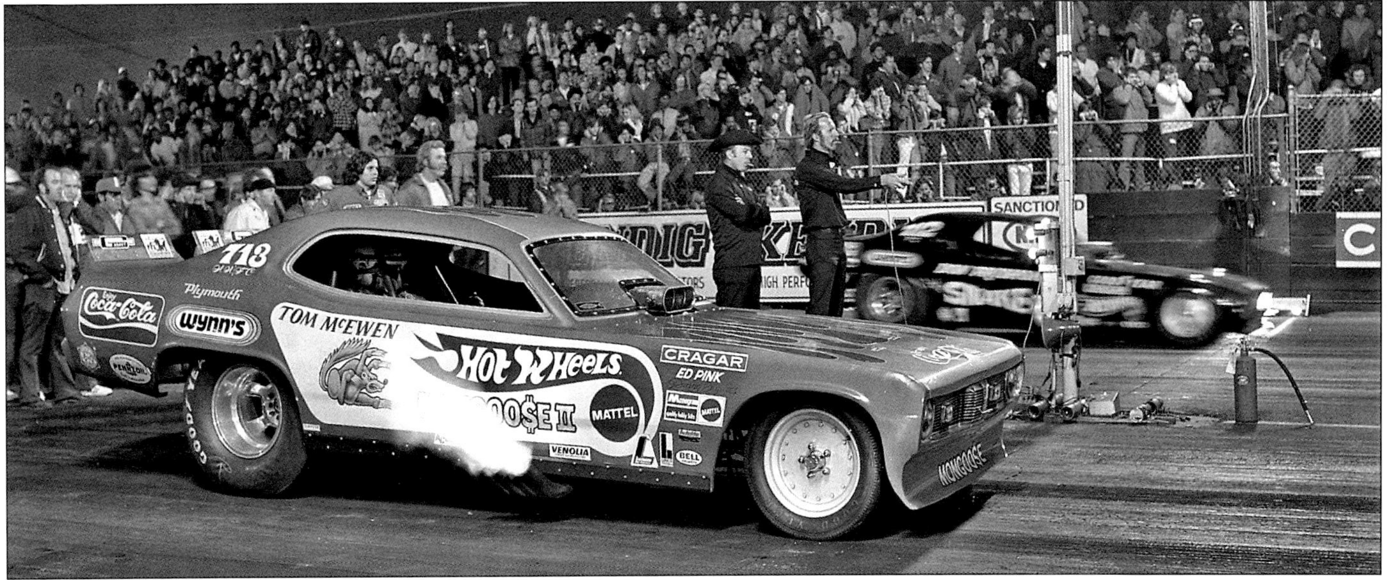

No one ever thought that when the curtain dropped for the final time for Funny Cars at Lions Last Drag Race, it would end with the greatest rivalry in drag racing history: Don Prudhomme and Tom McEwen. The final-round pairing also signaled the end of the Wildlife Photo Racing Enterprises. It was well past midnight when both cars staged and both left evenly at the green, but it was McEwen who closed the history book and upset the Snake with a career-best ET of 6.39 at 225 mph.

The mid-engine Funny Car was still in the early development stages when Robert Contorelli carefully engineered a more conventional designed with a sleeker and lower Mustang Mach I body. Contorelli's Mustang was built on a budget of $15,000, which included a Speed Products Engineering chassis. The 1,200-hp hemi engine was based on an Ed Donovan aluminum block built with early hemi heads maintained by Gene Oates. (Photo Courtesy Steve Reyes Photography)

Chapter Seven

Mid-Engine Marvels or Quarter-Mile Monstrosities of Technology and Safety?

During the early days of Funny Cars, when adding superchargers and nitro made more power, a handful of racers had the concept of placing the engine behind the driver. This was for balance of power and performance but mostly driver safety due to possible engine, blower, and transmission explosions and fires.

The idea became reality when several rear-engine Funny Cars arrived on the scene. Among those who took the chance of altering the face of Funny Cars was Lou Baney.

Baney had Ronnie Scrima and Pat Foster construct a steel-bodied Barracuda with backing from the Southern California's Plymouth Dealers Association's Hemi Cuda. In

Doug Thorley's Javelin 1 *was a marvel ahead of its time. The AMC was a strong runner with high-7-second ETs and a top speed near 200 mph. As with the early Hemi-Cuda, it was admissible to air flowing under the empty engine compartment, which lifted the front end at Irwindale, where it was destroyed.*

Eddie Pauling was one of the unique rear-engine owner/ drivers when he broke into the Funny Car ranks with his rear-engine Whinemaker *1966 Dodge Dart. Pauling experienced modest success with the Dart, and he decided to stay with the back-motor technology. Pauling built a new rear motor Mercury Cougar and kept the early 392 Hemi for power. He ran the* Whinemaker II *for several more seasons before building a more conventional front motor Mustang flopper for 1971.*

the early testing stages, the Barracuda showed promising results under load, which were documented with a movie camera that was mounted to the front end of the car.

AA/FD pilot Tom McEwen made a series of half passes at Lions to see how the car would handle under hard acceleration. When Baney gave the go-ahead to flat-blade the throttle for a full pass, the light front end of the 'Cuda bounced up and down the strip, allowing air to enter the empty engine compartment. This caused the car to go airborne in the lights and crash-land hard back on the track, destroying the body.

When Maynard Rupp noticed more money could be made match racing a Funny Car, he left the seat of the Logghe Brothers fueler and built the mid-engine, hemi-powered 1966 Chevelle, *Chevroom*. Maynard scored his share of match racing wins with his exhibition racer.

Doug Thorley had a thought that it was a lot easier to have an unrestricted view driving at 190 mph down the strip instead looking around a bulky supercharger, bug catcher, and the tin doghouse. So, when Thorley and AMC joined forces, they brought out a unique lightweight, rear-engine Javelin built by Woody Gilmore. The *Javelin 1* was originally equipped with a blown AMC 390-ci Wedge that exceeded expectations. Later, the Wedge was replaced with a late-model Keith Black Hemi that boosted power and torque.

Arizona's Eddie Pauling was one of early rear-engine owner/drivers for a Funny Car with his rear-engine *Ol' Whinemaker* 1966 Dodge Dart. Eddie's exhibition Dart

ran with limited success, but he wanted to stay with the rear-motor technology when Pauling built a more competitive rear-motor Mercury Cougar, relying on the power of the early 392 Hemi. The *Whinemaker II* ran for several more seasons before Pauling decided on going with a more conventional front-motor Mustang.

Three's a Crowd

The most ingenious contraption built around the early rear-engine movement was Tommy Stringfield's *Triple Trouble* Chevy II. The 1966 Chevy Nova was packed with not one or two but with three potent 367-ci small-block engines, totaling 1,128 inches of pure chaos! The torque of all three made mincemeat of the surface on the strip. The front engine was nearly pure stock, fueled with a single Holley carburetor, but the other two healthy fuel-injected motors sat side by side in the back seat area.

Adding into the mix, Stringfield crafted three side-by-side Pontiac differentials. The center unit was used in a conventional way through a 3-speed manual transmission, while the other units used a direct-drive unit linked up through a clutch operative system. The *Triple Trouble* weighed more than 2 tons and resulted in mid-11-second runs.

Not satisfied with the performance numbers, Stringfield removed the front engine and one of the two

One of the strangest creations belonged to Tommy Stringfield with his *Triple Trouble 1966 Chevy II Nova. It had a total of three 367-ci small-block Chevy engines, including two fuel-injected engines sandwiched together side-by-side in the back seat behind Tommy. Adding up to a whopping 1,128 inches of pure "hell," the Nova chewed up the surface numerous times through a heavy-duty 3-speed manual transmission.*

John Force

There have been many unconfirmed stories with the *Dragway Patrol* Mustang of Roy Mehus that was driven by a new, relatively unknown driver, John Force. Force eventually purchased the Mustang from Mehus, applied new paint, and re-lettered the body with the name *Night Stalker.*

As the owner and driver, Force's inaugural passes at Irwindale got him, the crew, and the car excommunicated from the track when the drive chain disintegrated on a burnout, which littered the track and showered starter Larry Sutton with broken links, rivets, and pieces of hot metal debris.

The *Night Stalker* was never a success on the track but has been remembered as a disaster to many in Funny Car. Force persevered and never backed away from his visions of being a professional driver and owner. Today, Force is a 16-time NHRA and one-time AHRA Funny Car champion driver and holds multiple NHRA World Championships as an owner in both Funny Car and Top Fuel Dragster.

The Dragway Patrol Mustang of Roy Mehus powers up to heat the hides with new driver John Force. The Mustang was designed by former owner Jack Chrisman to run and handle like a slot car, but the car never lived up to its potential. Force purchased the car from Mehus and went out on his own with his brother, Louie Force, in charge of tuning and maintenance.

For 1972, drag racing pioneer Jack Chrisman stepped away from a remarkable career driving conventional Funny Cars that put him well into drag racing's history books. Taking a totally different approach to racing, he built his rear-engine Sidewinder *SOHC 427 Mach I Mustang. Chrisman never made a pass in the car. He sold it to upcomer Roy Mehus, who hired Bill Finicle to drive. Unfortunately, Finicle crashed the car during testing, shown here at Orange County International Raceway. (Photo Courtesy Steve Reyes Photography)*

small-blocks from the back seat, removed the three rear ends, and replaced them with one conventional differential that was moved forward and relocated behind both front doors. The *Triple Trouble* received new life as the one most unusual-looking wheel-standers.

Funny Car History

Drag racing pioneer Jack Chrisman had driven nearly anything that was created to race on four wheels, including the Chrisman and Nicolini *Sidewinder #1* and *#2* dragsters. In 1972, Chrisman revived a somewhat different idea when he built his rear-engine SOHC 427 *Sidewinder* Mach I Mustang.

Chrisman was the first to wheel a 160-mph blown fuel Funny Car (Sachs & Sons *Super Cyclone* Comet). His new sidewinder measured out to 125- to 130-inch wheelbase with 85 percent of the motor toward the back axle. Chrisman never drove the *Sidewinder* and sold the car soon after completion to Roy Mehus and hired driver Bill Finicle.

The Funny Car rear-engine insurgence was short-lived. It died out in the mid-1970s without the effect on what the rear-engine dragster had revolutionized. One factor was the tight fit between the body and windshield that made most drivers claustrophobic.

The early cars were mostly Dodge Dart–bodied machines: the Dart Charger, Cotton Owens's the *Cotton Picker* Dodge Dart wagon, Don Garlits's Dart, and the *Polka Dot.*

The early 1970s brought out the likes of Robert Contorelli's Mustang, Billy Holt's *Alabamian* Vega panel wagon, Ken Riehle's *Hell Fire* Camaro, Motta and Williamson's Dodge Challenger, Jack Chrisman's SOHC *Sidewinder* Mach I, Slack and Hallman's Mustang, the *Dragway* Patrol Mustang, and the *Hindsight* Dodge Dart were among the movement but never lived up to expectations.

Most of the mid-engine floppers were great ideas to answer the increase of engine explosions and fires. However, overall, they were total disappointments with poor handling and performances.

Stan Bowman purchased Gas Ronda's Mach I and campaigned it as the *California Stud* for a season. He revamped the outdated chassis by cutting, altering, and modifying the chassis to rear-engine specifications and fitted a Vega panel wagon body.

When the rear-engine Top Fuel dragsters hit the scene in 1971, Jim Dunn applied the same science and principles of the dragsters to build the most successful rear-engine Funny Car in drag racing history. "Fireman" Dunn debuted his rear-engine 'Cuda in 1972 at Lions Grand Premiere, where handling problems kept him from competing. Over months of trying this and working to make the car more stable, Dunn finally turned the corner when he drove the 'Cuda to the runner-up position at the March Meet. He went on to win his first race in an NHRA Division 7 race at Utah.

Billy Holt's *Alabamian* Chevy Vega panel was one of the best-looking rear-engine cars that had the best equipment that money could buy. The chassis was fabricated by Don Hardy with power from a late 1,200-hp 426 Chrysler Hemi. Holt's partner and friend Wayne Mahaffy occupied the seat. During early testing secessions, Mahaffy lost control and crashed, demolishing the car. He escaped serious injuries but both Holt and Mahaffy had enough of the mid-engine experiment and built a front-engine conventual flopper.

Virginia Beach racer Mike Tucker purchased Ken Riehle's *Hell Fire* Camaro and dropped the car down into the BB/FC class. He renamed it the *Streaker.* It's unknown if Tucker's Camaro was a successful contender in the BB/FC field.

A few more entries of the mid-engine monstrosities came away from the West Coast with early Funny Car campaigners Dave Motta (*Sampson*) and Don Williamson (*Hairy Canary*). The duo built a sleeker, more aerodynamic 1972 Dodge Challenger that had a height of 44

The Hell Fire 1972 Camaro of owner/driver Ken Riehle was one of the mid-engine monsters built by Rollie Lindblad with power from a blown nitro Keith Black 472-ci Hemi connected to a 2-speed manual transmission. The Farmington, Connecticut, Hell Fire ran a best ET of 6.19 at 235 mph in its short life when veteran Funny Car driver Lew Arrington logged a few stints under the shell after a fire destroyed his Brutus Mustang. (Photo Courtesy Steve Reyes Photography)

Dave Bowman, the ex-AA/FD and Fuel Altered pilot, purchased and drove the former Gas Ronda Mach I Mustang in the 1971 campaign before configuring the outdated chassis and turning it into the California Stud mid-engine Chevy Vega panel truck. The Stud was one of the mid-engine Funny Cars that suffered from handling and performance problems.

Jim Dunn powers down the 1320 at Bakersfield during the 1972 March Meet. Dunn made his presence known from the mid-engine Plymouth when he chalked up a runner-up position after a broken clutch assembly failed against Ed McCulloch in the final round.

Billy Holt's new Alabamian *Chevy Vega panel rear-engine car was built by Don Hardy with a 1,200-hp 426 Chrysler Hemi. Holt's partner, Wayne Mahaffy, handled the driving duties, but during the early outings in the car, Mahaffy lost control and crashed. He ended up demolishing the car. Mahaffy wasn't seriously injured in the mishap, but the mid-engine Vega rebuild was scrubbed and replaced with a more front-engine conventual flopper. (Photo Courtesy Steve Reyes Photography)*

Dave Motta and Don Williamson diverted from building a conventional front-engine Funny Car and chose the rear-motor route with one of the slickest designs with this 1972 Dodge Challenger. Measuring only 44 inches high, the highly modified, aerodynamic Fiberglass Trends body from Frank Santos was mounted to a Kent Fuller 122-inch chassis. An early-model 440-inch Chrysler was built and maintained by Williamson (of the Hairy Canary *fame), which resulted with Motta turning low-7-second runs.*

inches. The Challenger ran several impressive numbers in the low-7-second range.

Bert Berniker's *Hindsight* Plymouth Duster was built by chassis fabricator Richard Ruth at his shop Competition Engineering in Sun Valley, California. With Keith Black motivation, Berniker put Don Baumunk behind the wheel. Baumunk clocked several runs over 200 mph before stepping out of the car for another venue. Replacing Baumunk was driver Jim Adolph and, in later stints, Dennis Geisler, who experienced a blow over at the

Mike Tucker cuts loose the hides in his Streaker *Camaro BB/FC. The Virginia Beach, Virginia, resident purchased the ex-*Hell Fire *fuel Funny Car from Ken Riehle and campaigned the flopper regularly on the East Coast.*

Veteran Funny Car pilot Jim Adolph attempts to put Bert Berniker's Hindsight *mid-engine Plymouth Duster into the stout field at the NHRA Supernationals at Ontario Motor Speedway. Unfortunately for Adolph and Berniker, the Duster couldn't grip the slick track and did not qualify.*

NHRA Winternationals in 1975 that caused considerable damage and ended the life of the *Hindsight*.

Jim Gets It Dunn

The highpoint of rear-engine marvels belonged to Jim Dunn, who was well recognized throughout drag racing during his 1972 campaign that was documented by Hollywood with the blockbuster *Funny Car Summer*. The full-length film portrayed a touring Funny Car team that endured a grueling summer match racing schedule.

Dunn raced for several years with the rear-engine 'Cuda, which found its way several times in the winner's circle. One of those times was the 1972 NHRA Supernationals at Ontario, when Dunn defeated Barry Setzer's Vega, becoming the one and only rear-engine Funny Car to win a national event.

One last consideration for the mid-engine "very bad idea" category was the project for Ed Lenarth's *Holy Toledo* sidewinder Gremlin-bodied Funny Car. Lenarth coaxed Bob Hightower into the seat of the Garvin and Lenarth experiment, but constant problems kept the car from achieving positive results. Hightower never ran the car with the AMC body. He ran it several times as a dragster at Irwindale and at Lions, both times ending into or over the guardrails.

The most successful mid-engine Funny Car in the history of drag racing belonged to "Fireman" Jim Dunn from La Mirada, California. Dunn shocked the Funny Car world in 1972 when he beat Pat Foster driving Barry Setzer's Vega at the NHRA Supernationals at the Ontario Motor Speedway. Dunn's performances caught the attention of cinemaphotographer Ron Phillips, who brought the life of the touring Funny Car star to the silver screen with his box office film **Funny Car Summer.** *The documentary depicted Dunn's life drag racing across the western states of America.*

Ed Lenarth's attempt to campaign a mid-engine Funny Car fell short of his expectations with the Hemi-powered Holy Toledo *sidewinder Gremlin flopper. Bob Hightower climbed into the seat of the Lenarth and Garvin experiment and attempted several test passes both at Irwindale and Lions, each ending with the same results. At Irwindale, the sidewinder's handling problems put Hightower into the rails. Hightower fared worse at Lions a few weeks later. The car shook violently when launching off the starting line and at 200 feet out suddenly careered into the guardrail. It vaulted up and over the rail, which resulted in considerable damage.*

Photographer Tom West captured the eyes of "Jungle" Jim Liberman coming toward the camera with one of Liberman's patented tire-annihilating sideways burnouts. You always had to be alert when Liberman was on the track. Even the 100-mph backups to the starting line were an adventure.

Chapter Eight

"Jungle" Jim Liberman: The Persona of a True Showman

In professional sports, each organization has a hall of fame to honor the best and most recognized athletes for their accomplishments. Drag racing has its own lore in each pro category. In Top Fuel dragsters, there was "Big Daddy" Don Garlits, and in Pro Stock were stars Bill "Grumpy" Jenkins (Chevrolet), Ronnie Sox & Buddy Martin (Chrysler), and Bob Glidden (Ford). However, the most recognized name in the history of Funny Cars was "Jungle" Jim Liberman.

Russell James Liberman was one of drag racing's brightest personalities. He brought smiles out of everyone. Going to the strip on a Saturday night to watch him perform was an experience. The magnetism he brought to the strip was compared to the Rolling Stones. His showmanship put fans into the stands early, marking their territory and grabbing the best possible view, as thousands stood along the fences four rows deep to watch him perform. Like P.T. Barnum, Liberman was the ringmaster, the strip was his stage, and the fans were his audience. People loved to watch him!

Co-owners and tuners Lew Arrington and driver Jim Liberman were the "Kings of the West Coast" in the early days of match-race, bashing with their hemi-head Pontiac-powered GTO. Whether running the best of three or best of five, *Brutus* was always up to the challenge and won more than 80 percent of its races.

Fans gather outside Irwindale Raceway on Irwindale Avenue to catch a glimpse of "Jungle" Jim laying down one of his long, smokey burnouts well beyond the 600-foot mark. The young Liberman was changing the flair and showmanship in Funny Car, and he was instantly becoming a cult hero to many of his followers.

Brutus

From the beginning, Liberman was one of the ordinary racers who drove the wheels off cars. He was dragging from A/MP Chevys to his first A/WB-injected Chevy II *Hercules*. Lew Arrington and Liberman co-owned the infamous *Brutus*, a Pontiac Tempest GTO that ran a crossbred 392-ci Chrysler Hemi with a pair of one-only Mickey Thompson hemi-Pontiac heads.

Arrington and Liberman both provided the expert tuning, but it was Liberman's lightning-fast reactions that put him behind the wheel and basically made him the one to beat! Liberman earned the title as the "King of California," being the number-one match racer on the West Coast in 1966.

From Fremont to Ramona, Liberman was the most-feared driver behind the wheel of a Funny Car. Arrington and Liberman understood the values of nitromethane and experimented with varied percentage loads that dropped their times of 9.50s to respectable 8.60s.

Along with successes on the match race trail, Liberman won his share of various premiere races, including the Funny Car Cavalcade and the Bash at the Beach Funny Car Extravaganza. Both races were at Lions Drag Strip with Liberman driving the *Brutus* GTO.

The Chevy IIs

Liberman didn't stop at the *Brutus* GTO. He built his first Funny Car in 1966: an S/XS stretched-nose Chevy II. At selected races, Liberman doubled up both his tuning and driving duties for both the *Brutus* and his Nova. This catapulted his career status to a national level.

In 1967, Liberman parted ways with Arrington and had the Logghe Brothers design and build his own Funny Car. Liberman managed to do everything while on his own. He had complete control from painting his car and building engines to

Wives were more valuable to a team than only being seen glamorized on the track while backing up the family Funny Car. In many ways, they dealt with the smallest things that basically went unnoticed to many. Prior to the pre-race pomp-and-circumstance festivities at the second annual Orange County International Raceway Manufacturer's Funny Car Team Championships, Bobbi Liberman quietly sits by herself on the hood of the GTO, providing an emergency equipment repair. Bobbi applied a bead of glue to the center of one of the cracked lenses in Jim's goggles. We will never know for sure if the repair worked because the Funny Car Championships were delayed a week when rain washed out the team championships.

Fans might not remember the race outcomes, but they remember where or what they were doing at the strip when the announcement blared out over the PA system: "Here comes 'Jungle' Jim Liberman out of the staging lanes, rolling up to the starting line." Fans ran toward the fences, lining up several rows deep while the grandstands filled with standing room only. The roar of the crowd was deafening. The power of "Jungle" Jim overtook the crowds with anticipation. The magic of his fire burnouts not only captivated every fan but the media was also overwhelmed. No fewer than 13 photographers stood in the other competitor's lane waiting to capture the shot of a lifetime. Liberman's opponent, Gene Conway, became a Liberman fan as well, watching him intently, not willing to take away any of his thunder while the Corvette idled, waiting to perform his burnout. In a fan's view, this was an unforgettable memory.

The incredibly talented duo of driver Kenny Safford and super tuner Gary Dyer of the Mr. Norm's Super Charger take notes of the crew prepping the super boss Camaro of "Jungle" Jim Liberman at Irwindale Raceway's East versus West Funny Car Championships. Liberman laid down one of his dazzling fire burnouts, but unfortunately, burnouts don't win races. Liberman lost to Richard Siroonian driving the "Big" John Mazmanian Plymouth 'Cuda with a smokey, sideways pass that produced an ET of 7.73 at 191.48 mph.

fabricating delicate parts, such as throttle linkages, and modifying fuel pumps and fuel injectors. He was also his own booking agent. He made all of the adjustments before computers were a thought, and he knew more about his car and conditions when he made half passes on the track.

Throughout his career, Liberman did not have a confidant or tutor, just a hero, which was Arnie Beswick. Like Beswick, an independent who paid his way without support from the factory and owned everything he drove, Jungle always worked hard and earned his rewards.

By the age of 21, match racing and appearance money was Liberman's livelihood. He made more money match racing than he did at any NHRA Nationals event. Keeping up his demand to be at several strips on the same day's schedule was brutal. Liberman decided in late 1968 to build a second car, and Logghe was once again chosen to construct the new car. Clare Sanders, of the *Lime Fire* Barracuda fame, was hired to drive the number-2 team Chevy II. The accomplished Sanders proved to be a great new hire for Liberman when she swept through an eight-car field at Cayuga, Ontario.

Liberman and Sanders Win First NHRA Eliminator Title

In 1969, for the first time in NHRA history, Funny Cars were recognized and had their own elimination bracket at each national event. Liberman and Sanders came out to Pomona for the ninth annual NHRA Winternationals, fielding their pair of identical Chevy II Novas. The cars were separated by their main sponsor names: Goodies Speed Shop and Steve Kanuka Racing Engines. The cars also had a different set of front wheels.

"Jungle" Clare qualified in the third position, but "Jungle" Jim did not make the cut in the 16-car field. Through three rounds of eliminations, the finals brought Ray Alley in his Engine Masters Barracuda against the blue Chevy II of Sanders. At the green, it was all Sanders from starting line to finish line, as she won the first-ever NHRA Funny Car Eliminator Title with an ET of 7.88 at 187.89 mph over the Barracuda's 8.11 at 187.11 mph.

Jungle Mania Defined

Liberman lived his life to its fullest. It was a vagabond life on the road, averaging six days a week racing in the summer months to sold out tracks. Always in demand, he was compared to a five-tool sports athlete, and he was the complete racer!

He was a natural when it came to mechanics. What others thought were trashed parts, he found a way to make them work on his own cars. He also built his own engines.

"It takes more than cubes and guts," Liberman said. "It takes experience, the know-how to make an engine hot and plenty more, knowing all of the little tricks that separate the men from the boys when the going gets hot!"

The name "Jungle Jim" was synonymous with his success on the strip. Promotors advertised over the airwaves and in the daily fish wraps to encourage all to attend the upcoming weekend meet. Just mentioning the name "Jungle" Jim Liberman brought in thousands of fans just to see him race.

I don't think anyone for sure can pinpoint the beginning of the hype on the name of "Jungle" Jim. The story is that a radio DJ from the West Coast was promoting an upcoming match race encounter with *Brutus* and said, ". . . the hottest GTO tiger out of the jungle along with the swingingest driver to tame a tiger, 'Jungle' Jim Liberman!"

The Irrepressible Liberman

Rich Guess, president of Goodies Speed Shop and the major sponsor for both Liberman and Lew Arrington's *Brutus*, opened his new store in San Jose, California, in grand style by hosting an open house. It included the

"Jungle" Jim Liberman demonstrates another hypnotizing fire burnout with an estimated 200 onlookers packing the staging lanes at Orange County International Raceway. Liberman was one of the top contenders on team General Motors, but overall the team lacked success, tallying only four points and ending in last place. As for Liberman, he went out to do his best and always put on a great show.

Jim Liberman was one of several racers who had a high level of proficiency. At the strip, he wrenched, tuned, rebuilt, and replaced his own motors at an amazing pace, but his talents didn't stop there. "Jungle" Jim was at his best impersonating a backup girl lining up his new Funny Car with driver Ron O'Donnell in the ex-Kirby Brothers and Kocela Beach City Chevrolet RS Camaro at Irwindale.

appearance of the wildest driver in drag racing, "Jungle" Jim with his Goodies-backed Chevy II on display.

Liberman took the opening to another level when he jumped into the car, fired it up, and performed a 150-foot burnout across the parking lot, ending up in a massive cloud of smoke. Not only did it create a scene but it also took him another 100 feet to stop the car. He then backed up and shut the car off. The fanatical crowd went out of its mind. Although the demonstration brought customers and the curious to the shop, the local authorities were not too pleased with "Jungle" Jim's mischievous activities, but no citations were issued.

Liberman was selected by *Car Craft* magazine's readers as the 1969 Funny Car Driver of the Year. He went on a three-week sweep, winning several major independent events including the third annual All-Chevrolet Eliminator title at Suffolk, Virginia, running an ET of 7.39 at 194.38 mph; capping the Mr. Chevrolet Eliminator title; and earning the "Quickest Chevrolet on Record" title with an unreal 7.28 ET at Capital Raceway.

The Fire Burnout

Liberman mastered the burnouts, blasting the tires sometimes the length of the quarter mile and either turning off the strip and onto the return road driving at high rates of speed back to the starting line or backing up at more than 50 mph to race his opponent. The crowd went crazy.

Along with his long, smokey burnouts, Liberman also perfected his fire burnouts. No matter where you were at the track, you stopped what you are doing and

ran to the fence to catch a glimpse or see the excitement he brought. All fans in the stands stood on their feet to watch this amazing show not only once or twice but several rounds at night.

The respect he had from his rivals in the other lane was deserved. Competitors would wait patiently until Liberman completed his spectacular fire burnouts.

Photographers stormed the lane in front of the opposition, knowing that people came to see Liberman, and they only had one chance to capture that one-of-a-kind money shot.

Liberman also had the knack for arriving at the track just before the closing of tech inspection, often dancing a fine line with the NHRA tech officials to allow him to race. He also pushed the limits several times by blowing past the starting line on his second burnout, each time extending a little farther down the strip while giving the fans a second chance of watching "Jungle" Pam back up the car.

Liberman earned stern warnings from the NHRA officials and was often threatened with being disqualified if he continued. One official finally had enough of Liberman's antics in the final round of a divisional race held at Maple Grove. After his second burnout that took him well down the track, the lead official ran down to the starting line to axe "Jungle" Jim against the Bob Banning Dodge of Tom Sneden. Sneden, knowing what was about to happen, followed suit and put his second burnout pass well past the tree too. At this point, the official threw up his arms in frustration and let them race.

Liberman's last run in his Chevy II–bodied Funny Cars ended in the later months of 1971. "Jungle" Jim's trademark blue Goodies Chevy was painted with a deep red paint.

Wild Yet Mild

Many in drag racing classified Liberman as the craziest man in drag racing, but a few knew he was extremely safety minded. He put together programs at various high schools, technical schools, and with the Boy Scouts on his own time away from racing, promoting safety in all forms including drag racing. Liberman demonstrated all the safety features of the Funny Car, including his racing apparel. He set up a movie projector to run drag racing films while setting up a real Christmas tree and reaction timer, giving kids the chance to see what it was like to compete of the starting line of a drag strip. If time permitted, a lengthy question-and-answer secession closed out the seminar.

At age 23, Liberman was appointed the lead Competition and Technical Director by Jesse Levine, the president of Automobile Racing Club of America (ARCA) to handle the club's aspects of speed and safety products both on and off the track. He gave back to the racing community. He was very approachable, signing autographs, answering questions, and even eating lunch with the fans when time permitted. He loved to perform and entertain, always giving the fans their hard-earned money's worth. He also took heart with kids, especially those who were under-privileged.

The business side of Liberman landed him a deal in 1975 with the 7-11 Corporation. He also teamed with comedian Jerry Lewis to raise money for Lewis's Muscular Dystrophy Labor Day Telethon. At Englishtown, New Jersey, the track's annual US All-Pro Funny Car Championships were sponsored by 7-Eleven and were on the same weekend as the telethon. It was a double win for the fans at Englishtown, watching Liberman compete in the show while record amounts of money were collected to help Jerry's Kids.

"Jungle" Pam

In the years to come, "Jungle" Jim added another piece of the puzzle when he brought on board a beautiful young woman named Pam Hardy. Hardy became a fixture in the camp when she took over the role of pouring the tire compounds in the water box, backing up the car after one of his burnouts, and kneeling around the car checking for any leakage.

Her attire consisted of her own version of "Daisy Duke" shorts and mesh haltered tops, leaving nothing to the imagination. Her appearance around the starting line often distracted the opposition in the other lane.

"Jungle" Pam Hardy directs Liberman back into his tracks at Irwindale Raceway. Jim and Pam were a major draw anywhere they went. Just watching Pam back up the car and kneel to look to check for any fluid leakage under the car and Liberman's pedal-to-the-metal, bonsai runs were well worth the admission price.

"Jungle" Pam was also instrumental in helping with the maintenance on the car, trading in her shorts and tops for a pair of overalls to thrash on the car between rounds.

When a driver was booked into a highly advertised match race or a highly paid guaranteed show, a well-planned-out route was in place, but sometimes, things don't go as planned. One possible disaster was avoided

Hectic turnarounds between rounds can lead to all kinds of miscues. When a disconnected oil line wasn't secured on fire up, an oil bath ensued along the side of the transporter, prompting cleanup by crewman Joey Oster. (Photo Courtesy Steve Delgadillo)

Jim Liberman's sleekest Funny Car was his 1974 Chevrolet Revell "slant nose" Vega at the Summernationals in Englishtown, New Jersey. Funny Car enthusiasts could own their personal version of "Jungle" Jim Liberman's Vega along with the other model team members when Revell jumped on board as a major sponsor. Liberman's folk hero status was at his all-time high in Funny Car racing along with "Super Crew" "Jungle" Pam and Bob McCoy. Bob Gerdes of Circus Custom Paint designed the wild flamed scheme with the jungle man character wearing shades and swinging on a vine.

He left us too young, but he will never be forgotten. A humble tribute to the greatest showman in drag racing is centrally located in the Famoso Grove at the Auto Club Famoso Raceway in McFarland, California. The placard and tree were dedicated by one of Liberman's hometown tracks located more than 2,700 miles away at Maple Grove Raceway near Mohnton, Pennsylvania.

One in the last line of Jim Liberman's Funny Cars was his Revell Chevy Monza. Liberman was voted the NHRA's 17th-greatest driver, even though he only won two NHRA Funny Car Eliminator titles. His first title was in 1969 as an owner when Clare Sanders drove the "Jungle" Jim Team #2 Chevy II past Ray Alley in the final round of eliminations. The other title was in 1975 at the NHRA Summernationals at Old Bridge Township Raceway Park, in Englishtown, New Jersey.

The 2010 California Hot Rod Reunion at Bakersfield held a special event with the Justice Brothers Spotlight, honoring none other than "Jungle" Jim Liberman. On hand honoring Liberman was number-2 team driver Clare Sanders, mechanic Larry Petrich, "Jungle" Pam, car owner Dave Baney, and driver Ron Huegli of the Goodies entry. It had been more than 51 years since Russell James Liberman climbed behind the wheel of his blue Goodies-backed 1969 Chevy II Funny Car, and these sentimental moments were shared with son James (Randy) Russell Liberman. It was amazing to witness Randy's emotions as he relived the path taken by his dad "loud pedaling" his way throughout hearts and memories.

when Liberman and Hardy were booked as the top draw at Atco Raceway in 1972. Minutes before to race time (8 p.m.), the traffic around the track was gridlocked with carloads of people trying to get inside the gate before the first round.

Liberman, a victim of the congestion, was unable to get inside the gate. Seeing this dilemma unfold, he pulled over the rig outside and quickly unloaded, fueled up, and fired up the car during the National Anthem. He drove his Funny Car through the gates and up to the starting line with massive header flames to a waiting Pat Foster in the Barry Setzer's Vega! The place went ballistic with the thousands of exuberant fans!

Liberman won his only NHRA National Funny Car Eliminator title at the 1975 Summernationals at Englishtown, New Jersey. In 2001, he was voted as the 17th top driver in drag racing history during the 50th NHRA Anniversary celebration. His popularity is strong as ever with several nostalgia teams building tribute Funny Cars to honor the true superstar he was.

Lasting Legacy

Liberman passed away right after midnight on September 9, 1977, when the Corvette he owned and drove lost control. He drove head-on into a public bus on Route 3 in West Goshen Township, Pennsylvania.

The impact impaled the charismatic king of Funny Car under the bus. It was reported that rescue responders took an estimated 50 minutes to remove his remains. "Jungle" Jim was just 32 years old.

Word spread like wildfire about his passing. Within hours, his house had been overcome with hundreds of friends and people who pillaged and looted anything inside, taking anything that wasn't bolted down. It was described as tomb raiders breaking into, robbing, and desecrating a tomb of a pharaoh. Toolboxes, tools, engines, car parts, and anything that meant a lot to Liberman was lost forever.

For many, it was the day drag racing died. It's been nearly 45 years since the passing of "Jungle" Jim, and after all these years, his popularity level remains on top. His T-shirts, diecasts, vintage programs, unbuilt plastic model kits, autographed handout hero cards, and photographs are still the top sellers at shows and racing events, demanding the big coins.

Revell, the plastic model car giant from the 1970s, distributed millions of Top Fuel and Funny Car All-Star Drag Racing Team 1/24- and 1/16-scale plastic kits worldwide. Revell claimed that its number-1 all-time selling Funny Car kit was the 1/16-scale "Jungle" Jim 1973 Vega. Even today, plastic kits are being reproduced as the companies try to keep pace with the high demand.

Life on the Road with "Jungle" Pam

"We were racing in Atco, New Jersey. We pull up into the staging lanes, and I did my usual thing, inspecting the track for debris. Those screws, nuts, and tools that were hurled at you by spinning tires could ruin one's day. A track official asked what I am doing on the track. No women were allowed on the track. I told him that I was part of the crew, and I will back up the car.

"'Oh no you will not!" the track official said. "No women on the track! Let's go talk with Jungle about this.'

"Jungle saw it all clearly. 'If she cannot be on the track, then I'm not racing,' he said.

"We raced.

"The next day, we headed over to Maple Grove for another night race with full track burnouts. After the first burnout, we waited and waited, and he was idling but not moving. Nuts! The reverser broke again.

"Sprinting down the strip to reach the car, waving to the guys on the line to try to push it back and nothing. Rocking the car finally got it into reverse. We bent over the hood of the Vega and continued pushing it back to the starting line when Jim motioned to me, pointing.

"'What?'

"With several more pointing motions at me, I shrugged my shoulders. Still frantically pointing, I looked down and see my blouse had come completely unbuttoned—and naturally without having the proper undergarments on.

"Thanks to Jim, he saved me from one the most embarrassing photo ops that I would have never lived down."